DALIT MOVEMENT
Role of B R Ambedkar

DALIT MOVEMENT
Role of B R Ambedkar

R.K. Bakshi

ADHYAYAN

ADHYAYAN PUBLISHERS & DISTRIBUTORS
NEW DELHI (INDIA)

Published by
ADHYAYAN PUBLISHERS & DISTRIBUTORS
4378/4B, 105, J.M.D. House, Murari Lal Street
Ansari Road Darya Ganj, New Delhi - 110002
Ph.: 011-23263018, 011-23277156, Fax: 011-23280028
Email: adhyayanpublishers@yahoo.com

DALIT MOVEMENT Role of B R Ambedkar

Edition 2010
ISBN 978-81-8435-224-5

Printed in India

Published by Harish Chandra Yadav for Adhyayan Publishers & Distributors, Laser Typeseting at A.V. Rao and Printed at Tarun Offset Printers, Delhi

Preface

Dr. B. R. Ambedkar has undoubtedly been the central figure in the epistemology of the dalit universe. For the dalit masses he is everything together; a scholar par excellence in the realm of scholarship, a messiah who led his people out of bondage and ignominy on to the path of pride, and a Bodhisatva in the pantheon of Buddhism.

It is not difficult to see the reason behind the obeisance and reverence that dalits have for Ambedkar. They see him as one who devoted every moment of his life thinking about and struggling for their emancipation, who took the might of the establishment head on in defence of their cause; who sacrificed all the comforts and conveniences of life that were quite within his reach to be on their side; who conclusively disproved the theory of caste based superiority by rising to be the tallest amongst the tall despite enormous odds, and finally as one who held forth the torch to illuminate the path of their future. It was he, who forsook his high pedestal, climbed down to their level, gave them a helping hand and raised them to human stature.

The present book describes the crucial role played by Dr. B.R. Ambedkar in shaping the destiny of the millions of people who were treated as untouchables. While tracing the socio-political history of the Ambedkarite dalit movement, it presents an account of dalits' endeavour, encounters and experiences. While highlighting its considerable achievements if dalit communities today, the book also explores the reasons for the limitation of dalit movement. The book will be of immense help to the researchers, academicians, development action planners, administrators, social workers and all those who are interested in development studies, particularly among the disadvantaged people of Indian communities.

Author

Contents

1

Life History of B.R Ambedkar

Dr. Bhimrao Ramji Ambedkar (1891-1956) was born in the British-founded town and military cantonment of Mhow in the Central Provinces (now in Madhya Pradesh). He was the 14th and last child of Ramji Maloji Sakpal and Bhimabai Murbadkar. His family was of Marathi background from the town of Ambavade in the Ratnagiri district of modern-day Maharashtra. They belonged to the Hindu Mahar caste, who were treated as untouchables and subjected to intense socio-economic discrimination. Ambedkar's ancestors had for long been in the employment of the army of the British East India Company, and his father served in the Indian Army at the Mhow cantonment, rising to the rank of Subedar.

Bhimrao started his school education in 1900 in the Government High School, Satara. At that time, his name in the school was Bhiva Ramji Ambavadekar. One Brahmin teacher named Ambedkar in the Satara High School loved Bhimrao very much. As a mark of love and respect for him, Bhimrao started calling himself "Ambedkar". Throughout his life, he remained grateful to the teacher who treated him kindly during his school days.

During his school days, Ambedkar had several humiliating experiences, which made him realize what the stigma of untouchability meant. Once, Ambedkar and his brother were going to Goregaon from Masur Railway Station. They hired a bullock-cart for this purpose. Hardly had the cart gone a few yards when the caste Hindu cart-man realized that the two boys in his cart were "untouchables". He threw them out on the road in a fit of rage, because he felt that they had polluted his wooden cart. Ambedkar and his brother calmed the cart man's anger by paying double the fare. Ambedkar's elder brother drove the cart, and the cart-man followed the cart on foot, as he was afraid of being polluted! Ambedkar and his brother could not get drinking water during the whole journey.

Similarly, barbers refused to cut Ambedkar's hair because of fear of pollution. Ambedkar's sister used to cut her brother's hair. Further, because of being an "untouchable" by birth, Ambedkar was forced to sit apart from other students in the school. He could not mix with other boys or play cricket and other games with them. His teachers would not touch his notebooks. Some of them would not even ask the "untouchables" to recite poems or put questions to them for fear of being polluted! When they felt thirsty in the school, they turned their mouths upward and somebody would kindly pour drinking water into their mouths. The "untouchables" were traditionally prohibited from learning Sanskrit. The Sanskrit teacher in Ambedkar's school refused to teach Sanskrit to the "untouchables". Ambedkar had no option except to study Persian as the second language in the high school.

In 1904, Ambedkar's father, Ramji, shifted to Bombay. Ambedkar joined the Elphinstone High School. In Satara Ambedkar was not allowed to play games, but he did not face any such restriction at Bombay. However, there were incidents, which made Ambedkar realize his "untouchable" status. The non-untouchable Hindu children used to keep their tiffin-boxes behind the blackboard in classroom.

Once, Ambedkar was asked to write something on the blackboard. Ambedkar's classmates were afraid that their food would be polluted by Ambedkar's presence near the board. They ran to the blackboard and removed their tiffin boxes from there even before Ambedkar could reach and touch the board! Ambedkar passed his Matriculation Examination in 1907. This event was celebrated by his family. In those days, a child coming from Mahar family passing the Matriculation Examination was a highly unusual event.

1.1. Discrimination on the Basis of Caste

Bhim began to notice that he and his family were treated differently. At high school he had to sit in the corner of the room on a rough mat, away from the desks of the other pupils. At break-time, he was not allowed to drink water using the cups his fellow school children used. He had to hold his cupped hands out to have water poured into them by the school caretaker. Bhim did not know why he should be treated differently—what was wrong with him?

Once, he and his elder brother had to travel to Goregaon, where their father worked as a cashier, to spend their summer holidays. They got off the train and waited for a long time at the station, but Ramji did not arrive to meet them. The station master seemed kind, and asked them who they were and where they were going. The boys were very well-dressed, clean, and polite. Bhim, without thinking, told him they were Mahars (a group classed as 'untouchables'). The station master was stunned—his face changed its kindly expression and he went away.

Bhim decided to hire a bullock-cart to take them to their father—this was before motor cars were used as taxis—but the cart-men had heard that the boys were 'untouchables', and wanted nothing to do with them. Finally, they had to agree to pay double the usual cost of the journey, plus they had to drive the cart themselves, while the driver walked beside it. He was afraid of being polluted by the boys, because they were 'untouchables'. However, the extra money persuaded him that he could have his cart 'purified' later! Throughout the journey, Bhim thought constantly about what had happened—yet he could not understand the reason for it. He and his brother were clean and neatly dressed. Yet they were supposed to pollute and make unclean everything they touched and all that touched them. How could that be possible?

Bhim never forgot this incident. As he grew up, such senseless insults made him realise that what Hindu society called 'untouchability' was stupid, cruel, and unreasonable. His sister had to cut his hair at home because the village barbers were afraid of being polluted by an 'untouchable'. If he asked her why they were 'untouchables', she could only answer -that is the way it has always been." Bhim could not be satisfied with this answer. He knew that -it has always been that way" does not mean that there is a just reason for it—or that it had to stay that way forever. It could be changed.

Ambedkar was married, at a young age of seventeen years, after doing his matriculation. His wife, Rami, later renamed Ramabai, was only nine years old at that time. She was the second daughter of her then deceased father, Bhiku Walangkar, who worked as a porter. The marriage was solemnized in the open shed of the Byculla Market of Bombay.

1.2. Scholarship and Academic Excellence

At this time in his young life, with his mother dead, and father working away from the village where Bhim went to school, he had some good fortune. His teacher, though from a 'high' caste, liked him a lot. He praised Bhim's good work and encouraged him, seeing what a bright pupil he was. He even invited Bhim to eat lunch with him—something that would have horrified most high caste Hindus. The teacher also changed Bhim's last name to Ambedkar—his own name.

When his father decided to remarry, Bhim was very upset—he still missed his mother so much. Wanting to run away to Bombay, he tried to steal his aunt's purse. When at last he managed to get hold of it, he found only one very small coin. Bhim felt so ashamed. He put the coin back and made a vow to himself to study very hard and to become independent.

Soon he was winning the highest praise and admiration from all his teachers. They urged Ramji to get the best education fro his son Bhim. So Ramji moved with his family to Bombay. They all had to live in just one room, in an area where the poorest of the poor lived, but Bhim was able to go to Elphinstone High School—one of the best schools in all of India.

In their one room everyone and everything was crowed together and the streets outside were very noisy. Bhim went to sleep when he got home from school. Then his father would wake him up at two o'clock in the morning! Everything was quiet then — so he could do his homework and study in peace.

In the big city, where life was more modern than in the villages, Bhim found that he was still called an 'untouchable' and treated as if something made him different and bad —even at his famous school.

One day, the teacher called him up to the blackboard to do a sum. All the other boys jumped up and made a big fuss. Their lunch boxes were stacked behind the blackboard—they believed that Bhim would pollute the food! When he wanted to learn Sanskrit, the language of the Hindu holy scriptures, he was told that it was forbidden for 'untouchables' to do so. He had to study Persian instead—but he taught himself Sanskrit later in life.

1.2.1. Higher Education

The Maharaja Sayajirao Gaikawad of Baroda had announced scholarship for higher studies to any promising untouchable student. Ambedkar welcomed the opportunity and joined Elphinstone College, Bombay. One of his teachers, Professor Muller, lent him books and gave him clothes. However, the overall environment was humiliating. The college hotelkeeper, who was a Brahmin, would not give him tea or water. Nonetheless, Ambedkar concentrated all his energies on his studies and passed his B.A. examination in 1912 with English and Persian as his subjects.

1.2.2. Baroda State Service

After his graduation, Ambedkar joined the Baroda State Service. He had hardly served for fifteen days when his father died on February 2, 1913. The higher office in Baroda State was manned by upper caste Hindus. The idea of pollution by touch was so strong that even the peons in his office used to throw office files at him from a distance! He could not get residential accommodation in any decent locality. He was staying with Pandit Atma Ram, an Arya Samajist. The social conditions were highly unfavorable and it was difficult for him to continue in service. He therefore decided to resign his post at the earliest opportunity.

1.2.3. Higher Education in USA and UK

Ambedkar got another opportunity to pursue higher education when the Maharaja of Baroda decided to send some students to the U.S.A. for higher studies at Columbia University. Ambedkar was one of them. In third week of July 1913, he joined Columbia University, New York, as a Gaikawad Scholar. He was the first Mahar to study in a foreign university. Ambedkar joined a cosmopolitan club where some of the Indian students lived. He could now move freely and could continue with his daily routine in an atmosphere of equality. This was a very new experience for him. In June 1915, Ambedkar obtained his M.A. degree for his thesis on "Ancient Indian Commerce". In May 1916, he read a paper on "Castes in India, their Mechanism, Genesis and Development" at the Anthropology Seminar of Dr. A.A. Goldenweizer. It was published in the Indian Antiquary, in May 1917. It was also published in the form of a brochure, the first published work of Ambedkar. In the paper, Ambedkar described endogamy as the "essence of caste". He expressed the view that the caste was a "closed class".

In June 1916, Ambedkar submitted his thesis for the degree of Ph.D. entitled "National Dividend for India: A Historical and Analytical Study". It was published eight years later as The Evolution of Provincial Finance in British India. Ambedkar left Columbia University in June 1916 to join London School of Economics and Political Science as a graduate student. In October 1916, he was admitted to Gray's Inn for Law. However, he had to return to India after spending a year in London, because the scholarship granted to him had lapsed. In London, he had been working on a thesis for the M.Sc. (Economics) degree.

1.2.4. Back to Baroda

In July 1917, Ambedkar was made Military Secretary to the Maharaja of Baroda with a view to be groomed for the post of the State's Finance Minister. However, he could not get accommodation in any hotel or hostel in Baroda. He took shelter in a Parsee hotel and stayed there incognito. He received similar treatment in his office. Peons flung office files on his table. Drinking water was not available in his office. The humiliations reached a climax, when one day a group of Parsees armed with lathis forced Ambedkar to vacate the Parsee hotel where he was living. No Hindu or Muslim was prepared to give him shelter in the city All this was unbearable to him. He sent a note to the Maharaja; but the Diwan expressed his inability to do anything in the matter. Ultimately Ambedkar left Baroda and went to Bombay in November 1917.

1.2.5. Bombay: Sydenham College

In Bombay Ambedkar tried to mould his life afresh. He started a business firm offering advice to dealers in stocks and shares. Nevertheless, he closed permanently as the customers were not ready to come to an "untouchable" for advice. In November 1918, he joined as Professor of Political Economy in Sydenham College, Bombay. He served the college from November 1918 to March 1920. As his fame spread, students from other colleges attended his lectures. However, the social treatment remained unchanged. "The high-caste Professors objected to his drinking water from the pot reserved for the professorial staff". Gandhi's travails in South Africa are well known. It is a pity that Ambedkar had to face similar, or even worse, treatment in his own country!

1.2.6. Mooknayak

In January 1920, Ambedkar started a Marathi fortnightly Mooknayak (Spokesman of the Voiceless) to champion the cause of the depressed classes in India. In the editorial of the first issue, he remarked that the existing newspapers were catering only to the interests of certain castes. He said, "devoid of power and knowledge, the non-brahmins and the depressed classes cannot make any progress."

1.2.7. Depressed Class Conferences

In the meantime, different conferences of depressed classes were being organized in Maharashtra. Ambedkar attended the conferences of the depressed classes held at Nagpur (1918) and Kolhapur (1920) under the presidentship of Sahu Maharaj. At the later conference, Sahu Maharaj declared that Ambedkar had the potential for becoming an all India leader.

1.2.8. Back to UK for Higher Studies

In September 1920, Ambedkar rejoined the London School of Economics and Political Science and entered Gray's Inn to qualify as a barrister. He had saved some money with the cooperation of his wife for this purpose while working at Sydenham College. He accepted some financial help from Sahu Maharaj as well. In June 1921, the University of London accepted his thesis "Provincial Decentralization of Imperial Finance in British India" for the M.Sc.

(Econ.) degree. In 1922-23, he spent some months studying Economics in the University of Bonn in Germany. In March 1923, he submitted his thesis "The Problem of the Rupee—its Origin and its Solution" for the degree of D.Sc. (Econ.). Ambedkar was called to Bar in April 1923. Thus Ambedkar became M.A, Ph.D., M.Sc., D.Sc. and Bar at Law.

1.2.9. Back to India

On returning to India Ambedkar started practicing at Bombay High Court. In July 1924, he founded the Bahishkrit Hitakarini Sabha (Society to Serve the Interest of Outcastes), an educational and cultural organization aimed at improving the conditions of depressed classes. The motto of the organization was "Educate, Organize and Agitate".

Ambedkar was also gaining foothold as a lawyer. He fought a successful defense in a libel case filed against some non-Brahmin leaders who had published a pamphlet against Brahmins declaring that the Brahmins had ruined India. However, for a regular income between 1925-28, he had to depend on his pay as a teacher in Batliboi Accountancy Training Institute.

1.3. Fight for Dalits

1.3.1. The Mahad Conference

In 1927, the Governor nominated Ambedkar to the Bombay Legislature. In 1927, itself the Mahar conference was organized which marked the emergence of Ambedkar as an important leader. The conference ended with his first act of public protest. The protest consisted simply of the assertion of the right of untouchables to draw and drink water from an open public tank in Mahad, a small town in the Konkan region of Maharashtra.

In 1923, the Bombay legislative Council had passed a resolution recommending that "the untouchable classes be allowed to use all public water-places, wells and dharamshalas which are built and maintained out of public funds or administered by bodies appointed by Government or created by statute."

The Bombay Government issued a directive in 1923 to give effect to this resolution. Inspite of the resolution, many local boards and municipalities including Mahad Municipality did not grant civil rights to the depressed classes. In 1926, the Bombay Legislative Council passed another resolution denying financial grants to such defaulting municipalities and local boards. Finally, the Mahad Municipality threw open the tank (which was famous for its tasty water and hence known as Chowdar) to all communities. Dr. Ambedkar organized the Dalits to assert their rights to drink and take water from the tank. Thousands of delegates attended a conference of "untouchables" at Mahad on March 20, 1927. In his presidential address, Ambedkar stressed the necessity of rooting out ideas of highness or lowness. The conference passed a resolution appealing to caste Hindus and the Government to make the resolution regarding public water-places a reality.

After the Conference, all the delegates marched in a procession to the Chowdar Tank to assert their rights. Ambedkar also walked down the steps of the tank and drank a handful of water from it. There was a rumor that "untouchables" had entered the Vireshwar Temple. The caste Hindus came to the pandal of the Conference and attacked the delegates. Stray individuals were beaten. They had to run into Muslim houses for shelter. Ambedkar was forced to take shelter in a police station!

After this event, the "untouchables" in that area were forced to face social boycott. They were dislodged from their land and assaulted in many villages. Ambedkar urged his followers to take aggressive steps to wrest the right to drinking water at public water-places, and to force their entry into public temples.

1.3.2. Bahishkrit Bharat

The Mooknayak, which Ambedkar had started earlier, had ceased publication. In 1927, he started another Marathi periodical Bahishkrit Bharat. The periodical intended to be a fortnightly came out intermittently for over two years. Through this journal, Ambedkar clarified his own ideas on the various aspects of the movement that he had initiated.

1.3.3. Mahad Satyagraha and the Burning of the Manusmriti

At Mahad, a satyagraha conference was organized on December 25, 1927. Earlier Periyar had organized a Satyagraha at Vaikkom in 1924. Ambedkar was watching these developments very carefully. In one of his editorials before Mahad Satyagraha Ambedkar has touchingly referred to the Vaikkom struggle.

In his speech at satyagraha conference at Mahad, Ambedkar attacked the varna system as being at the root of inequality. He emphasized that Hindu society should be organized on two principles: equality and absence of caste system. Among other resolutions a resolution was passed to burn the Manusmriti, which according to Ambedkar perpetuated the social, economic, religious and political slavery of the untouchables. Accordingly, the Manusmriti was burnt publicly on December 25, 1927. By another resolution, it was demanded that priestly profession among Hindus be democratized, allowing everyone who desired to have an opportunity to become a priest.

The report that Manusmriti had been burnt as a part of the Mahad Satyagraha gave rise to strong revulsion and much criticism in the caste-Hindu press. Justifying this action, Ambedkar wrote in the 3 February, 1928 issue of the Bahishkrit Bharat that his reading of the Manusmriti had convinced him that it was insulting in its treatment of the Shudras and that it did not even support the idea of social equality. To burn a thing is to register protest to the idea it represented. By so doing, one expected to shame the persons concerned into modifying their behavior. He said further that it would be futile to expect that anyone who revered the Manusmriti could be genuinely interested in the welfare of the untouchables. He compared the burning of the Manusmriti to the burning of foreign cloth recommended by Gandhi.

1.3.4. Nasik Temple Entry Satyagraha

The Nasik Satyagraha for the entry of untouchables to the Kalaram Temple began in March 1930. It went on for six long years until April 1936. Ultimately it ended without gaining its specific objective. When the Nasik Satyagraha petered out, Ambedkar spoke thus in the Yeola Conference on 13 October 1935:

> "Even this movement to obtain our ordinary rights as human beings and achieve equality in Hindu society has failed. Thus the time has arise to take the final decision. This weak and lowly status that we occupy is because we are a part of the Hindu society. Therefore, would you not wish to embrace another religion, which will give you equal status, equal rights and fair treatment? Give up your links with Hinduism. Enter a religion where you will obtain peace and dignity. But remember to select only that religion in which you will get equal status, equal opportunity and equal treatment. It was not my fault that I was born an untouchable. But I am determined that I will not die a Hindu."

Even before the Nasik Satyagraha began in 1930, Ambedkar had begun to look upon the temple entry as relatively unimportant part of his programme. He seems to have said this to the Nasik leaders who came to invite him to accept the leadership of the Sătyagraha. He is reported to have told them that he was more interested in securing political rights for the untouchables than in gaining them entry to temples.

1.4. Ambedkar in Politics

Ambedkar was a political leader and led an active and eventful life. He struggled for separate electorates for the depressed classes. He was a member of Bombay Legislative Council from 1927. He deposed before the Simon Commission in 1928. He attended the Round Table Conferences in 1930 and onwards as a representative of the depressed classes. At the Second Round Table Conference, he repeatedly clashed with Gandhi. In 1932, he signed the historic Pune Pact as a representative of the depressed classes. In July 1942, he joined the Viceroy's Executive Council as Labor Member. Ambedkar was an elected member of the Constituent Assembly of India. He was elected to the Drafting Committee and ultimately, elected its Chairman. Ambedkar was included in the first cabinet of the independent India as the Law Minister. He resigned in September 1951 from Nehru's cabinet owing to differences with him. After resigning from Nehru's Cabinet Ambedkar contested Lok Sabha election as an opposition leader in 1952 and 1954. He was defeated in both these elections. However, in March 1952, he was elected to the Rajya Sabha.

Ambedkar's views and attitudes had hardened against orthodox Hindus, despite a significant increase in momentum across India for the fight against untouchability and he began criticizing them even as he was criticized himself by large numbers of Hindu activists. Speaking at the Yeola Conversion Conference on October 13 near Nasik, Ambedkar announced his intention to convert to a different religion and exhorted his followers to leave Hinduism. He would repeat his message at numerous public meetings across India.

In 1936, Ambedkar founded the Independent Labour Party, which won 15 seats in the 1937 elections to the Central Legislative Assembly. He published his book *The Annihilation of Caste* in the same year, based on the thesis he had written in New York. Attaining immense popular success, Ambedkar's work strongly criticized Hindu religious leaders and the caste system in general. He protested the Congress decision to call the untouchable community *Harijans* (*Children of God*), a name coined by Gandhi. Ambedkar served on the Defence Advisory Committee and the Viceroy's Executive Council as minister for labour.

Between 1941 and 1945, he published a large number of highly controversial books and pamphlets, including *Thoughts on Pakistan*, in which he criticized the Muslim League's demand for a separate Muslim state of Pakistan. With *What Congress and Gandhi Have Done to the Untouchables*, Ambedkar intensified his attacks on Gandhi and the Congress, charging them with hypocrisy.

In his work *Who Were the Shudras?*, Ambedkar attempted to explain the formation of the Shudras i.e. the lowest caste in hierarchy of Hindu caste system. He also emphasised how Shudras are separate from Untouchables. Ambedkar oversaw the transformation of his political party into the All India Scheduled Castes Federation, although it performed poorly in the elections held in 1946 for the Constituent Assembly of India. In writing a sequel to *Who Were the Shudras?* in 1948, Ambedkar lambasted Hinduism in the *The Untouchables: A Thesis on the Origins of Untouchability*:

> The Hindu Civilisation.... is a diabolical contrivance to suppress and enslave humanity. Its proper name would be infamy. What else can be said of a civilisation which has produced a mass of people... who are treated as an entity beyond human intercourse and whose mere touch is enough to cause pollution?

While he was extremely critical of Muhammad Ali Jinnah and the communally divisive strategies of the Muslim League, he argued that Hindus and Muslims should segregate and the State of Pakistan be formed, as ethnic nationalism within the same country would only lead to more violence. He cited precedents in historical events such as the dissolution of the Ottoman Empire and Czechoslovakia to bolster his views regarding the Hindu-Muslim communal divide.

However, he questioned whether the need for Pakistan was sufficient and suggested that it might be possible to resolve Hindu-Muslim differences in a less drastic way. He wrote that Pakistan must "justify its existence" accordingly. Since other countries such as Canada have also had communal issues with the French and English and have lived together, it might not be impossible for Hindus and Muslims to live together.

He warned that the actual implementation of a two-state solution would be extremely problematic with massive population transfers and border disputes. This claim was almost prophetic, looking forward to the violent Partition of India after Independence.

Despite his increasing unpopularity, controversial views, and intense criticism of Gandhi and the Congress, Ambedkar was by reputation an exemplary jurist and scholar. Upon India's independence on August 15, 1947, the new Congress-led government invited Ambedkar to serve as the nation's first law minister, which he accepted. On August 29, Ambedkar was appointed chairman of the Constitution Drafting Committee, charged by the Assembly to write free India's new Constitution.

Ambedkar won great praise from his colleagues and contemporary observers for his drafting work. In this task Ambedkar's study of sangha practice among early Buddhists and his extensive reading in Buddhist scriptures was to come to his aid. Sangha practice incorporated voting by ballot, rules of debate and precedence and the use of agendas, committees and proposals to conduct business. Sangha practice itself was modelled on the oligarchic system of governance followed by the tribal republics of ancient India like the Shakyas and the Lichchavis. Thus although Ambedkar used Western models to give his Constitution shape, its spirit was Indian and indeed tribal.

The text prepared by Ambedkar provided constitutional guarantees and protections for a wide range of civil liberties for individual citizens, including freedom of religion, the abolition of untouchability and the outlawing of all forms of discrimination. Ambedkar argued for extensive economic and social rights for women, and also won the Assembly's support for introducing a system of reservations of jobs in the civil services, schools and colleges for members of scheduled castes and scheduled tribes, a system akin to affirmative action.

India's lawmakers hoped to eradicate the socio-economic inequalities and lack of opportunities for India's depressed classes through this measure, which had been originally envisioned as temporary on a need basis. The Constitution was adopted on November 26, 1949 by the Constituent Assembly. Speaking after the completion of his work, Ambedkar said:

> "I feel that the Constitution is workable; it is flexible and it is strong enough to hold the country together both in peace time and in war time. Indeed, if I may say so, if things go wrong under the new Constitution the reason will not be that we had a bad Constitution. What we will have to say is that Man was vile."

Ambedkar resigned from the cabinet in 1951 following the stalling in parliament of his draft of the Hindu Code Bill, which sought to expound gender equality in the laws of inheritance, marriage and the economy. Although supported by Prime Minister Nehru, the cabinet and many other Congress leaders, it received criticism from a large number of members of parliament. Ambedkar independently contested an election in 1952 to the lower house of parliament, the Lok Sabha but was defeated. He was appointed to the upper house of parliament, the Rajya Sabha in March 1952 and would remain a member until his death.

1.4.1. Political Thoughts and Isms

1.4.1.1. Capitalism

Capitalism is the basic economic system of the modern age. "It involves the method of enterprise and a rational capitalistic establishment; and the spirit of capitalism illustrates that attitude which seeks profit rationally and systematically", observes Max Weber.

It is the organisation of business upon a large scale by an employer or company of employers possessing an accumulated stock wherewith to acquire raw materials and tools, and hire labour so as to produce an increased quantity of wealth which shall constitute profit.

From various definitions of capitalism Dr. S.K. Srivastava concludes that, "Capitalism or capitalist civilization is that stage in the development of Industry and legal institutions in which the majority of workers find themselves divorced from the ownership of the means of production in such way as they become mere wage earners whose subsistence, security and personal freedom depend upon capitalists who can be counted on fingers, control the entire organisation of land, labour and machinery; and undertake business and production purely from the point of view of private gain".

Hence, the salient features of the capitalism are:

(i) Private property,

(ii) Ownership of means of production,

(iii) Economic freedom,

(iv) Vital role of entrepreneur, and

(v) Competition accompanied by oligopoly.

Mr. V.B. Singh lays stress on the motive of profit making and points out the following characteristics of capitalism:

(i) Profit constitutes the motivating force for the advancement of economic activities;

(ii) The profit realised is not controlled by the State or the public bodies, but by individual entrepreneurs; and

(iii) Profit is generally invested in the production of wealth, so as to get further profits.

Mainly because of this motive of profit making the capitalists, in the words of Karl Marx, started misappropriating the 'Surplus Value' produced by the labour. It resulted in inequalities of income; division of society into classes like rich and poor, employers and employees and haves and have-nots; social unrest; unemployment; class-conflict leading to class struggle and class-war; cut-throat competition;

unplanned production; loss of moral values and trade cycle. Hence, there emerged a socialistic thought which aimed at replacing capitalism by limiting or abolishing private property; establishing collective ownership on the means of production by way of nationalisation and by establishing a class-less society based on equality and justice. Marxism, which embodies Socialism and Communism, criticized and described in detail the evils of capitalism and stood against it every tooth and nail.

Dr. Ambedkar was a staunch democrat and a committed socialist. He therefore agrees that the 'have-nots' are always exploited by the 'haves' and joins hands with Karl Marx in overthrowing the supremacy of the 'haves'. But, he does not accept economic relationship as the be-all and end-all of human life and thus rejects economic motive as the driving power behind all human activity.

Hence, the mis-appropriation of the Surplus Value by the owners of private property cannot be the only reason of exploitation. Dr. Ambedkar does not therefore believe in the abolition of private property as the only remedy to bring an end to the exploitation, poverty and sufferings of the have-nots. On the contrary, he defends an individual's right to private possession of wealth and property and stands for a greater security of the individual's economic interests, with the help of state control.

He believes in individual liberty and wants the capitalists to co-operate with the state for the betterment of economic and social affairs.

He is opposed to the annihilation of capitalists as it would be, in his opinion, an act of violence. He believes in non-violent method of socio-economic change without depriving anybody of his personal liberty may he be capitalist or an owner of private property. But he maintains that the primary function of a growing society is an effective check on economic exploitation and therefore seeks "to eliminate the possibility of the more powerful having the power to impose arbitrary restraints on the less powerful withdrawing from the control he has over the economic life of the people.

Obviously, he is against the concentration of wealth in a few hands and seeks to put "an obligation on the state to plan the economic life of the people on the line which would lead to highest point of productivity without closing every avenue to private enterprise, and also provide for equitable distribution of wealth."

1.4.1.2. State Intervention

Dr. Ambedkar, though disagreed with Karl Marx and defended an individual's right to liberty and private property never favoured capitalism as the best form of economic system. Being a democrat he wants individual liberty through democracy and being a socialist he wants social emancipation through socialism.

F. M. Stern wrote a book titled as 'Classless Capitalism' and tried to impress that American Capitalism is not only classless but also democratic and thus superior to the kind of capitalism known to the rest of the world. He further observed that the "American Capitalism is dominated by two seemingly unconnected movements; one is shrinking demand for human labour per unit of production and the other is rapid expansion of the market for the products of modern industry. These two movements must-and in the final outcome do-balance each other." Siding totally with the capitalistic process he believed in market mechanism but did not favour State intervention.

Dr. Ambedkar maintained that the State can prove itself an ideal agency to protect, both democracy and socialism by resorting to timely intervention and adequate controls. He says, "It is true that where the State refrains from intervention what remains is liberty.....but this liberty is liberty to landlords to increase rents, for capitalists to increase hours of work and reduce rate of wages. This must be so. It cannot be otherwise. For, in an economic system employing armies of workers, producing goods en masse at regular intervals some one must make rules so that workers will work and the wheels of industry run on. If the State does not do it, the private employer will.

Life otherwise become impossible. In other words what is called liberty from the control of the state is another name for the dictatorship of the private employer." He favours state intervention against capitalism but not to the extent of communism.

Dr. Ambedkar, as a practical democrat with an ardent faith in a democratic way of life, has opposed monopoly and dictatorship in its shape and form. He is against complete nationalisation and state control of the economy. He advocates State Socialism and state ownership in the fields of agriculutre, industry and insurance with a view to see that the dictatorship and capitalism do not stand in the way of democracy and socialism and their rapid success in India.

Land holding in India, according to Dr. Ambedkar, is not only a matter of property but also a matter of social states.

The traditional village economy, based on agriculture, is the root cause of socio-economic inequality and injustice. He therefore advocates nationalisation of agricultural land with collective farming where agriculture becomes a State Industry.

Dr. Ambedkar is not opposed to the private sector of the economy. He suggests that some spheres of production, except in the basic industries, should be operated through the state or through private enterprise or under both the state and private control. He realizes that the private enterprise cannot bring about rapid industrialization of Indian economy because of its motive of maximum profit and absolute backwardness of the traditional village economy of the country; and even if it attempts to industrialise the economy, it would produce inequalities of wealth, exploitation of workers and such other evils of capitalism. Hence, he is in favour of nationalisation of basic and key industries only. So also he advocates nationalisation of insurance with a view to give

(i) greater security to the individuals and

(ii) adequate funds to the State for financing economic plans.

Thus, Dr. Ambedkar seeks to establish a balance between State ownership and private enterprise. He is neither in the camp of pure or Scientific Socialists or of the communists who advocate total nationalisation and complete state monopoly, nor favours capitalism which stands for free and un-controlled private enterprise.

Dr. Ambedkar wants "to retain Parliamentary Democracy and to prescribe the state socialism by the law of the constitution, so that it will be beyond the reach of Parliamentary majority to suspend, amend or abrogate it".

Lord J.M. Keynes propounds a theory of state capitalism as opposed to state socialism and wants the state to function within the general requirements of the capitalist system. Thus, as regard to state intervention in economic life of the people Dr. Ambedkar comes close to Lord J. M. Keynes, but with a different attitude.

Keynes propounded, revised or reformed Capitalism whereas Dr. Ambedkar advocated a new kind of State Socialism. Both are the reformers of capitalist system; but when Keynes fundamentally remains a capitalist, Ambedkar turns to be an individualist and socialist in his socio-economic philosophy. This attitude towards human interest brings Dr. Ambedkar very near to J.S. Mill who outlines a comprehensive programme of social policy observes, Dr. D. R. Jatava.

To Dr. Ambedkar, Capitalism and Brahminism, an integral part of Hinduism, are the twin enemies of Indian society as Brahminism is also based on exploitation and inequality. In his attack on Hinduism Ambedkar comes closer to Karl Marx who regards religion as the opium of the people and wants to overthrow the supremacy of religion and capitalism.

1.4.1.3. Capitalism Versus Democracy

Capitalism is said to have been changing and capitalism today is not the classical capitalism of earlier times. But the profit-motive remains and its evil effects cannot be ignored. Even in case of India the British Government did not stop the squeezing of the masses by the landlords and exploitation of the labourers by the capitalists, might be because of the fear of resistance and their own ideology of capitalistic economy. Hence, to believe that capitalism will be replaced by social outlook and socially oriented planning or to effect reforms in capitalism will not bring any fruits.

F. M. Stern believes that American Capitalism is 'Classless Capitalism' without which dignity and prosperity for all cannot be realized. He also talks of 'Democratic Capitalism' based upon change and growth, strives to expand production, to create new ideas, new wealth and greater property for all; but, also admits that economic and social equality for all can probably never be attained.

Dr. Ambedkar said, "Those who are living under the capitalistic form of industrial organization and under the form of political organization called Parliamentary Democracy must recognize the contradictions of their systems.....In politics equality and in economics inequality."

It is thus obvious that capitalism cannot sustain the democratic principle of equality; and democratic society cannot justify exploitation and inequality. How can there be fraternity and justice without equality? So also there is no trace of morality and ethics in the ideology of capitalism. Dr. Ambedkar therefore could never support capitalism in its shape and form.

1.5. Conversion to Buddhism

Ambedkar had started moving away from Hinduism in 1935 itself when he had publicly declared that he was not going to die as a Hindu. In 1936, he had attended the Sikh Missionary Conference. In 1936, Ambedkar also wrote and published Annihilation of Caste, his undelivered presidential address to the Jat-Pat-Todak Mandal Conference at Lahore. At the end of his written address, Ambedkar reiterated his resolve to give up Hinduism.

In 1944, during a visit to Madras, Ambedkar had spoken about "Rationalism in India—Revolution and Counter-Revolution". This theme had stayed in his mind. It found expression in his talk to Buddhist Association in 1951 and was to form the basis of a book named Revolution and Counter Revolution in Ancient India, which remained unpublished during his life. In May 1950, Ambedkar contributed an article "Buddha and the Future of his Religion" to the Mahabodhi Society Journal in which he expressed his preference for Buddhism. Ambedkar started writing his book The Buddha and His Dhamma on 14 October 1951. It was finally published in 1957 after his death. In the third week of December 1954, he started writing The Riddle in Hinduism, which, too, was published after his death.

Meanwhile on 24 May 1956, Ambedkar formally announced on the day of Buddha Jayanti that he would embrace Buddhism in October 1956. The actual conversion took place in Nagpur on 14 October 1956. Ambedkar embraced Buddhism along with his wife and lakhs of his supporters. After his conversion Ambedkar declared:

> By discarding my ancient religion which stood for inequality and oppression today I am reborn. I have no faith in the philosophy of

> incarnation: and it is wrong and mischievous to say that Buddha was an incarnation of Vishnu. I am no more a devotee of any Hindu god or goddess. I will not perform Shraddha. I will strictly follow the eight-fold path of Buddha. Buddhism is a true religion and I will lead a life guided by three principles of knowledge, right path and compassion.

On 15 November 1956, Ambedkar went to Katmandu to attend the World Buddhist Conference. He delivered a lecture on "Buddha and Marx". In less than two months after his conversion to Buddhism Ambedkar died at his Delhi residence on 6 December 1956.

1.6. Making of Indian Constitution

After the war Babasaheb was elected to the Constituent Assembly to decide the way jthat India—a country of millions of people—should be ruled. How should elections take place? What are the rights of the people? How are laws to be made? Such important matters had to be decided and laws had to be made. The Constitution answers all such questions and lays down rules.

When India became independent in August 1947, Babasaheb Ambedkar became First Law Minister of Independent India. The Constituent Assembly made him chairman of the committee appointed to draft the constitution for the world's largest democracy. All his study of law, economics, and politics made him the best qualified person for this task. A study of the Constitutions of many countries, a deep knowledge of law, a knowledge of the history of India and of Indian Society—all these were essential. In fact, he carried the whole burden alone. He alone could complete this huge task.

After completing the Draft Constitution, Babasaheb fell ill. At a nursing home in Bombay he met Dr. Sharda Kabir and married her in April 1948. On November 4, 1948 he presented the Draft Constitution to the Constituent Assembly, and on November 26, 1949 it was adopted in the name of the people of India. On that date he said: "I appeal to all Indians to be a nation by discarding castes, which have brought separation in social life and created jealousy and hatred."

1.7. Later Years

In 1950, he went to a Buddhist conference in Sri Lanka. On his return he spoke in Bombay at the Buddhist Temple. In order to end their hardships, people should embrace Buddhism. "I am going to devote the rest of my life to the revival and spread of Buddhism in India."

Babasaheb resigned from the Government in 1951. He felt that as an honest man he had no choice but to do so, because the reforms so badly needed had not been allowed to come into being.

For the next five years Babasaheb carried on a relentless fight against social evils and superstitions. On October 14, 1956 at Nagpur he embraced Buddhism. He led a huge gathering in a ceremony converting over half a million people to Buddhism. He knew that Buddhism was a true part of Indian history and that to revive it was to continue India's best tradition. 'Untouchability' is a product only of Hinduism. Only seven weeks later on December 6, 1956 Babasaheb died at his Delhi residence. His body was taken to Bombay. A two-mile long crowd formed the funeral procession. At Dadar cemetery that evening, eminent leaders paid their last respects to him. The pyre was lit according to Buddhist rites. Half a million people witnessed it. Thus ended the life of one of India's greatest sons. His was the task of awakening India's millions of excluded and oppressed to their human rights. He experienced their suffering and the cruelty shown to them. He overcame the obstacles to stand on an equal footing with the greatest men of his time. He played a vital role in forming modern India through its Constitution. His work and mission continue today—we must not rest until we see a truly democratic India of equal citizens living in peace together.

References

Bikshu Sangharakshita, *Ambedkar and Buddhism*, Windhorse Publications, Mar 1989.

Keer, Dhananjay, Dr. *Ambedkar Life and Mission*, Bombay, Popular Prakashan, 1995.

Robert Pen, *Evaluating Ambedkar's Social Philosophy in the Context of Casteism in India, SDB.* 63-70, 1995.

Zelliot, Eleanor, *Dr. Ambedkar and the Mahar Movement' Ph.D. Dissertation*, University of Pennsylvania, 1969.

2

Dalit Identity in Ambedkar Era

The Indian caste system describes the social stratification and social restrictions in the Indian subcontinent, in which social classes are defined by thousands of endogamous hereditary groups, often termed as jtis or castes. Within a jti, there exist exogamous groups known as gotras, the lineage or clan of an individual, although in a handful of sub-castes like Shakadvipi, endogamy within a gotra is permitted and alternative mechanisms of restricting endogamy are used (e.g. banning endogamy within a surname). However, none of the Hindu scriptures endorse caste-based discrimination.

Although generally identified with Hinduism, the caste system was also observed among followers of other religions in the Indian subcontinent, including some groups of Muslims and Christians. The Indian Constitution has outlawed caste-based discrimination, in keeping with the socialist, secular, democratic principles that founded the nation. Caste barriers have mostly broken down in large cities, though they persist in rural areas of the country, where 72% of India's population resides. Nevertheless, the caste system, in various forms, continues to survive in modern India strengthened by a combination of social perceptions and divisive politics

According to the ancient Hindu scriptures, there are four "varnas". The Bhagavad Gita says varnas are decided based on Guna and Karma. Manusmriti and some other shastras mention four varnas: the Brahmins (teachers, scholars and priests), the Kshatriyas (kings and warriors), the Vaishyas (agriculturists and traders), and Shudras (artisans, service providers).

This theoretical system postulated Varna categories as ideals and explained away the reality of thousands of endogamous Jtis actually prevailing in the country as being the result of historical mixing among the "pure" Varnas - Varna Sankara. All those, including foreigners, tribals and nomads, who did not subscribe to the norms of the Hindu society were contagious and untouchables. Another group excluded from the main society was called Parjanya or Antyaja. This group of former "untouchables" Dalits) i.e. downtrodden, was considered either the lower section of Shudras or outside the Varna system altogether. Passages from scriptures such as Manusmriti indicate that the varna system was originally non-hereditary.

Several critics of Hinduism state that the caste system is rooted in the varna system mentioned in the ancient Hindu scriptures. However, many groups, such as ISKCON, consider the modern Indian caste system and the varna system as two distinct concepts. Many European administrators from the colonial era incorrectly regarded the Manusmriti as the "law book" of all the Hindus, and thus concluded that the caste system is a part of Hinduism, an assertion that is now rejected by most scholars, who state that it is a social practice, not a religious belief.. Manusmriti, was in any case a work of reference for the Brahmins of north India, especially Bengal and was largely unknown in southern India.

Although many Hindu scriptures contain passages that can be interpreted to sanction the caste system, they also contain indications that the caste system is not an essential part of Hinduism. The Vedas placed no importance on the caste system, mentioning caste only once (in the Purush Sukta) out of tens of thousands of verses. Most vedic scholars believe even this to be a subsequent and artificial insertion. In fact, none other than B. R. Ambedkar concluded after a thorough study that this is a much later interpolation and gave strong scholarly evidence to support his conclusion. In the Vedic period, there was no prohibition against anyone, including the Shudras listening to the Vedas or participating in any religious rite.

In Early Evidence for Caste in South India, George L. Hart stated that "the earliest Tamil texts show the existence of what seems definitely to be caste, but which antedates the Brahmins and the Hindu orthodoxy". He believes that the origins of the caste system can be seen in the "belief system that developed with the agricultural civilization", and was later profoundly influenced by "the Brahmins and the Brahmanical religion". These early Tamil texts also outline the concept of equality. Saint Valluvar has stated "pirapokkum ella uyirkkum", which means "all are equal at birth". Likewise, Saint Auvaiyaar has stated that there are only two castes in the world: those who contribute negatively and those who contribute positively. From these, it can be inferred that the caste system is more of a socio-economic class system.

Traditionally, although the political power lay with the Kshatriyas, historians portrayed that the Brahmins as custodians and interpreters of Dharma enjoyed much prestige and many advantages.

Fa Hien, a Buddhist pilgrim from China, visited India around 400 AD. "Only the lot of the Chandals he found unenviable; outcastes by reason of their degrading work as disposers of dead, they were universally shunned... But no other section of the population were notably disadvantaged, no other caste distinctions attracted comment from the Chinese pilgrim, and no oppressive caste 'system' drew forth his surprised censure.". In this period kings of Sudra and Brahmin origin were as common as those of Kshatriya varna and caste system was not wholly prohibitive and repressive.

The castes did not constitute a rigid description of the occupation or the social status of a group. Since British society was divided by class, the British attempted to equate the Indian caste system to their own social class system. They saw caste as an indicator of occupation, social standing, and intellectual ability. Intentionally or unintentionally, the caste system became more rigid during the British Raj, when the British started to enumerate castes during the ten year census and codified the system under their rule.

The Harijans, or the people outside the caste system, had the lowest social status. The Harijans, earlier referred to as "untouchables" by some, worked in what were seen as unhealthy, unpleasant or polluting jobs. In the past, the Harijans suffered from social segregation and restrictions, in addition to extreme poverty. They were not allowed temple worship with others, nor water from the same sources. Persons of higher castes would not interact with them. If somehow a member of a higher caste came into physical or social contact with an untouchable, the member of the higher caste was defiled, and had to bathe thoroughly to purge him or herself of the impurity. Social discrimination developed even among the Harijans. Sub-castes among Harijans, like dhobi, nai etc., would not interact with lower-order Bhangis, who were described as "outcasts even among outcastes".

Sociologists have commented on the historical advantages offered by a rigid social structure, such as the caste system, and its lack of usefulness in the modern world. Historically, the caste system offered several advantages to the population of the Indian subcontinent. While Caste is nowadays seen by instances that render it anachronistic, in its original form, the caste system served as an important instrument of order in a society where mutual consent rather than compulsion ruled; where the ritual rights as well as the economic obligations of members of one caste or sub-caste were strictly circumscribed in relation to those of any other caste or sub-caste; where one was born into one's caste and retained one's station in society for life; where merit was inherited, where equality existed within the caste, but inter-caste relations were unequal and hierarchical. A well-defined system of mutual interdependence through a division of labour created security within a community. In addition, the division of labour on the basis of ethnicity allowed immigrants and foreigners to quickly integrate into their own caste niches. The caste system played an influential role in shaping economic activities. The caste system functioned much like medieval European guilds, ensuring the division of labour, providing for the training of apprentices and, in some cases, allowing manufacturers to achieve narrow specialisation. For instance, in certain regions, producing each variety of cloth was the speciality of a particular sub-caste. Also, philosophers argue that the majority of people would be comfortable in stratified endogamous groups, and have been in ancient times.

2.1. Dalitisation

When the old Indian agrarian production became a little more productive the division of labour was established as basic structure of the society; but in India the productivity remained on a low level during centuries so that the new non-productive jatis had to keep down the costs of the material production and the necessary services; they needed cheapest labour. Yet, they achieved that aim by creating totally oppressed jatis which they could extensively exploit. Through such a Dalitisation the varna jatis established the most cost-saving system of exploitation at all—even more cost-saving than slavery. The slave-holder had to buy and to maintain his slave and couldn't send him away just as he wished—even if the slave became unable to work. The varna jatis could deal with the Dalits according to their particular interests and use them according to demand—without any responsibility. Not being even property of the varna exploiters the outlawed people were transformed through the process of Dalitisation from god-like human souls into cheap and downtrodden working bodies—unable to get themselves out of their cruel situation during centuries. The Dalitisation and even the creation of the varna system was a long lasting more or less uncontrolled social process of complex social interactions. Deriving it from a book or an ideology or religion is an absolutely naive view of real history. Such an interpretation is produced by the old brahmanical belief in the power of thought, spoken and written words and mantras.

The Dalitisation got its shakti from the real unfathomable social process wallowing through the history and determining the historical chances of the people. The brahmanas and even Manu only tried to codify, to explain and to justify a found system that the social process had produced long time ago.

In India that reversion would have happened earlier if the invaders and colonialists hadn't have artificially maintained the antiquated Dalitisation. Under the new social conditions ultimately dissolving the traditional system of exploitation there isn't any need of the Dalit system—anymore. Nevertheless, although officially propagating the abolition of the 'caste'-system the so-called Savarnas try to maintain the out-dated varna system even to-day. The ongoing process of nationalisation of the Indian society which is intensively promoted by the Hindutvavadis successfully starts to completely eradicate that fossil system from Indian society.

The Dalits are becoming increasingly aware of their lack of rights in the last decades and making the betterment of their social conditions a central point of Indian policy. So they are starting to play an important active and passive role in the Indian society. Not least, because of their millions of votes they have become a powerful vote bank. All political parties in India are highly interested nowadays in having their share of that cake. Even the Dalits of the Neo Buddhist Religion are getting some ideological and political influence in India to-day. Yet, within the Indian Buddhist minority they have become the most powerful group—not only numerically constituting the majority of the Indian Buddhists but also being politically very active, well trained and aggressive.

These Neo Buddhists go back to the so-called 'Father of the Indian Constitution' Dr Bhimrao Ramji Sakpal, alias Ambedkar (1891-1956): therefore, they are called Ambedkarites.—Ambedkar belonged to the Mahar jati, which is one of the higher ranking jatis of the Untouchables in Maharashtra. Unlike the mass of his jati associates Sakpal succeeded with the help of his brahmanical school teacher in making an academic career. His brahmanical guru lent him even his own brahmanical name Ambedkar. By means of a scholarship from the Maharaja of Baroda Ambedkar could attain the degree of a Bachelor of Arts from Bombay university in 1912. A state scholarship of the principality of Baroda permitted him to study afterwards at Columbia university in New York from where he graduated as a Master of Arts.

A scholarship granted by the Maharaja of Kolhapur enabled him to study law at London so that he could take a degree as a Barrister-at-Law and a doctorate in economics. He has lived again in Bombay since 1923 launching into a very intensive activity as an attorney and teacher. However, he didn't make a career for himself, but became completely committed to the interests of the Untouchables: by means of upbringing, agitation and organisation of the Dalits. That commitment made him the recognised leader of the Indian Untouchables and brought him the highest public offices of the colonial and free India. He became a member of the British Viceroy's Council, the chairperson of the constitution committee and a minister of justice of the first free Government of India.

Ambedkar has mostly been known as a political leader of the Untouchables up to 1950. He set up three political parties to advocate the interest of the Untouchables in the public. His latest foundation, the Republican Party, is still active in Mahahrashtra, mainly as a communal party of the Mahars—however allied with the Congress party.

Politically set against the Indian National Congress of Mohandas Karamchand Gandhi (1869-1948) and Jawaharlal Nehru (1889-1964) and compared to the Muslim league of Mohammed Ali Jinnah (1976-1948), the founder of the Indo-Islamic state of Pakistan, unsuccessful, Ambedkar put in order to help his jati associates more effectively on the religious card.

Concerning the religious background of Ambedkar we have to take notice that his family belonged to the Kabir Panth. This Bhakti religion didn't acknowledge any jati and varna boundaries in religious, not yet in practical respect, and worshipped the Nirguna Rama. The origin from a Ram Bhakti Hinduism strongly denying the ruling varna system by religion and interpreting the Holy in the Nirguna way determined his further religious and political development.

The confrontation of his Untouchable jati with the Savarnas which caused also him the usual humiliations was nevertheless more lenient for him. It's true, the support of progressive high jati Hindus made him take an almost unprecedented social rise. However, as a leader of the Mahar community and of the other Untouchables he used his entire intellectual ability, ideological power and political influence for their interests and aspirations which he formulated programmatically, legitimised religiously and realised politically.

Seeing clear-sightedly that in the traditional Indian context the religious motivation is the most important issue for the liberation fight even of the Indian Dalits Ambedkar intensively looked out a useful socio-religious ideology. The Kabir Panth, the traditional religion of his family, did not come into consideration since it represented only a small frozen quietistic community without any political interest and therefore for a modern mass liberation fight equipped not at all.

First, he planned to convert together with his jati associates to Sikhism. The then vice president of the Golden Temple Managing Committee in Amritsar, Sardar Dalip Singh Doabria, requested him for this purpose pointing out to the allegedly egalitarian character of the Sikh religion. That primary option may have stemmed from the fact, that the founder of Ambedkars family religion, Kabir, may have been initially been a Sikh. The essential reason to put Sikhism into consideration was the cultural one: the religion of Guru Nanak to the Hindu Culture.

However, Ambedkar protruded more and more with pro-Buddhist statements since India had become independent; he required his political and social supporters, particularly his jati associates, to start celebrating Buddha Jayanti, Buddha's Birthday, every year. Under the title 'The Buddha and the Future of His Religion' he published in the Maha Bodhi Journal a programmatic article in the same year. He wrote, that Buddhism is the only religion that suits for the world, emphasising 'reason, morality, liberty, equality and fraternity'.

Ambedkar established a new Buddhist dharma. Picking up the ideals of the French Revolution he created a religious-bourgeois social ideology denying the Marxist ideology and the egalitarian neo casteism of M. K. Gandhi. His turn to such a social bourgeois Buddhism—never found in India and elsewhere before—finally led to his personal religious conversion: Ambedkar took in Nagpur (Madhya Pradesh) diksha from the eldest Buddhist monk of India, U Chandramani Mahastavir, at the 14th of October 1956, some weeks before his death in December, in this way joining Buddhism ritually and officially.

The convert immediately founded the Bharatiya Bauddha Mahasabha ('Indian Buddhist Union'), seemingly imitating the Hindu Mahasabha. Together with Ambedkar some hundred thousand followers mostly Mahars converted to that Ambedkariten Neo Buddhism. Because of this mass conversion the number of the Indian Buddhists increased from 1956 to 1951 up to 3 250 000 members. No doubt, by means of the Ambedkar movement the Indian Buddhism took an enormous upswing. Since those times uncountable Buddhist events have been performed and new Buddhist institutions, associations and monasteries were established at many places. The Neo Buddhism inspired also the small minority of traditional Indo-Buddhism mostly existing in the Himalayan areas.

That mass conversion was certainly a big success for the increase of Buddhism in India, nevertheless the other side of the coin consisted in the split of the Dalit masses which were mostly Hindus and not interested to leave their traditional religions and to join the new Buddhist community. Ambedkar's attacks on the Savarna Hinduism had biographically seen their first origin—as above suggested—in Kabir's Avarna Hinduism.

To fight that Savarna Hinduism which discriminated against the Untouchables Ambedkar as a son of a Kabirite family didn't need any radical religious conversion. Such a fight has been and is particularly today a possibility within Hinduism itself. Ambedkar's turn to Buddhism wasn't so much a consequence of the non-political attitude of his original religion but far more because of substantial political reasons.

In his view the National Indian Congress under the leadership of M. K. Gandhi was incapable and too reluctant to change the living conditions of the Untouchables. He saw that Gandhi's political movement was ready to give the Muslims a lot of advantages but refused to concede the same to the Hindu Untouchables. The Hindu modernists, the so-called Hindutvavadis, absolutely committed to a united, jati and varna free Hindu nation, completely agreed with Ambedkar on this issue. Yet, their political influence was still very small in those times so that Ambedkar didn't ask them for support.

The actual political leadership of the Hindu masses was controlled by the open and hidden Savarna jatis of all Indian religions including Christians and Muslims. Their very successful organisation was the already mentioned Indian National Congress led by a Gujurati Vaishya Bania, M. K. Gandhi, and a Kashmiri brahmin, Jawaharlal Nehru. The Indian National Congress represented above all the great land owners and agriculturists who were mostly Savarnas and who were not naturally interested to grant any human and social rights to the Dalits. In addition, the ruling socio-economic class successfully prevented with the aid of the Indian National Congress the national upbringing, so that the lower jatis couldn't get any higher professional qualification to escape poverty nor develop a consciousness of emancipation to eradicate their deep implanted inferiority complex.

The ruling class of free India also refused the introduction of a general compulsory military service fearing the military and intellectual arming of the masses. This service could have made an important contribution to the national education particularly to the Dalits and would have reduced the one-sided bondage of the military on the higher jatis.

At last, the compulsory military service would have reinforced the unity of India. All those progressive developments the ruling class didn't and don't want till today; to maintain it's socio-economic power it used and uses the splitting of the Indian masses into minorities, castes and religions imitating successfully the fundamental strategy of the British raj: ruling by dividing. Therefore, M. K. Gandhi couldn't never initiate any revolutionary crusade against the Savarnas to free the Untouchables from the retching grip of their oppressors. Moreover, Gandhi didn't just refuse the jati system as such but merely the mental discrimination against single jatis, primarily against the Untouchables. In spite of Gandhi's Harijan ideology and in spite of a lot of anti-caste-discrimination laws, the influence of the jati system in general and of the Savarnas in particular, has increased more and more during the decades of the Nehru dynasty.

Although Ambedkar identified the Savarna Hinduism as the most powerful enemy of the Untouchables yet he kept in a decided manner a firm hold on the Indo-genous dharma which he and the Hindutvadis call 'Hindu Culture'. Therefore, Islam and Christianity were as serious alternatives out of question. Indeed, he compared himself with that Moses, "who liberated his people from slavery" and highly respected Jesus Christ; but he was repelled by the Christians because they "never fought for the removal of social injustice" and practised themselves in southern India the Savarna system.

Ambedkar especially took exception to the fact that those Untouchables who converted to Christianity became "selfish and self-centred": "They don't care a snap of their finger what becomes of their former caste associates so long user system they and their families, or they and a little group who have become Christians, get ahead". The Christian converts even denied their jati associates, they were contemptible traitors of their caste association. Therefore, he didn't want any increase of the number of such Christians. In addition, the increase of Christians would only reinforce the power of the British colonialism. Moreover, Christianity might be only ninety percent a copy of Buddhism.

Ambedkar's choice finally fell for three reasons to Buddhism. He said: "I prefer Buddhism because it gives three principles in combination which no other religion does. Buddhism teaches Prajna (understanding against superstition and supernaturalism), Karuna (love), and Samata (equality). This is what man wants for a good and happy life ". That picture of Buddhism is nothing else than an idealising construction for political reasons, devoid of any historical and actual evidence.

The primary motive of Ambedkar's conversion was not so much of religious but of social and political nature. His main intention consisted in developing the worldly emancipation of the Untouchables. No wonder that a half million of his jati associates, the Mahars, accepted to follow him. Anyway, a change of religion by a caste and to follow a caste leader into an other religion is a very typical phenomenon within the Indian caste system. These masses mostly hadn't any relation to Buddhism before their conversion and followed Ambedkar for reasons of personal loyalty only. In such a way, a convert explained: "We became Buddhists because Dr. Ambedkar told us so". An other one said: "I got thinking about economic and social betterment and then I just followed Ambedkar to Buddhism". A third one confessed: "I had no other incentive but blind love for Ambedkar and the people. This is true for many".

Ambedkar's Buddhism obviously appears to be "a religion of liberation of the oppressed in society". On the one hand, through this definition Ambedkar's Neo Buddhism became the strongest rival of Christian and Muslim social ideologies and on the other hand, the sharpest opponent of the Savarnas. The Savarnas prevented very successfully with the help of the Indian National Congress the emancipation of all the Dalits.

Because of the numerical dominance of Hindus within the Indian Savarna community Ambedkar developed an abstract anti-Hinduism blaming the Hinduism as such for the delusion of untouchability. Therefore, the anti-Hindu turn stems from the fact that the ruling class of India under the political leadership of the Indian National Congress suppressed the emancipatory power of the Hindus and abused the Hindu tradition for the tacit justification of the continued Savarna practise in spite of their contrary political declarations.

Facing the numerical reality that the vast majority of the Untouchables are also Hindu, Ambedkar had to propagate religious conversion. The Dalits were told to become Buddhists and leave Hinduism if they want to be worldly liberated. That undifferentiated anti-Hinduism must necessarily fail. It isolates the Neo Buddhism from the Hindu Dalits and let it become in the long run a cast religion:

predominantly as cast religion of the Mahars. Such developments happened in the Indian religious history very often. However, that self-isolation would be only a repetition of the old caste models: both the religion as well as other cultural elements are limited to one's own caste. The restriction to the caste horizon is currently secured by an aggression Ambedkar mobilised against the Hinduism in general.

The Ambedkarites represent in the contemporary India the strongest Buddhist power. Even if the traditional Indian Buddhists separate themselves from them, in such a way, they increasingly emboss the picture of Buddhism in the eyes of the Hindus, of the Muslims and Christians: as a religion destroying relationships, preaching intolerance and using religion for political purposes. In spite of that extreme anti-Hindu propaganda the modernist Hindus don't condemn the mass conversion of Hindu Untouchables to Buddhism.

The Hindutvavadis understand Buddhism as a part of the Hindu dharma. Such a conversion is seen only as a change within the Hindu fold. Therefore, the Hindus accept a such conversion earlier than the mass conversions to Christianity and Islam. The two other religions are unacceptable because they don't belong to the dharma. Ambedkar also joined the Indian Buddhism, because of its actual non-existence. By this he could solve three difficult problems:

1. Under any circumstances didn't Ambedkar want to separate his movement from the Indo-genous dharma; therefore, his reason for choosing Buddhism as religious alternative was his strong attachment to the Hindu Culture.
2. Since there didn't actually exist any ritually pure Buddhist castes in India anymore, in case of conversion Ambedkar didn't have to reckon on any caste conflict with Buddhist Savarnas. Therefore, in Sri Lanka Ambedkar's Buddhisation of the Singhalese Dalits would have been made fail by the Buddhist Goyigama jatis.
3. Although Ambedkar interpreted Buddhism in a very unusual way he hadn't even to fear any religious conflict since a powerful Buddhist orthodoxy didn't exist in India. It seems as if the old Indian dharma uses Ambedkar's movement as a historical possibility of the dharmic re-integration of the Untouchables, which was prevented by the very anti-modern caste system.

Ambedkar's decision to convert to the Buddhist wing of the Indo-genous or Hindu dharma and his decisive rejection of any religion of non-Indian origin on one side, and the absence of any remarkable mass conversion to Islam or Christianity since his conversion on the other side is a success of the Indian dharma nobody was expecting before. The Christian and Muslim ideologists, missionaries and extremists were believed the dharma religions would vanish and the Hindu people convert to their adharmic faiths. Ambedkar has obviously rendered the Hindu Culture great service stopping the downfall of the dharma in India in general and the advance of Communism, Christianity and Islam within the Dalit fold in particular.

The anti-Hindu Ambedkarism simply shows the overwhelming intellectual power of the Indian dharma tradition making dialectical progress with his evolution through the cunning of the dharmic reason. Ambedkar knew that his dharmic option for the Sikhism and later on for Buddhism and against Islam and Christianity was completely in accordance with the Hindutvavadis placing greater importance to the affiliation to the Hindu Culture in general than to the affiliation to a particular traditional or new Hindu sect.

In his fight to liberate the Dalits Ambedkar never left the Hindu Culture option. Even when Ambedkar was reflecting the possibility to join Sikhism he made a clear statement that only a religion of the Hindu Culture could be an alternative for the depressed castes: "Looking at these alternative faiths purely from the standpoint of Hindus, which is the best—Islam Christianity or Sikhism? Obviously, Sikhism is the best."

By this choice they have not to leave the Hindu Culture: "If the Depressed Classes join Islam or Christianity, they not only go out of Hindu religion, but they also go out of Hindu Culture. On the other hand, if they become Sikhs they remain within Hindu culture". He ironically doubt, Ambedkar's historic choice was a clear vote for the Hindu Culture. In spite of vehement attacks on the Savarna Hinduism he never planned to eradicate the Indo-genous or—using Ambedkar's and the Hindutvavadis' term—Hindu Culture.

The basic value of the Hindutvavadis as mentioned above is the maintenance of Hindu Culture in an united Hindu nation; in their opinion is the most important factor weakening the Hindu Culture the creation of the caste system. Therefore, it's quite logical that the destruction of the caste system and the eradication of the untouchability are fundamental aims of the Hindutvavadis.

Therefore, Hindu nationalism is nothing else than the political will to strengthen the Indian nation by unification; but the unity can only be reached through a casteless society of equal citizens. That fundamental interest of the Hindutva movement makes clear that in spite of some important differences there is nevertheless an basic ideological convergence between Ambedkar and Hindutva: the maintenance of Hindu Culture.—Ambedkar wanted the destruction of the caste system by caste-motivated reasons, the Hindutva wants the same by national ones.

Due to this common interest it is no wonder that "Ambedkar had intimate relations with the Hindutvawadis" of the Hindu Mahasabha and its president V. D. Savarkar. Both ones were joined together in the decisive will to extinguish untouchability from the Hindu society. The judgement of the Hindutva movement on the untouchability was classically formulated by Savarkar as follows: "This system of untouchability is unwarrantable and suicidal, hence only for the sake of humanity we the Hindus should eradicate it". With the official of the Hindu Mahasabha, Munje, Ambedkar exchanged extensively letters; once he asked him concerning his possible conversion for advice.

Later on he criticised Savarkar for not doing enough to defend the Hindu interests in face of the British-Muslim conspiracy! During the second world war, however, both ones played the military card: "Savakar blessed Ambedkar's programme of militarisation. He expressed confidence that under the able leadership of Ambedkar the Mahar brethren would exhibit their military merits and strengthen the 'collective power' with their militancy". That the chief of the Hindu Mahasabha appreciated the military arming of the Untouchables, shows very clearly about the narrow kinship between Ambedkar and Hindutva.

If the Hindutva would have been the enemy of the Dalits how could the leader of an radical Hindu organisation accept the military power of the Untouchables? That the chief of the Hindu Mahasabha the military arming of Untouchables greeted, no doubt, shows clearest the narrow kinship between Ambedkar and Hindutva. Over and above that Savarkar declared in order to stop the Pan-Islamism conjured by Mohammed Ali Jinnah, such an alliance "would be retaliated by hatching pan-Hindu-Buddhism." The "Hindu-Bouddh unity from Jamnu to Japan" would put an end to the machinations of Jinnah.

There is no doubt, Buddhism was by the Hindutva seen as is an integral part of Hindu Culture from the very beginning. In the frame of this understanding of the Bauddha dharma as part of the more general Hindu dharma the conversion of Ambedkar was nothing else than a change of an apartment within the same house. Therefore, it's not surprising that Ambedkar writing the Indian constitution co-operated narrowly with the Hindu Mahasabha. Together with the Hindutvavadis he fully shared the idea of 'Hindu nationalism'; just this ideology was his essential motive not convert to Islam and Christianity: "Conversion to Islam or Christianity will denationalise the Depressed Classes".

Ambedkar's criterion of Indian nationalism didn't consist in the identification with the abstract Indian Nation but with the Indo-genous dharma; therefore he excluded Christians and Muslim from but included Hindus and other dharma people into the Indian Nation. Under any circumstances the Untouchables shouldn't leave the Indian dharmic nation but become her fully acknowledged members.

To surmount the traditional social isolation of the Untouchables in India Ambedkar realised sharp-sightedly that this was possible only by the integration of the Dalits into the Hindu fold, into the majoritarian dharma society; otherwise the converted Dalits would give up or loose the solidarity of all the other Hindu Dalit castes. Conversion to adharmic communities has made the Dalits fully helpless victims of their oppressors inside and outside their new community.

Beyond that: conversion to adharmic communities weakened the possible power of the Dalit community as a whole and was therefore nothing else than a disastrous betrayal of the solidarity of the Untouchables. Logically, the dharma nationalism was an essential item for the emancipation of the Untouchables. Separating the Untouchables from the Indo-genous dharma didn't mean nothing else than their denationalisation. The Untouchables shouldn't under any circumstances been alienated form the other parts of the Indian dharma society. It's obvious: Ambedkar believed in the emancipate power of the Indo-genous dharma for the Dalits: neither Christianity nor Islam could give the Dalits the chance to become free. Therefore it was very clear that Ambedkar didn't want to strengthen Muslims or Christians although they always disseminated to be egalitarian and casteless religious communities !

Although Ambedkar knew that all these communities were caste ridden nevertheless his basic argument against them didn't consist so much of their casteistic reality but in their adharmic character! Even if they would have been casteless he wouldn't have accepted a conversion to them. The argument of the denationalisation stated here reveals that Ambedkar took the Indian Muslims and also the Indian Christians as communities, that didn't belong to the country, to the nation, reveals him as a very exclusive and extremist Indo-genous nationalist.

After having excommunicated Christians and Muslims from the Indian nation, the question arises: Who, then, did according to Ambedkar belong to that Indian dharmic nation? The Hindus, the Sikhs and the Buddhist, those people only who follow the Indo-genous dharma, called by the Hindutvavadis Hindu dharma. However, the absolute dominance of the Indo-genous dharma went in the thinking of Ambedkar even further. Even the caste aspirations have to be subordinated to the dharma! He calculates: "On the other hand, if they embrace Sikhism, they will not only not harm the destiny of the country but they will help the destiny of the country."

Destiny, however, means dharma, the Indian dharma, which besides Sikhs and Buddhists in spite of sharp criticism also the Hindus also belong to. The Untouchables aren't allowed to damage that dharma—therefore only a religious change within "the destiny of the country" comes into consideration. Only following the Indo-genous dharma, the Dalits can build a more advanced India. Ambedkar then appeals to the non-Muslim, the actual Hindu nation: It might be exactly the same way in interest of India, that the Untouchables, if they must change their belief, the Sikhism accept.

Therefore, the common nation of the Hindus, the Buddhists and Sikhs, the Indo-genous religious communities, must have an interest next to it, that the Untouchables don't desert to the Christians who were collaborating with colonial rulers and the Muslims who are only interested in their communal domination. The exclusion of the two exogenous religious communities, which are denationalised, and therefore doesn't belong to the nation shows very clearly, that Ambedkar's nationalism wasn't based on racial, caste or religious but on cultural criteria, on the Indo-genous culture or the dharma arising from the soil of India—which as we said above the Hindutvavadis call 'Hindu dharma' or 'Hindu Culture'.

Regarding the Indo-genous culture as the highest value and connecting the liberation of the Dalits with the dharma he prevented the massive emigration of the Untouchables from the Indo-genousn culture. Indeed, it isn't wrong to say that Ambedkar kept the Hindu Dalits from leaving the Indo-genous dharma by becoming adharmic Christians or Muslim; but he did more, no less: he even tied ideologically the Dalits to the dharma—paying as price the justified denunciation of the Savarna Hindus who oppressed the karuna ethics of the Hindu dharma. As rulers the Savarnas forced the varna Hindus into the discrimination of the Dalits.

Within the traditional Indo-genous religious communities there was actually hardly any varna caste which could escape that prejudice. The Hindutvavadis being no caste but a voluntary organisation and only a small group lacked any political importance in those times.—So, adopting the Buddhism as a new caste religion of the Mahar Untouchables Ambedkar found a brilliant compromise. Buddhism almost absent in India and therefore not controlled by Savarnas belonged nevertheless to the dharma.

Converting to that religion one would be liberated from the ideological dominance of the Savarnas and got hold of the dharma. Considering the Savarnas' ideology that the Dalits don't belong to the dharma society Ambedkar succeeded in integrating the Untouchables into the dharma society for the first time. His identity wasn't based on religion, jati, varna or language but on the Indo-genous culture. Therefore, his Neo Buddhism only seems to have been anti-Hindu. It was anti-Savarna. Rather, Ambedkar started a social movement, which will most effectively get rid of the socially grounded deformation of the dharma in future. Reason is that his movement basically agrees with the Hindutvavadis to maintain the Indo-genous culture, the dharma, and to reach this aim through a social revolution, that is the eradication of untouchability and the whole caste system. That objective convergence of the Dalit and Hindutva interests will inevitably bring together both movements. Therefore, the newly made political coalitions between the BJP and Dalit parties are very logical; they will continue even if the Dalit leaders influenced by the Congress ideology are very inconsistent in political affairs. Nevertheless, the egalisation of the Indian and particularly the Hindu society propagated by the Hindutvavadis and pre-formulated in Swami Vivekananda's socio-political programme of Brahma-nisation including all castes and people is backed by the Dalit movement.

2.2. Identity Formation

Dalits are an earth dependent eco people. That there is a story of violence against this essential identity of the Dalits is undeniable. However, our point of departure is not the depressing story of what Brahminism has done to them over the past millennia. We do not want to become once again a victim of Brahminic oppression and subsequently help its establishment by keeping Brahminism in our focus. The dominant religions have certain characteristics and certain strategies vis-à-vis the indigenous people.

i) They consider themselves as revealed and their scriptures are supposedly written under divine inspiration. The revelation supposedly comes from god who is a metaphysical being.

ii) Each religion considers itself as superior to the others by virtue of the power of their god manifested through deeds of valour. These manifestations are usually destruction of nature, of innocent people, conquest of territories and subjugation of nations.

iii) Each of these religions have developed discourses of purity and impurity by which they have oppressed people of other religions.

iv) The dominant religions have established a bipolairty of Moksha (heaven) and Naraka (hell) and have brought insurmountable misery to the people. The ultimate goal of human existence on earth is heaven. Human existence is only a temporary phase, a pilgrimage, a necessary evil etc. All religions have promised heaven to the people and have deprived them of their earthly means of existence thus causing an existential dilemma.

v) The dominant religions have created a dichotomy between the soul and body. While body is physical the soul is spiritual. What belongs to the physical realm is temporary and what belongs to the spiritual realm is eternal. Whatever belongs to the body is essentially evil and therefore, human beings should strive to camouflage their existence with spiritual aspects.

According to the dominant religions the zenith of human existence is the attainment of heaven. Man in his physical existence is essentially evil and must purify himself during this life on earth so as to reach heaven which only the pure can attain. This is salvation, that the soul is cleansed of all impurities. Each religion has the ingredients of what can be constructed as the patented prescription for this soul cleansing. Based on such assumed identity will be the subjugation of the people to a multitude of normative standards and prescriptions dogmatically and ritually imposed on the people, of course with a host of promises of rewards and threats of punishment. The punch line is the eternity that is attached to these promises and punishments.

The common consequences are there for all to see. It is said of the Christians that they entered Africa with the Bible and the natives had only their land. After the natives became Christians through the shenanigans of the Christian powers the black Africans had Bible in their hand and the White Christians had the land of the natives in their hands. "You came to our country with Bible in your hand when we had our land in our hands. Now we have your Bible in our hands and you have our land in your hands". Such a political transformation came about by first diluting and later transforming the cultural identities of the natives. In country after country the natives became slaves of the invading Christians whose missionaries were sent as a strategy for 'softening' the rugged natives into submission.

The arrival of the Aryans into India was an unprecedented assault on the identity of the people of India as was the later arrival of Christians and Muslims. Thence started a long history ascribed identity for the Dalits. Brahminism also evolved through its discursive practices, dogmatization and ritualisation a technology for the absorption of the ascription so that establishment of a hegemony became much easier than anticipated. The discursive practices of Brahminism were aimed at the objugation of the indigenous people, especially the Dalits through inexplicable ascription. Ascription of base characteristics to the Dalits were made through religious discourses so that acceptance of such ascription would become easy both by the dominant caste and the Dalits themselves. Such communicative incompetence is continued and sustained till today. "When the Aryan and non-Aryan religions, one refined and the other vulgar, the one good and the other base, met there was the tendency for the bad to beat the good out of circulation." The chain of hegemonisation moved stealthily beyond social relations and expanded to alienation of the people from their material resources and appropriation of these resources by the dominant caste groups.

A necessary prelude to establish and enjoy a dominant power relation in the caste society was the creation of a new cultural identity to a people or transforming their existing identity to suit their needs. One African Bishop beautifully summed up the consequence of such transformation in identity by saying that 'when the whites came to our land with Bible in their hand we had our land in our hands. Now, the whites have our land in their hands and we have their Bible in our hands'. Brahminism had done this millennia ago to the Dalits, the natives of this land.

Till Babasaheb came on the stage Dalits by and large lived with two types of identities. One was ascribed identity and the other was assumed identity. Examples of characteristics ascribed to the Dalits that ultimately went to establish an identity which was not theirs abound in the Vedas and the two epics. The contextualisation of an ascribed identity to the Dalits cannot be ignored. While ascribing low and mean characters to the Dalits Brahminism contextualised its mean efforts by simultaneously ascribing qualities of superiority to itself.

1) The Brahmana caste is sprung from the gods: the Shudras from the Asuras.
2) The Shudra has sprung from non-existence.
3) The Shudra is a servant of another (and cannot be anything else.
4) A Shudra and an outcaste are burial ground
5) The wicked Shudra race is manifestly a burial ground.

6) One may know that bearing grudges, envy, speaking untruths, speaking evil of Brahmins, backbiting and cruelty are the characteristics of a Shudra.
7) Even if freed by his master, the Shudra is not released from servitude; for this is innate in him; who then can take it from him.
8) Let the Brahmin's name be auspicious, a Kshatriya's full of power, let a Vaishya's mean wealth, a Shudra's however be contemptible.
9) A once-born man who insults members of a twice-born caste with gross invectives, shall have his tongue cut off; for he is of low origin.

The Shudra is impure. He is not to be respected. The life of a Shudra is of no value.

Brahminism has ascribed impurity to the Dalits because of beef eating though this caste indulged in beef eating till the time of a vigorous conflict between Brahminism and Buddhism.

Till then meat eating had nothing to do with purity. The moment hegemonic discourses started beef eating became impure. Brahminism did not allow the Dalits to have any other food.

Brahminism did not allow the Dalits to have education in an attempt to keep them in eternal darkness of ignorance. Once it succeeded in its attempt it ascribed lack of intelligence to the Dalits. It ascribed an identity of savagery to the Dalits through the images of Rakshasas propagated through the epics.

The centrality of ascription on Dalits is around an uncivilized but carefully crafted discourse of Impurity, low origin, servitude, lack of civilization etc. It does not need any big explanation that this has led to the establishment of an identity through its continuous battering of the dalit mind. Such a battering has taken place along with a total denial of educational opportunities to the Dalits so that they may not develop the capacity to develop a counter discourse. Such ascription were simultaneously coupled with ascription of superiority to the dominant castes.

Based on the ascription Brahminism also went about developing and establishing normative order and normative prescriptions purported at objugating the Dalits and make them actively assume the ascribed identity. Ascription have a double effect:

i) They develop and establish societal attitudes about dominant castes which establish an identity and position of superiority. They also establish attitudes about other castes which promulgates an identity and position of inferiority, subservience and inhumanity.

ii) Ascription lead to the internalization of these value framework. The dominant castes internalize values of superiority and begin to believe they are in fact a most privileged people for having been born as Brahmins and begin to look upon other human beings as eugenically inferior and begin to treat them so.

2.2.1. Assumed Identity

Internalization of ascription leads to the evolution of another identity which is the assumed identity. The dominant groups have barraged the Dalits with an uninterrupted creation of myths first, about its own purity, valour, spirituality, superiority etc. second, about the weakness, impurity, untounchability, lack of intelligence etc. The objugated groups have generally consumed such myths of the dominant groups without being critical enough of the myths. The objugated groups were never even allowed to develop appropriate tools for their critical analysis. As a consequence these groups assumed such myths as truths and began to live by the precepts attached to these myths. Machiavellian efforts have been made in this country to perpetuate the Brahminic chicanery of objugating the Dalits by submerging their historical and innate identity by forcefully or deceitfully ascribing a false identity on them. Babasaheb Ambedkar refused to accept this Brahminic ploy and philosophically argued that Dalits are not Hindus.

2.3. Impacts of Brahminisation

The project of Brahminisation of the country is not a modern phenomenon. It is as old as the arrival of the Aryans in the Indian scene. All the ascribed identity that we are speaking of was aimed at Brahminisation of India. The emergence of the Nation-State is a capitalist phenomenon. Much before that there were theocratic states which ruled by the then kings under the normative prescriptions of the Brahminic social order. The Brahmin-Baniya combine of the colonial era sought vigorously to hinduise India in the context of the post colonial emergence of the Indian nation. The effort here was to ascribe a Hindu identity to the whole nation despite a pharisaic profession of secularism. According to Jaffrelot Hindu nationalism is a cultural strategy to defend Brahminic hegemony. Hindu Nationalism can be defined as an ideology that seeks to imagine or construct a community on the basis of a common culture a culture configured by a particular notion of Hinduism. The Brahminisation project actually started not at the turn of the century is commonly stated by scholars. The first Project of Brahminisation was the establishment of an ideological hegemony which did not find a counter polarity. The second Project of Brahminisation was the consolidation of a normative order based on the dominant ideology. This too did not have a counter polarity. The third Project of Brahminisation was Hindu Communalism with a clear opposite pole in Buddhism. He ordained that there should be a respect to other creeds. The fourth phase of Brahminisation is the Nationalist discourse of the Brahmin-Baniya combine which can be traced from 1920.

Babasaheb gives an identity to the Dalits which rejects all the ascription of Brahminism while simultaneously makes a cultural and political assertion of the innate identity of the Dalits. Babasaheb's identity of the Dalits is that they are Dalits.

i) This identity rejects all the discourses of purity and impurity
ii) It rejects all the ascription of superiority and inferiority based on the discourses of purity and impurity
iii) It rejects the characterization of Dalit rulers as Rakshasas
iv) It rejects the ascription of lack of intelligence to the Dalits
v) It rejects the ascription of lack of civilization to the Dalits
vi) It rejects the identity of subservience ascribed and ordained on the Dalits
vii) It rejects the Hinduisation of Dalits

The rejections of these converge into a positive identity formation of the Dalits which find repeated expressions in Babasaheb's writings. This is the identity of the Dalits as a protesting people. Protest is a positive assertion of an oppressed people.It asserts the cultural innatism of the Dalits, that they are a people, a broken people. This is what they are historically and in the depth of their being. It has also a socio-political positioning of the Dalit communities in the Nation-State.

2.4. Re–visioning Dalit Identity

The next millennium will be declared as Ambedkar Era for the cultural and political assertion of the Dalits. The dalit assertions in the Ambedkar Era will have many dimensions.

In the name of Hinduism the project of Brahminisation has alienated the Dalit people from their original religious forms and spirituality. As a people the Dalits are different and are not Hindus. Dalits have gone to other religions in search of equality and dignity. They went to Christianity but have found a reassertion of the same caste system in the Church. Their untouchability still remains alive in many churches. In the recent past the Dalit Christians have to put up a relentless battle not only for their political rights but also for their religious rights within the church. The most unfortunate thing is that the Dalit Christians consider themselves superior to the Dalits. Christianity has untiringly shown heaven to the Dalits as something that they should aim for while keeping them in misery on this earth. Dalits have not found their liberation in Islam too. Islam has kept the Dalits where they were when they entered that religion. Therefore, the identity of Hindu Dalits, Christian Dalits, Muslim Dalits etc. will be rejected. There will be only Dalits. Dalits have converted themselves to established religions like Christianity, Islam, Buddhism, Sikhism etc. in an attempt to assume an identity that will in the line of their protest identity. However, the need is to establish an identity based on the innate qualities of the Dalits.

The Dalits are an eco-people having a close relationship with Mother earth. In the dalit world view Earth is not a resource to be exploited but a Mother who provides and protects. She has a place for all. She provides livelihood for all and protects all her children. Weapons of war are alien to her children as there is no effort to hegemonise either her children or all that lives on her lap. Dalitism moves away from a 'man' centred world to a nature centred world.

Unlike the dominant religions which hold out promises of heaven or condemns people to hell after this life Dalitism advocates a religion that will take people back into the womb of Mother Earth who will resurrect them in some other form. Dalitism has not hegemonised. Each people based on their community identity have a right to evolve their own systems of governance. The concept of the nation state which is a by product of capitalism is alien to Dalitism.

Mother Earth is resilient. She has borne all sorts of evil designs by the male man. The Dalits share this characteristic of resilience. They have endured nearly 3500 years of continuous oppression, marginalisation and exploitation. Like Mother Earth they have braved dominance of the male order silently. The Shakti of Mother Earth has filled all live veins of their being. Yet every now and then Mother Earth chooses to teach a lesson to the treacherous humanity. The Dalits need to imbibe this characteristic of Mother Earth. Shakti is manifested not only in resilience but also in resistance and retaliation to establish justice in the world. The Brahminic forces should not any more lay their hands on the Dalits. They have made the Dalits untouchables. Untouchables they will be in the new era. If any one touches them for exploitation they will be taught a fitting lesson.

Mother Earth is all inclusive. She does not discriminate her children. Everybody is welcome to dwell on her. Her hospitality knows no bounds. When a stranger enters a dalit colony he/she will experience the same type of inclusiveness. Anyone can enter the dalit colony and seek any type of help. There will be water and food even for the most strange person. Only then will their identity be known to the Dalits. They will first ask for the caste or religious identity of a stranger and only then will they give even water to drink. In the cities when it is difficult for the Dalits to find a rented house.

For the Dalits there is neither heaven nor hell. We come from the womb of Mother Earth and go back to her. It is only Brahminism and capitalism that digs her womb and burst nuclear bombs. This is an arrogant assertion of male domination which emanate from the patriarchal principles of Capitalism and Brahminism. The prominence given to women in dalit culture has been corrupted by the influx of Brahminic paradigms among the Dalits. During the Ambedkar Yuga the Dalits will purify themselves internally and restore the place for women that rightfully belongs to them. The dalit panchayats will be led by dalit women. The dalit sanghas should have dalit women as leaders. Dalit women will be preferred as candidates in the reserved constituencies. Dalit women will not only have equality but also high esteem and veneration.

None of the existing religions has brought equality and dignity to the Dalits. We have embraced different religions in search of equality and dignity but have been incessantly discriminated against in all these religions. No gods have incarnated till now on behalf of the Dalits. In the Ambedkar Era all these hegemonic religions will be rejected by the Dalits. The Dalits will establish their own religion based on the values of freedom, equality, dignity for all human beings at all times. It will not claim to be purer than any other community, not superior to any other community.

All dominant religions have shown heaven as the ultimate goal of this life thus showing to people an escape route from their responsibilities in this present life. Hinduism has shown rebirth and Karma as a way out of all responsibilities to humanity. In the dalit religion salvation is of this earth. Transcendence and mysticism of the Dalits belong to this life on this earth. It is in living a full life in the here and now that the excellence of one's birth is achieved. Establishing the terrestrial rights of all people will be the achievement of bliss. Ambedkar Era will make an all out effort to get redemption from the sins of the dominant forces of the world. Redemption for the Dalits is not from their own sins but from the above mentioned sins of the world.

Salvation in the Ambedkar Era will mean the destruction of all the evil ascription that the Brahminism has made to the Dalits. The Brahminic ascription will be consciously removed from dalit psyche by rediscovering the submerged intrinsic goodness of the Dalits as a people and by establishing external symbols that will constantly remind the dalit communities what they are in essence in the core of their being.

Land can be restored to Dalits not by the goodness of the Brahminic forces, nor by a change of heart on their part, nor by their generosity. The restoration should take place through appropriate and stringent laws without loopholes to serve the convenience of the rich. The enactment and implementation of such laws will not come from the Brahminic forces nor from their admirers. If they have to do so the Dalits will have to establish the mutually complimentary bipolarity of power as resistance and power as participation. Governance is the arena of battle. Dalits will establish their legitimate space not only in the processes of allocation of values but also in influencing these processes of allocation. In order to achieve this effectively in an overwhelmingly Brahminic-political context the Dalits will claim a right to elect their own leaders all by themselves.

Brahminism has sought to keep the Dalits in eternal darkness while simultaneously giving a supreme position to learning to its own clan. If there is one sin that Brahminism should not be absolved of it is this sin of denying knowledge to people which is the height of absolutely ungodly and demonic arrogance. Dalits are a people who are naturally intelligent. Ambedkar Era will strongly stand in favour of educating all dalit people, especially the dalit children. The government bears a significant responsibility. The Brahminic forces should repent and atone for their sins by opening the floodgates of education to the Dalit children.

2.5. Ideological Identity

It needs to be recognized at this stage that one of the greatest difficulties in reconstructing Dalit culture and history is the lack of written history. Whatever has been left within the Dalit communities has a mixture of Brahminism though only a long time research will bring out the truth whether it is Dalitism that is mixed with Brahminism or the other way about. Clifford Geertz perceives ideology as "schematic images of social order" i.e. symbols and metaphors consciously constructed as a means of rationalizing change in a modernizing society. Changes have to come in favour of the Dalits an the changes have to be rationalized through the creation of symbols and metaphors. What Babasaheb has given to the Dalit community as a heritage will be the foundations of a Dalitology that will develop in the Ambedkar Era. Dalitology is the Science of Dalits. The liberation philosophy of Babasaheb will not be allowed to fossilize into an immovable monument. Rather it will be the Ratha that will have to be carried forward by Dalit Intelligentsia of the country from where Babasaheb has left. It should be constantly on the move. It is a philosophy filled with the pains and aspirations of the Dalit people and it will keep living. It is liable to creative criticism and further growth. This will be the core character of Dalitology, that it will never claim itself superior, nor the ultimate truth nor will it hegemonise any other people.

2.6. Political Identity of Dalits

The Dalit identity is wrought with serious political fundaments. It is an all embracing identity of a people who have been discriminated, oppressed and exploited in the name of caste. It does not apply to all the economic poor. Musafir writes that when the Aryans arrived in India there were ten tribes. The Aryans in applied the policy of divide and rule, propounded the theory of casteism and converted all our ten tribes into about 6000 castes and also sowed the seeds of discrimination among our people. It is here that the Dalit identity assumes a political character. In any tribal culture there are different communities with their own identities. Yet these identities do not split us into different personalities. The Dalit communities, though many, are one because of the oppression and untouchability they have suffered together as one people. This does not take away their other identities. An individual becomes a strong personality when all the multiple identities are recognized and strengthened. The need in the Ambedkar Era is to strengthen the identities of the different communities that go to make a common identity called Dalit. The multiple identities are the constituent elements of one common identity called the Dalit. The Dalit identity will be weakened in as much as the other identities of the communities are not strengthened.

It is political in character because the Dalit identity essentially leads the Dalit people into occupying their rightful space in governance. This country belongs to the Dalits and they should be governing it, creating and providing space for all who live in it. The capitalistic emergence of the Nation State is the antithesis of governance. Stopping short of the common identity called the Dalit and glorifying only the constituent identities to the detriment of this common identity will further shrink the available space within the Nation–State politics. Babasaheb, Kanshiram, Mayavati, B. Krishnappa, Krishnaswamy and other luminaries have shown the way. There may be many others coming in the same direction. Let thousand flowers bloom. It only makes the garden more beautiful.

References

Prakash, Prem, *Ambedkar, Politics and Scheduled Castes,* 1993.

Vidyasagar I.S., *Concept of Humanism of Dr. Ambedkar*, Jaipur, ABD Pub., 2005.

Suman R.D., ed., Dr. Ambedkar: Pioneer of Human Rights. New Delhi: Bodhisattva Publications, Ambedkar Institute of Buddhist Studies, 1977.

Thomas Pantham and Kenneth L. Deutsch ed., "The Political Thought of Dr. B.R. Ambedkar," in *Contemporary Indian Political Thought*, Delhi: Sage Publications, 1986.

Tripathi, Sridhar, *Encyclopaedia on Ambedkar*, 5 Vols, Book Details, 2007.

3

Origin of Dalit Movements

The mythologized history of India does not provide many clues to the direct rebellions of the oppressed masses against their oppression. But it is inconceivable that they did not take place at all over a long period of two millennia that nibbled at their existence every moment with a 'divine' contrivance called caste. The extraordinary success of this contrivance of social stratification is as much attributable to its own design that effectively obviated coalescence of the oppressed castes and facilitated establishment and maintenance of the ideological hegemony as to its purported divine origination. Thus the caste system held society in a metaphysical engagement and at the same time in physical alienation with itself. Materially, it provided for the security of every one through caste professions and psychologically an aspirational space for every caste including the non-caste untouchables to feel superior to some other. Right from the early revolts like Buddhism and Jainism down to the Bhakti movement in the medieval age, one finds articulation of opposition to the caste system materialising in a religio-ideological idiom. This trend in fact extends well down to modern times that marks a new awakening of the oppressed castes and the birth of the contemporary Dalit movement.

The religious discourse is thus a common feature of all the anti-caste movements. For example, the Satnami movement of the Chamars in the Chhattisgarh plains in Eastern Madhya Pradesh that eventually became an independent religious sect; the Dravid Kazhagam movement of Periyar EVR Ramaswamy Naicker which created a stir by publicly burning the effigy of Rama and celebrating the virtuousness of Ravana; the Nadar Mahajana Sabha in Tamilnadu the

Ezhava movement of Narayana Guru which culminated in establishment of a new religious sect called Sree Narayan Dharma Pratipalana Yogam in Kerala and the most pervasive Dalit movement led by Babasaheb Ambedkar curiously reaching its climax of mass conversion to Buddhism; they all signify an overriding hatred for the religious code of Manu and a proposition of an alternate faith for themselves. The most articulate expression of this dejection is found in Ambedkar's own analyses that holds overthrowing of 'Hindu' religious ideological hegemony as a necessary condition for the liberation of Dalits.

Notwithstanding the views of some people who contend that the caste system was not a rigid system that had disallowed inter-caste movement of people, the fact remains that it does not have any evidence of having brought in a change in the forces of production or in the relations of production till the advent of British rule. With its quasi-autonomous villages it remained in a fossilised form for centuries. This feature of the Indian society precisely impelled Marx to disdainfully comment that India did not have history and to commend the British colonial rule for waking it up from its slumber to Western modernity. The first cultural shock this Indian society received was through the Moslem invaders. Egalitarian Islam initially treated all Indians equally but soon the imperative of their political strategies made them realise the utility of the intrinsic divisions existing in the Indian society and they not only decided to compromise their egalitarian zeal but also allowed adulteration of their cultural broth with the poison of caste.

Bhagawan Das quotes Ibn Batuta, a Moslem scholar who accompanied Mahmud Ghaznavi stating that the Moslem invaders at first treated all Indians alike but later took advantage of the cleavages existing in Indian society. The compulsions of politics overtook religious spirits, which meant the Brahminic social order, based on castes remained largely unhindered and even influenced the emergent Moslem society with the Hindu converts. It was the Moslem invaders who first opened the gates of their cities to these 'Untouchables'. Many 'Untouchables' and low caste people embraced Islam and joined the invaders, partly to avoid persecution and partly in search of better status and fortunes. Those who embraced Islam and joined the armies of Moslem invaders imitated the customs and manners of their new masters.

There were even some high caste Hindus including Brahmins who converted to Islam for various reasons. These converts coming from diverse castes brought in their respective cultural modes of living into the emergent Moslem society and along with it the caste divisions. First of all, the conversion enabled them to come out of their caste professions, which had been the mainstay of their low social status. Secondly, in renouncing their religion they must have had a sense of revenge against the ignominy heaped upon them and a vague sense of belonging to the ruling community. Thirdly, the opportunity to wield the sword in itself meant many things to them: it meant notional raise in their caste status catapulting them from a non-caste untouchable to that of Kshatriya—a penultimate rung in the caste hierarchy.

It is a moot point whether these conversions could be called a social movement insofar as technically the latter insists upon an organisation striving for some collective goal of social change. It certainly reflects a spirit of rebellion at least at the individual level to defy the caste code and embrace a different faith. Insofar as caste society had the intrinsic organisations of castes that governed their respective caste behaviours and managed the community life within the caste framework, it is a difficult proposition to say that this rebellion materialised without any organisational backing. In all probability these kinds of people's choices particularly in large numbers, get exercised only with social connivance. As could be seen from the later instances of conversions, the religious conversions never took place in any significant scale without there being a social movement to support it. In this sense, one could surmise the existence of some movement of untouchables that spearheaded the conversion to Islam.

The above overview highlights the following:

i) Indian society as a whole never accepted hierarchy as a basic value system.

ii) The anti-caste movements essentially were against the creed of Brahminism that had ordained the iniquitous social structure.

iii) They were always articulated in terms of constituting an antitheses to oppressive aspects of the 'Hindu' religion.

iv) They invariably materialised in the form of denouncements of these aspects and in corollary, adoption of a different faith,

v) Which in their perception was better.

vi) These movements invariably needed certain extraneous enablers especially the political congeniality.

3.1. Origin of Dalit Movement

Unlike the Moslem invaders, who had ruled India on the strength of their developed feudalism, far superior to the priest-ridden Indian system, the British conquest of the country was based on their superior technique of production and social form, that was much more efficient than the technique of feudalism. The British colonisation with its bourgeois liberal ethos coupled with the imperatives of their ruling strategy, created space for working up subaltern identities, mainly in terms of caste and religion. The institutional changes, cultural changes, economic changes, and emergent social changes that came in during the colonial rule gave impetus to the aspirations of the lower castes. The development opportunities that these changes created came into conflict with traditional social relations, which still shackled them through caste bondage.

There appears to be some kind of capability threshold that takes into account a balance of all resources with a social group, below which social movements are not possible. The colonial rule lent various opportunities to the disadvantaged sections and pushed them up past this threshold. It was thus natural that the first of the social resistance movements was by the Shudra castes. Because, as the labouring caste, they constituted an immediate interface with the parasitic upper castes, and in terms of resources they got over the threshold sooner than, say, the more oppressed untouchables. These movements broadly exposed the fraud perpetrated by Brahmins in the name of religion. Although, the Dalit movement was significantly influenced by the non-Brahmin movement of backward castes, it soon drifted away from the latter. With the advent of Ambedkar, it soon secured national prominence.

Around this time, there was a strong revolutionary movement all across the globe that drew its inspiration from the Bolshevik revolution in Russia in 1917. It claimed its ideological strength from the theories of historical materialism, dialectical materialism and scientific socialism propounded by Karl Marx. The Russian revolution had ignited hope of emancipation in oppressed humanity. The leadership of this communist movement however came from the middle class educated youth who for historical reasons had to come from the upper castes, the majority being the Brahmin itself. Their comprehension of the philosophy of communism was acutely constrained on one hand by the lack of systematic political education compounded by the non-availability of much of the original literature, and on the other by their class and caste consciousness. It rested on the dictums like class struggle, dictatorship of proletariat and notions of the base and superstructure without the underlying dialectics that lent it its specific meanings. This movement was essentially pitted against British imperialism that brought them nearer some sections of the nationalists and tended to ignore the caste as a super structural identity. On its part, the Dalit movement not only did not find any answer to their specific caste exploitation but on the contrary total apathy about it in the communist movement. In their strategic formulation, the open anti-State stance of the communists moreover did not found favour with the Dalits.

As Gail Omvedt perceptibly observes, the autonomous Dalit movement had to engage with three forces in colonial society:

i) It developed in opposition to the socially and culturally pervasive and historically deep-rooted hegemony of Brahminical Hinduism.

ii) It had to contend with the hegemony of the nationalist movement, which under the leadership of the Congress, strove to take over the agendas of several subaltern movements while restraining their democratic and egalitarian potential.

iii) It had to face a difficult relationship with the communist movement which otherwise should have been its natural ally.

While dealing with Brahminical hegemony, the autonomous Dalit movement naturally perceived an ally in the backward castes. The anti-Brahmin movement launched by the creative and visionary genius of Mahatma Phule in Maharashtra in many ways inspired the Dalit movement. In spite of the difference in time period marking out different transitory phases in the history of the country; differences in dispositions, equipment and social backgrounds between Phule and Ambedkar, one finds essential similarities in their characterisation of the social structure and the movements they launched and led. Both

Phule and Ambedkar regarded British rule positively for introducing modernity into the moribund Hindu society but simultaneously both showed its limitations; both repudiated the claims of nationalists that India was a nation; both had no faith in the Indian National Congress; both came to characterise and oppose it similarly; The pious formulation of Phule and to a certain degree of Ambedkar hoped to bring together all the Untouchables and the Shudra castes in opposition to Brahminism. Howsoever underestimated or grossly overlooked the contradictions between the Shudra backward castes and the non-caste Dalits may be in the village setting where precisely the caste problem is to be confronted, the Shudra castes came to share the mantle of Brahminism in relation to Dalits. This legacy of Manu could neither be overcome by the powerful non-Brahmin movement of Mahatma Phule, who had certainly shown how to bring them together during his life time; nor by the Dalit movement despite its significant investment for bringing about a broad unity of all the labouring people during Ambedkar's time. Immediately after the death of Mahatma Phule his Satyashodhak Movement lost its anti-caste zeal. Even the attempts for reviving and revitalising it under the patronage of Shahu Maharaj of Kolhapur could not succeed and by 1920 it completely lost its anti-Brahminism character and degenerated into a political addendum of ruling class.

The majority from the Shudra castes, as marginal or small farmers or artisans labouring in the jajmani-balutedari system, is variously exploited and is poor. A minority of them, as big farmers and middle farmers, were well off. Some of them were vested with the traditional powers of village administrators. These people of the farmer castes came to don the role of exploiter in the village setting. During the post-independence period the imperatives of electoral politics provided the motive force for the consolidation of the middle castes. These castes received disproportionate benefits from the policies and programmes implemented during this period. Many of the benami transfers also went to them, as they were the confidants of the former landlords. The green revolution, as numerous studies concluded, clearly benefited the bigger farmers who again belonged to these castes. The empowerment of a section from these Shudra castes impelled them to create a formidable constituency for themselves in nexus with the capitalist class and to wield significant political power.

The contradiction between them and the Brahmins that impelled the non-Brahmin movements during the colonial times were overcome in this process, which enabled them to assume the hegemonic role in the rural setting.

All the castes under this generic Shudra caste-group were not well off economically and equal socially. Many of them, the artisan and service castes, were as poor as Dalits and lay at various rungs in the caste hierarchy. However, they could be bracketed together socially in caste terms and economically as farmers as most of them had land. The caste divisions between them were really imperceptible in hierarchical terms. In relations to Dalits however they were placed socially and culturally clearly apart as the caste Hindus. All these Shudra castes came to pose as a single block in opposition to Dalits for mainly two reasons. One, their superiority in the caste hierarchy to Dalits lent them power over them to extract more and more economic surplus and two, the assertiveness of the majority Dalit caste induced by their political consciousness and their economic betterment made them vulnerable and defensive. These dynamics achieved two things for the rural rich. One, it obfuscated their exploitative relations with their own caste fellows and two, it provided them the requisite mass base to claim political power.

While the caste identity consolidated the middle castes into a powerful block, the same identity was used to catalyse disablement of Dalits by dividing them into various caste groups. Historically, all the Dalit castes were not economically equal. Most of them had a specific caste calling and so had a reason to perceive a stake in the system. Paradoxically, they constituted the interface between the village and town, which enabled them to acquire a self-identity as humans particularly during the alien rule. With nothing to lose, they therefore were the first to rebel against the caste system. There is enough evidence that the other Dalit castes also initially made common cause with this anti-caste movement. But, with the advent of parliamentary electoral politics the ruling class could easily engineer their detachment from the Dalit mainstream movement. Later, the contradiction between the middle caste hegemony and the Dalit struggle accentuated this division and put a cap on the prospects of Dalit unity.

This debacle embodied a larger debate relating to class vs. caste and the concomitant question of how to wage class struggle and also how to annihilate castes. Insofar as the working class in India collectively come from the Dalit and Shudra castes, it is important that they come together to become a class. In the same manner, the question of annihilation of castes is intimately linked to the coming together of the Dalits and lower-rung Shudra castes against the upper caste hegemony in every sphere of power. But the protagonists of class comprehended it in a restrictive manner and hence failed to tackle caste, which was the tangible and lived reality of the Indian proletariat. They were inevitably led to ignore it till they were compelled to acknowledge its existence by continual blows from concrete reality.

Unfortunately, this essentially anti-class, anti-caste agenda got juxtaposed against the class agenda of the communists and unleashed a sterile debate, which refuses to die even today. Caste or class, both these categories, to be workable, need to expand their boundaries to represent the current mode of exploitation in the country. This process would essentially bring out a large interface between them. This ought to happen however through the medium of concrete struggle based on caste or class-consciousness and not through any wishful amalgamation of caste and class conceived in the brains of some intellectual.

Insofar as the Shudra castes largely represent the class of have-nots together with the Dalit castes, and simultaneously functions as the nearest representative of Brahminism and also as the exploiting class, the need to apply a class filter to it cannot be overemphasised. The same principle is applicable to Dalits insofar as there is an evidence of class formation among them. It therefore needs to be understood that mere caste identity is not only going to be inadequate but is also going to prove dysfunctional. The prerequisite for this to happen is both, a strong Dalit movement which while fighting the remnant Brahminism is capable of orienting itself as a class assimilating the toiling masses from all the other castes, and a strong communist movement which incorporates into its class struggle the agenda of the struggles against social and cultural discrimination. The Dalits as the most proletarianised people will have to be the vanguard of both these struggles.

The opposition to Brahminical Hinduism led naturally to its rejection by Dalits but not of the religion itself. On the contrary, it gave rise to the Dalit-obsession of religion that curiously refuses to wane even when the organised religions ceased to ordain social affairs as they did many years before. As we know religion is a product of particular socio-economic phase in history that served the purpose to resolve certain crises on the basis of accumulated knowledge available then. The religious resolution invariably took the form of suppression of man's desire to seek a good life by promising him a better afterlife. Marx dismissed religion outright as a vestige of superstition and a tool of social control used to enslave the masses. For Marx, religion existed not to console, but to control; it was "the opium of the people,"-a drug that dulled the will to throw off the chains of oppression. When Dalits rejected Hinduism, it might have been necessary to fill the void. Buddhism, howsoever radical in its pristine form, came to be an organised religion with its package of aberrations. In its pure form, it may not even qualify to be a religion but in its popular form, with its own mythology, rituals, and mumbo jumbo, it was no different from any other. The consequence of this change has been in terms disorienting the Dalit masses from the material world where their real problems are rooted.

3.2. Hegemony of Nationalist Movement

The second factor would seem out-of-date as it relates with a specific moment in the past. However, there are a few vital questions that crop up in its conjunction that are still consequential to the discourse of revolutionary change in India and that should impel us to its discussion.

The first is about what constitutes a nation. The Dalit movement dismissed the premise of the mainstream nationalist movement that India was a nation. Ambedkar, for instance, repudiated the notion of a nation in a caste society and challenged it saying that each caste was a nation. Phule, who was Ambedkar's preceptor, had said that "unless all the people in the Balisthan, including the Shudras, Ati-Shudras, Bhill, Koli etc. become educated and are able to think over and unite, they cannot constitute a nation."

Despite these fore warnings and subsequent nationality movements bloodying the bosom of the country, the ruling classes are yet not awake to India's multinational character. The vested interests still keep on exhorting the gullible masses to sacrifice for the nonexistent nation or dismiss genuine peoples' movements calling them anti-national.

Nation, inasmuch as it is a phenomenon associated with the capitalist development, the pre-capitalist caste has to be antithetical to the concept of nation. Dalit movement by squarely posing this problem has indeed contributed to India's nation building efforts. The Indian National Congress, which spearheaded the national struggle for independence, represented the emerging Indian bourgeoisie's drive for overall political and economic control, whereas the Dalit movement under Ambedkar sought to strengthen the most disadvantaged people in the Indian society and set in the process of internal consolidation of the Indian nation.

With Ambedkar's taking upon a role of a constitution maker and a position in the Nehru cabinet, many of these lofty theoretical standpoints that could provide a framework for the Dalit movement got shifted to background. Notwithstanding his lamentations and exhortations against the post-independence political system, the emergent framework of the Dalit movement could not escape distortion in the powerful vortex of ruling class parliamentary politics. Ambedkar's programme for annihilation of caste system thus was completely way laid by the ruling class.

In the context of nation, the question here is what should be the relationship between the Dalit and nationality movements. The nationality struggles invariably land up using certain primordial identities in their anxiety to secure themselves uniqueness but are essentially underscored by the exploitations experienced by a set of people. As Ambedkar argued, Dalit struggle has the characteristics of a nationality struggle. It thus gets linked to the struggles of all the oppressed nationalities the world over. The alliance of Dalit movement with the genuine struggles of other oppressed nationalities will have a congenial acculturation impact and strengthen the Dalit movement.

3.2.1. Imperialism

The second question is about the struggle against the British imperialism. It is a common feature of anti-caste movements that they did not support the freedom movements and to some extent saw the colonial rule in congenial terms vis-à-vis their objectives of eliminating caste disability and gaining a due share of power. In most of the decisive battles that established British colonialism in the country, Dalit soldiers had played a heroic role. It is said that while the Brahmins mourned the fall of Peshawa in Koregaon battle, all others celebrated the event as their liberation by distributing sweets all over Pune. It was the spontaneous revelry of the oppressed over the downfall of the oppressor. The British did many positive things: foremost, they admitted Dalits into their army, they made them compulsorily educated, they introduced a modern legal system, which at least in principle disowned caste as the basis for law; they opened up new employment opportunities for the 'Untochables' in the European families, in mills and factories, in the railway and in shipping; and later they introduced political reservation for them.

It was not for any love for Dalits that the colonial rulers did favourable things to them. Most of it sprang from their strategic imperative and somewhat from a sense of superiority as victors. They did not hesitate reverting them when these reforms proved an impediment in their colonial interests. As for the anti-caste movements, it would be wrong to say that they were for the continuance of colonial rule. They were aware of the limitation of the alien rule. Ambedkar had squarely exposed the exploitative character of the colonial rule not only in his scholarly treatises but also in public.

Thus, although the anti-caste movement in general and Dalit movement in particular acknowledged the positive aspects of colonial rule and tactically sought to make use of their contradiction with the bourgeoisie nationalists to exert pressure on the latter to agree for desired reforms and devolution of power to the lower castes, it never was so overwhelmed as not to see its long term interests lying in the demise of alien rule.

Today the menace of imperialism has engulfed the entire world through its credo of globalisation, which is being promoted through its agencies like the IMF and the World Bank. The underlying economic philosophy of these programmes is to rely more on market forces, dismantle controls, reduce the role of State, liberalise prices, and replace the public with private sector. The experience with this package all over the globe is uniformly anti-people and directly proportional to the degree of their marginalisation. Dalits being the most marginalised people in India, their movement ought to have been concerned with these policies. While accepting the proven fact that globalisation hits poor people the hardest, some intellectuals expect that it might do good in terms of removal of social disability of Dalits. The argument though not entirely misfounded, betrays inadequate learning from the experience with the capitalist operations of over a century in this country. As capitalism has made skilful use of caste, globalisation, which is essentially capitalism in the era of information and communication technology, is not going to impact it positively. Of particular relevance to Dalits are certain implications of these policies of the free market.

One, the competitive advantage based investment would drive the corporatisation of agriculture and agri-business. The resultant consolidation of farms by the big agro-MNCs to have economies of scale is going to spell doom for the hopes of land reform. In so far the caste question is linked to this material key; it impels one to rethink the consequences. Two, the privatisation of the public sector and reduction of government jobs through the minimalist State that globalisation envisages, will directly hit the job-prospects of Dalits. It has many negative implications in terms of exploitation of Dalit women, Dalit culture and most importantly their hopes to struggle out their own emancipation. Dalit movement will have to understand the yawning contradiction between them and the imperialist agenda and devise strategies to counter it in their movement.

The third question that could be discerned from this moment is about the attitude of the Dalit movement towards the State. The Dalit movement reflects distinctly an attitude of one who looks at the State as an impartial, sans caste and class arbiter in the quarrel of classes and castes. Some times, the State is seen as the one genuinely interested in the welfare of downtrodden masses; a benevolent entity. This pro-State attitude could be understood when we see that the very birth of the Dalit movement was attributable to the factors provided by the State. The Colonial State comes out to be the basic enabler and catalyst of the Dalit movement. One of the first struggles that were launched at Mahad for reclaiming Dalit rights to access the public tank was basically to restore the writ of the State. Even later struggles cared not to violate the legal framework and thus tacitly expected the support of the State.

While contending with the hegemony of the nationalist movement under the nationalist bourgeoisie and while opposing the hegemony of Brahminism, the Dalit movement had essentially to take stock of its resources and opportunities held out by circumstances. In the Mahad Satyagraha, Ambedkar categorically explains his strategic calculation that he could not fight the formidable enemy with his meagre resources on several fronts. Their battles were essentially formulated on the strength of the State provision, the strategy being to use the existing law to assert the Dalit rights and expand the former to support the new ones.

Later, with the political reforms the Dalit movement forsook mass struggles and adopted the electoral path to secure political power. Political power was rightly seen as the key to all the problems. However, the concept of political power was acutely constrained by the framework laid down by the State. It was a well thought out strategy, to use the alien State as the bulwark to secure gains for Dalits from the competing camps. But the fact remains that the liberal democratic thought driving the contemporary Dalit movement did neither have any significant variant of this strategy nor any alternate concept of political power in its repertoire. As a result, the Dalit movement, which was conscious of its compulsions during the early days, got stuck in the traps laid out by the ruling classes.

The Dalit movement linked the concept of State power with its claim of equality. The gamut of reservations basically sprang from this. If Dalits are represented in various parts of State machinery in the ratio of their population then it is assumed that due share of power is enjoyed by Dalits. The flaw in this schema is on account of the State character. The State irrespective of whether it is a welfare State or any other kind of State, admittedly is a coercive organ of the ruling class against the ruled ones. If therefore the ruled classes opted to be the part of such an organ voluntarily, it has to be beneficial to the latter. Generally, when it is difficult to win over an adversarial class in direct confrontation, the ruling class always adopts the strategy of co-opting. It very well knows that the co-opted minority would be submerged by its majority. In simple language, it is a pure bribe to buy-in an opponent. The Dalit strategy of becoming a part of this exploitative mechanism out of their volition in ultimate analysis thus serves the ruling class interest.

There is no denying the fact that following the strategy of sharing State power in the prevailing circumstances certainly brought significant gains to Dalits. Through the mechanism of reservations in education, employment and politics, many Dalits are catapulted to positions which otherwise would have been unthinkable to them. But the buy-ins are always associated with gains. This class has completely distorted the ideology of Dalit liberation. Dalits as the native proletarian class cannot be liberated by sops granted in a prison. Their liberation is only conceivable in dynamiting this prison and constructing a new shelter in its place as per their own desire.

The profile of a Dalit notwithstanding the changes that has befallen to some due to the post-independence buy-ins is that of an illiterate, half-fed landless labourer utterly dependent upon his high caste patron who is constantly preyed upon by all kinds of vultures. He is the victim of a complex system evolved over several millennia.

3.3. Dalit Movement and Communism

The third factor is about its unsatisfactory relation with the communist movement. This factor will stand as the single most unfortunate paradox of contemporary Indian history. It stemmed from, not so much the ideological differences, which certainly existed in the form of certain unclear theoretical constructs in the mind of Ambedkar—the one who shaped the Dalit movement—as from the attitudes of the communist leaders towards the Dalit movement. These leaders working in Bombay in the Trade Unions dogmatically regarded the caste question as an unimportant superstructural issue, which would automatically disappear when the revolution takes place. The Dalit movement put the question on its head and asked that with the castes intact how would the revolution itself take place. The economic condition of Dalits was much worse than their savarna counterparts. Ambedkar observed that the communists used these TUs for their political gains rather than for the welfare of the working class. Whenever they took precipitate action to strike work, the workers tended to suffer differentially, owing to their caste-wise placements.

Ambedkar's objection to this 'irresponsible' TU behaviour was on two counts: (i) they were driven by raw 'economism' to the detriment of prospects of enhancing the political consciousness of the working class, (ii) they were using the working class as cannon fodder in the promotion of their political interests. Ambedkar's writing on communism or Marxism is heavily imbued with his annoyance with the Bombay-Communists. They cite examples of the parliamentary communist parties to show the lacuna or inapplicability of Marxism. It is necessary for them to understand that Marxism intrinsically solicits criticism but it presupposes its careful study.

Much of the misunderstanding got reinforced during the course of the petit bourgeoisisation of the Dalit movement. The vested interests used the stray quotations of Ambedkar to denigrate communism. It was a deliberate distortion. For, although Ambedkar could not discuss the philosophy of communism in the manner it deserved, he was never antagonistically disposed towards it. Rather, he acknowledged the beauty of communist philosophy and said that it was closer to his own. Preoccupied with the mission of liberating the Dalits, he insisted, quite like Marx, that the test of the philosophy was in practice, and opined that if communists worked from that perspective, to win success in India would be far easier than in Russia. He always regarded it as the ultimate benchmark to assess his highest ideal—Buddhism. With bitter experience with communist dogma and vulgarity of his times, he did sound polemically against Communism and appeared at times even professing its doom but it all underscored his wrath against the dogma that occupied the communist practice. After the collapse of communism in erstwhile Soviet Union and Eastern European countries, the anti-communism argument is gleefully put by certain people to claim Ambedkar right. It not only reflects their ignorance of both communism and Ambedkar but also and more importantly, alienates Dalits from the ideology that is specifically dedicated to have-nots of the world.

3.4. Ambedkar and Dalit Movement

Dalit movement has a rich history of rationalism and humanism. In fact, the historical evolution took place with Buddha's revolt against Varnashram dharma. Buddha not only rejected supremacy of Brahmins but also of the Shastras. Sanskrit was the language of the Brahmins and knowledge their sole domain and Buddha not only demolished their knowledge base of Brahmins but also popularized among the masses by sermonizing in Prakrit.And this tradition of revolt continued at the later stage also. All the indigenous reform movement and religions in India had inherently revolted against the Brahmanical value system, which gave divine sanction to untouchability and caste system. After Buddha, Mahavir Swami rejected the notion of caste and violence in the brahmanical structure. Even the birth of Sikhism is related to the caste prejudices rampant in varnashram dharma system. In the 15th century Kabir talked of rejection of caste system and talked of one God. He attacked rituals and Shastras and talked of a society based on equality.

Yet the brahmanical system continued by hook or by crook. The brahmanical literature degraded Dalits and talked very cleverly about the pre-birth theory. They promoted Gita which in return promoted not only violence but also caste system. The Brahmin intellectuals carefully planted their own people among Dalits to justify their position.

One is ashamed that even today we have gurus like Dronacharya who supported Varna Vywvastha and denied Eklavya, a Dalit to become the number one arch of his time. Accordingly, Dalits were not supposed to learn arms and only the Kshatriyas had a right to learn military training according to Varna Vyawastha. We could have accepted such norms in the primitive time and forgot about it but in the post independence India, the government followed it and formed not only Arjuna Award for best sports person but Dronacharya award for best coaches, indicating nothing has changed the mindset of our rulers. The result is that we have coaches like Dronacharya today who differentiate between their subjects and the condition is that our sports are in the worst shape.

While Mughal rule in India was a status quoits one, the emergence of British power made a lot of difference for the downtrodden people. They brought a sense of liberty for the marginalized communities. Jyoti Ba Phule belonged to Mali community of Maharastra. Pune's Chitpawan Brahmin would not allow any Dalit and backward to join schools. Women and particularly of Dalit community could never dream of going to school. Phule realized that unless the community get educated they would not be able to emancipate themselves. So he started a massive work of education by starting various schools in and around Pune. The Brahmins opposed education movement among Dalits which they had denied for years. Phule exposed the brahamnical literature, wrote plays about the exploitation of the farmers and appreciated Christian missionaries for their noble work in school education.

Taking inspiration from Phule, Baba Saheb Dr Ambedkar also talked the importance of education. But education must be rationalists and reasonable. Education agitate our mind. It gives us thought about what, is good and what is bad. Hence Education is root of every movement. Agitation on certain thing is a uniting factor. It became the famous word of Ambedkar " Educate, agitate and organise'. Ambedkar was one of the tallest intellectuals of the country, a scholar who understood the crookedness of the Shastras. He was an iconoclast and questioned the very essence of Shastras. In his letters to Gandhi he says that we should amend Shastras because they talk of caste system. Gandhi said that we had to believe in Shastras if we want to call ourselves Hindu because if we challenge the very foundation of Hinduism, which is the Shastras, then we have no business in calling ourselves Hindu. In fact, this led to bitter dual between Ambedkar and Gandhi. Ambedkar not only said clearly that he was born as a Hindu but would not die as a Hindu.

Ambedkar read Gita and Ramayana and questioned the wisdom. He was among very few intellectuals of his time who never considered Rama and Krishna as idol for Indians. How can be a person who maltreat his wife, be considered an ideal man, he opined. Gita, he suggested, openly justify killing and Varnavyavastha. He cites example of Krishna's sermon to Arjuna when the latter refuses to attack his own brotherns and relatives, "Oh Arjuna, you are not killing them.. You are just killing their bodies, for soul is immortal, ever present. It cannot be burnt, neither could it be dried." Ambedkar wondered that if a person murder some one, if would be easier for his lawyer to make his presentation in the court saying my client has not killed any one. He just killed his body the soul is immortal. Are these arguments valid?

Ambedkar fought for the dignity of Dalits. The Hindu Varnavyavastha snatched the dignity from Dalits. It degraded labour. The person who works hard to earn his bred was considered lowest while the Brahmins with their narrow minded tainted vision became

'Bhoodevatas', gods on the earth. The bloodsucking Gods had inherently anti Dalit bias. So angry was Ambedkar with the Hindu law book, which he considered as the source of caste system and discrimination against Daltis in India that he launched a movement against it.

On December 25th, 1927, Ambedkar launched a Satygrah in Mahad town of Maharastra for the water rights of Dalits and against the Manu Smriti. He burnt Manu Smriti terming it a document of discrimination with a number of his supporters. It was an act of great courage to do so in the den of violent Chitpawan Brahmins in Maharastra. It is interesting that Ambedkar fought for the rights of Dalits and had a broader vision forhis community. Unfortunately, when he started thinking of giving them a vision in 1955, he died. It was time when he embraced Buddhism and gave them an identity. Many people question Ambedkar's motivation to embrace Buddhism. Ambedkar has his own definition of Buddhism. He wanted his people to give an identity so that they get out of Varna System. Whatever we say, as long as we are a part of the Varna Vyawastha, whatever we do reflect our caste identities. Ambedkar, Phule and Periyar, all, wanted their followers to be provocative and proactive. Reject caste system and for that complete break up from the Hindu social order and embrace a better system.

Ambedkar wrote many thing over a period of 30 years. Some time he was living in deep anguish, elsewhere working with the government or framing constition and at the end as a Buddhist. And on each of these occasions he had different moods. There was a time when he became frustrated with the Varnavyavastha and he tore the Shastras. Then a time came when Ambedkar's main concern was to ensure fare participation of Dalits in political life of the country and he succeeded in getting separate electorate for them which he had to withdraw to 'save' the life of Gandhi, in 1932, known as Poona Pact. Then as a constitutionalist when he drafted constitution and later worked very hard to ensure fare deal for women in the Hindu Code Bill. In the last phase of his life when Baba Saheb embraced Buddhism, his main concern was providing a political alternative to Dalits.

It is also interesting to note that that Dr Ambedkar was a humanist to the core of his heart. Even when his so-called followers have converted him as a caste man or narrowly interpreted his ideologies and perception, Ambedkar could be termed an international humanist. A person who the persecuted all over the world today look to get inspiration. The narrow minded political fringes in the name of Dalit vision should think that Ambedkar first formed Indian Labour Party and later Republican Party of India and at no point of time he formed vision based on caste. Even on his 'thought on Pakistan' Ambedkar suggested that there should a party representing poor Hindus and poor Muslims, entirely secular, only that could save India. Muslim communalism only feed Hindu communalism.

Very unfortunately Dr Ambedkar's untimely death paralyzed the entire Dalit movement. His followers went to different streams. There are so many Republican Party of India that it is difficult who can we call as original party. The Ambedkarite movement (if it ever was), remained confined to 'Sarkari babu log', who will throng the parliament street in Delhi or Diksha bhoomi in Nagpur on December 6th and April 14th every year. It looked Ambedkar never spoke beyond reservation and varnya vyavastha. His writings of 30s were used more then the writings in the later stage perhaps to gain political leverages but that had hurt the movement.

While there is no denying fact that Ambedkar's popularity among the Dalits is not due to the 'Sarkari Babu Log' but the poor Dalits who consider him his emancipator. But hate campaign in the name of Ambedkar are uncalled for. There are many reasons for the same. Ambedkar is a uniting factor for Dalits. No doubt that he has become an icon from North to South from Hindi heartland to the southern Tamilnadu. To be frank, Ambedkar's reach to areas beyond his traditional domain is not just spreading of his ideology but using him as point of entry to gain a separate political status by the elite Dalit groups.

The worst fact is the Ambedkar is mainly known among the working class Dalits and enlightened and numerically powerful communities like Mahars in Maharastra, Chamars and Jatavs in the North India, Namshudras in West Bengal, Malas in Andhra and a few others in Tamilnadu. While Mahars hold sway in Maharastra and the Jatavs and Chamars outnumber any other community in the north contributed fairly to Ambedkarisation process. That helped people under the banner of Bahujan Political Party which used it as a vehicle to spread its wing.

When Mayawati became the chief minister of Uttar-Pradesh, analyists mistook it as a great revolution in the Dalits of Uttar-Pradesh. The fact of the matter is while it may be proudly said that a Dalit woman became chief minister of Uttar-Pradesh and that every Dalit felt proud of her being there at the chair yet the fact of Mayawati's ascendancy to Lucknow's thrown are different then what we perceive. They have very little to do with Ambedkar's movement and more to do with Mayawati's Chamar caste. The Chamar consolidation behind Mayawati ensured that she has an important role to play in Uttar-Pradesh. While it gave Mayawati a substantial chunk of seats in Uttar-Pradesh and increased her bargaining capabilities, it made her vulnerable also. For the past two decade no government in UP got to work full terms of five years. Mayawati's on tally in the assembly could never reached beyond 25% of the total seats of the assembly. Mulayam Singh Yadav has the same status quo situation. Both have realized that their respective vote bank remain in their pocket and will not ditch them however both now think to go beyond their traditional vote banks and are now flirting with the Brahmins and Thakurs. So the narrow Dalit politicisation in UP has also resulted in increasing power of the Brahmins and Thakurs being wooed by both the SP and BSP. This is an unfortunate trend being followed everywhere. The reason for this is the politics of power in the villages. BSP's over dependence on Chamars and a few other communities antagonized the other dalit communities, Mulyam Singh dependence on Yadavs and Thakurs also created problems for other backward communities and the need was to involve all the oppressed Dalits and backward together. This experiment of UP was sought to be taken elsewhere by disgruntled Ambedkarite who started crying foul on Periyar. Simply because the Dravidian parties are not taking them into consideration does not make a case to say that Periyar was anti Dalit.

This irony of the Dalits movement is that it has not resolved its own contradictions because Ambedkar is used as tool to hit at others and not resolve our own contradictions. Ambedkar's use is condemning brahmanical literature and values is no doubt useful in bringing people together but his positive writing for an alternative vision need to reestablished. It is easier to unite the communities on agitational mode against some one but very difficult to manage it when you get power or share in power. Dalits are facing it now. The elite Dalit groups who enjoyed reservation and power now refuse to accept this reality that those living in villages, living as landless, powerless without participation in political life are to be catered. They have no emotion other then selling Ambedkar's portrait and their own self. Today, this growing chasm between different Dalit group is just not an upper caste ploy but their own contradiction. In politics every opponent is ready to hit you when you are weak. Dalit movement failed to resolved many issues important to it and now face flak from all over.

The politics of identity never helps. The Dalits vision is to fight against hegemonies but in this process of breaking hegemonies, if we create our own hegemonies then the movement will break. In our efforts to break brahmanical hegemonies we created hegemonies in our own self and therefore Valmikis (Swachchkars), Madigas, Kuhmhars, Mangs and hundreds of other communities ask question for their fare representation. And a typical elite answer is that they have been allured by the upper castes. But the fact of the matter is that there is a wide gap between the numerically powerful communities in Dalits and the minorities.

The irony of the entire movement is that rather then working on the collective wisdom, the movement though claim to work for all communities, has by and large remain confined to a few individuals who used their community identity to gain the political clout. The Ambedkarite movement rarely talk of violence and violation of human rights. Their obsession with Manu Smriti and Hindu Gods to joke at took a perverted turn as one of the major problem that the Dalits face is to get acknowledgement from the caste Hindus. That a majority of Dalits despite all the facts, go the temples of the Brahmins and follow the same rituals. But these issues are seldom addressed in true sense. They are used as a rhetoric to lumpen the brahmanical system. The system will not go unless we want to get rid of it. The reason for not raising the issue of violence of Dalits is that many 'intellectual' feel 'uncomfortable' on this issue as they used their identity to get the entry into the media and would talk of 'philosophy'. Today, the same intellectuals have left all the work of the brahmanical system and now target the backward communities. Why has the Dalit movement changed its track from anti brahmanical campaign to anti backward campaign?

Iit has nothing to do with social movement which we all need to secularise and democratize our societies. The entire campaign is a power game. In this power game no body want to leave anything for others. In these power games we don't talk of philosophy. No doubt the backwards have become radical Hindutva people and have physically hit the Dalits and there is a need to draw a line. Like a few Dalit powerful communities, there are few backward powerful communities. The fight between a powerful Dalit community and a powerful backward community cannot be allowed to create a permanent rift between two groups. It has to be seen that the categorization of castes into backwards and schedule castes had its own flaws. There are oppressed backward communities which should have been in the Scheduled castes.

The non ambedkarite groups, mainly the NGOs, self-styled civil society people don't talk of philosophy. They bring a bundle of individual cases and weep all the time that Dalits are beaten up. One should remember that no movement can succeed without a philosophy and there would be no takers for a philosophy unless it is popularized in the movements. So issue of a broader secular democratic Dalit movement and atrocities on Dalits need to be worked at the same level. Narrowing Ambedkar's vision to a limited people and communities will damage the entire Dalit movement. Dalit movement is at the crossroad and need various answers.

Ambedkar wonderfully exposed the religious myths attached to Dalits. He tore apart the fundamentals put forward by the Brahmins in their holy texts. But at the same point of time one need to understand Ambedkar fully when he decided to embrace Buddhism with millions of Dalits. Ambedkar's genuine anti Brahmin or anti varna sentiments got exploited by the religious groups for the purpose of prosiletisation. Embracing any tradition or religion is the fundamental right of an individual but the fact remain that where does it help Dalits as an institution. When we challenge the institutions of holy religious text, question their finality and even burnt them when we feel they go against humanity, is it possible that we have the same elsewhere? Dalits have every reason to believe and tear apart the Hindu verna vyavastha but should they keep quiet when the other faiths also become tormentors? Should they not support those who are victims of their own faiths? If I like ' Why I am not a Hindu', I am sure we should not forget the cry of legendary Bertrand Russell long ago who wrote " Why I am not a Christian' and a few years back another fellow came up with resounding ' why I am not a Muslim'. Faiths have always been like that. They thrive on miracles and mischief.

If Rama and his brothers were mocked by Ambedkar about how they were born, similar is the case of Christ. It is no point blaming one and keeping quiet on others. Today's favorite things are blame game. A progressive Dalit movement cannot stand on the selective criticism of a few religious texts and conspicuously keeping quiet on other. A movement cannot be build on superfluous philosophy of negativism. It has to provide its own alternative to the people. Dalits have their own distinct identity and culture and those claiming to provide them an alternative God really misquote Ambedkar and kill their revolutionary spirit as suggested by many Dalit activists.

The high voltage of political power among Dalits in Uttar-Pradesh is due to its politicization process while the religious conversion has made them apolitical. The tribals in India became the victim of this apolitical process by NGOs and religious groups going there and taking over the leadership. The result was the tribals remain isolated and exploited. Dalits on the other side remained politically mobile and hence their leadership took over and negotiated in their own terms and conditions. There is another fact that the number of so-called NGOs among Dalits in South is more then what we imagined in the north but the account of political power in the Dalits in the North is much higher then the South. And this is the process of turning them apolitical and more religious ultimately resulted in their exploitation. In the south the conversion process was higher then the North. The Chamars and Jatavs of Uttar Pradesh rarely converted. They always claimed to be Buddhists. In Maharastra, the Mahars became neo Buddhists and the awareness level among them was superb. Buddhism did not take away their politicization process initiated by Dr Ambedkar but the conversion to other faiths actually made them apolitical resulting in more exploitation.

Ambedkar's legacy is very rich and need to be protected by us all. Dalit movement itself is a revolt against the obnoxious brahmanical values but at the same point of time, should express solidarity with all oppressed masses of the world. The movement should build bridges with likeminded groups, secular and democratic organizations, and avoid becoming another cult group. It should broaden its ideas and perception and reach those masses where it has not reached. It should avoid becoming politically correct. Identity will never work and those who have harped thesis of ' I ' only speak for them and nobody else has a business to speak for or on behalf of Dalits should resist such things. Nobody speaks for others. We all speak our own perception.

Tsunami discrimination against Dalits showed that how things take a dangerous if you make a community apolitical. Our political masters want them to be apolitical. But like them the agenda supported and furnished by the religious groups also end up in nothing. Dalits remained pitiable condition in Tamilnadu and Pondicherry. Their leaders were complaining outside India to the UN and to the Church while the ground level the higher ups among the backward communities ganging up against them. In fact the fishermen who happened to be Christians also refused to eat along with their fellow Christian Dalits. Why did the issue not become a hot issue accept a few headlines. We should have taken head on the prejudiced system. A religious community cannot fight a democratic battle. If we want to compare ourselves with the history of strong movements for civil rights by the blacks in the US, we will have to study the politicization process of the blacks, their fights for the right and broad spectrum of the movement. Moreover, the reach and ideological perspective of the movement were very clear. They revolve around more on the issues of human rights, civil liberties and attracted a very wide range of activists all over the US while the irony of the Dalit movement is that it remains more on the books, with the elite castes and with the organized sector and very little is done for the people sitting on the margin, in the villages.

These are dangerous and superficial ideas by those who have done little for their work. A movement based on negativism will never work. Identities have served the pocket of political masters and their 'intellectual' chums. They will not help the minorities among the marginalized. They are not based on democracy and participation. They are the collective ego of the powerful elite among them. A movement san respect for individual and without a corrective philosophy would not work. Dalits have their own cultural values and system, a system which need to explored and new values added to them. It is time for us to provide our own democratic secular progressive vision and rather then just work on an agitation mode forever. We need to introspect and bring the last man into our mainstream, otherwise these contradiction are powerful enough to destroy the legacy of a powerful man, named as Ambedkar. If we consider ourselves grateful to his legacy, time has come to redefine the Dalit movement.

REFERENCES

Kuber W.N., *Dr. Ambedkar: A Critical Study*, People's Publishing House, New Delhi, India.

Kusum Sharma, *Ambedkar and Indian Constitution*, 1992.

Omvedt, Gail, *Dalits and the Democratic Revolution: Dr. Ambedkar and the Dalit Movement in Colonial India*, 1993.

Pandey B.N., ed., *The Leadership of Babasaheb Ambedkar*, Leadership in South Asia, University of London symposium, New Delhi: Vikas, 1977.

Valerian Rodrigues, *The Essential Writings of B. R. Ambedkar*, July 2004.

4

Dalit Movements in Modern India

The term "Dalit" has different meanings for different people. The most common use of the term is to define people who were once known as "untouchables", seperated from the rest of society by the caste system. The word Dalit is today common across most Indian languages, meaning poor and oppressed people. As it refers to those who have been broken, ground down by those above them in a deliberate way, there is also clearly an inherent denial of pollution, karma and justified caste hierarchy to the word itself. Though use of the term Dalit in public discourse is of relatively recent origin – the 1960s – it is supposed to have been used first by Jotirao Phule (1827-1890) in his attempt to work for dalituthan, that is, the uplifting of the exploited sections of society. While Dr. Ambedkar did not popularize the word Dalit, his philosophy has remained a key source in its emergence and popularity. Marathi literary figures and neo-Buddhists began to use the word in their writings and contributed to the literary initiatives in replacing Harijan (man of God) and achchuta (untouchable) with Dalit, in the 1970s. They expressed their anger, protest and aspiration through this new word, rejecting the Hindu caste system and objecting to Gandhi's belief that caste Hindus' "charitable spirit" would be enough to overcome Untouchability.

While the word "Dalit" stems from opposition to terms bestowed upon Dalits by the non-Dalits—terms that legitimised their discrimination and deprivation—it has today essentially emerged as a political category. Dalits in legal parlance are called Scheduled Castes (SCs), and are identified as such by the President of India under Article 341 of the Constitution.

This constitutional identity, however, is exclusive and fails to capture the true picture. Dalits who have converted from Hinduism to another religion no longer qualify as SCs, although their status in society often remains the same. Moreover, Dalit movements in contemporary India are not uniform and each articulates a particular identity, be they Christian Dalits, Neo-Buddhists or Muslim Dalits. Hence, Dalit should not be seen as a term just describing a caste community. Rather, it should be viewed as a symbol of change and liberation, as a progressive ideology, helping the Dalit movement to achieve its end results. Increasingly used as a suffix, Dalit is a part of the identity of a person that holds certain values—those pertaining to equality and humanism.

Ambedkar did indeed give birth to a movement that encom passed all the needs of human society—economic, social, cultural, political and spiritual. He sought a total transformation and in doing so, attempted to make use of the best scholarship, the greatest insights of his time. Yet, like other social movements, the 'post-Ambedkar Dalit movement'—a term many use for the Dalit movement in independent India—has today come under an eclipse.

Babasaheb Ambedkar has undoubtedly been the central figure in the epistemology of the dalit universe. It is difficult to imagine anything serious or important in their collective life that is totally untouched by Ambedkar. For the dalit masses he is everything together; a scholar par excellence in the realm of scholarship, a Moses or messiah who led his people out of bondage and ignominy on to the path of pride, and a Bodhisatva in the pantheon of Buddhism.

It is not difficult to see the reason behind the obeisance and reverence that dalits have for Ambedkar. They see him as one who devoted every moment of his life thinking about and struggling for their emancipation, who took the might of the establishment head on in defence of their cause; who sacrificed all the comforts and conveniences of life that were quite within his reach to be on their side; who conclusively disproved the theory of caste based superiority by rising to be the tallest amongst the tall despite enormous odds, and finally as one who held forth the torch to illuminate the path of their future. He was their own among these few. It was he, who forsook his high pedestal, climbed down to their level, gave them a helping hand

and raised them to human stature. It is a commonplace occurrence to see dalits right from the humble landless labourer in villages to the highly placed bureaucrat in corridors of power, emotionally attributing their all to him.

It is thus natural for dalits to place him at the centre as their beacon and conduct their collective affairs as directed by its beam. This beam however is not monochromatic like a laser beam, to use an analogy from physics, but is composed of many light frequencies, the filters for which are controlled not by the masses but by some others. They manipulate this beam as per their desire, sometimes letting some frequencies pass and some times some other. They could selectively amplify some part and de-amplify the other and present an entirely different spectrum. What reaches the masses, thus, is not the holistic and true picture of 'Ambedkar' but its part, sometimes a distorted part, carefully filtered out and amplified by the 'technicians'. This fragmented and false Ambedkar is what reaches the masses. Because for the masses icons come handy. They are sans complexity of the main body, practical useable artefacts. Iconisation of the great heroes and their ideas at the hands of masses is thus inevitable. Human history is replete with such icons; rather it is largely made of them.

It is premised on a hypothesis that the history of post-Ambedkar dalit movement is largely influenced by the icons of Ambedkar that were produced by the socio-political dynamics of post-independence India. The process of iconisation, whatever be the motivation, has to have the basis, howsoever tenuous, in the material reality, in the facts about the subject. Being essentially a simplification of a complex reality, it involves the playing up of facts as per one's proclivities and propensities.

4.1. Types of Social Movements

Sociological theories distinguish social movements along two axes, whether they seek radical or limited change, and whether they focus on the entire society or on specific individuals. Alternative social movements see limited change among specific individuals, largely through remodelling lifestyles and behaviour (e.g., the hippie movement). Redemptive social movements try to change certain spheres of society (e.g., religious conversions). Reformist social movements attempt to change the entire society, but in limited ways, while revolutionary social movements, finally, attempt radical change in the entire society.

In terms of this paradigm, the anticaste movement, which began in the 19th centuiy under the inspiration ofjyotiba Phule and was carried on in the 1920s by the non-Brahman movements in Maharashtra and Tamil Nadu and then developed under the leadership of Dr Ambedkar, had characteristics of all four types of social movements though at its best it was revolutionary in terms of society and redemptive in terms of individuals. In partial con-text, the 'post-Ambedkar Dalit movement' has had revolutionary practice. It has provided alternative ways of living, at some points limited and at some points radical and all-encompassing, ranging from changes in behaviour such as giving up beefeating to religious conversion. It has focused on changes in the entire society, from radical revolutionary goals of abolishing caste oppression and economic exploitation to the limited goals of providing scope for members of Scheduled Castes to achieve social mobility. But, on the whole, looking at the 50 years since independence (though slightly over 40 years since the death of Ambedkar), this movement has been reformist. It has mobilised along caste lines but made only half-hearted efforts to destroy caste; it has attempted and achieved some real though limited societal changes, with gains especially for the educated sections among Dalits, but it has failed to transform the society sufficiently to raise the general mass out of what is still among the most excruciating poverty in the world. Though this movement has carried forward the challenge of e-powerment and brought anticaste issues into the political agenda, it still seems unable to become a decisive political force, leaving Dalits and other suppressed caste groups forced to bargain for concessions with the dominant political parties it characterises as *'Manuwadi'*, dominated by upper castes and the ideologies of Brahmanic Hinduism. The day promised by the 'new sun' seems still far away.

To understand what has happened, we can begin looking at some aspects of Dr Ambedkar's transformatory anti-caste movement.

4.2. Ambedkar's Movement

Babasaheb Ambedkar made his entry into the political and social life of

India in the period immediately after the First World War and the Russian Revolution. It was an era marked by social and political upheaval and the increasing hegemony of Marxist socialism in movements for social liberation. Though Ambedkar organised and led one of these movements as an autonomous movement for Dalit liberation, rejecting the leadership and ideological hegemony of non-Dalit socialists, he was influenced by Marxism throughout. His own theory which begins from the heritage of indigenous radicalism and stands in the tradition of Phule's revolutionary challenge can appropriately be compared to it.

Marxism was a totalistic and unified theory of change. The industrial working class, according to it, was both the most op-pressed class in society and at the same time the most capable of leading other social groups to revolution. This thesis was backed by a comprehensive analysis of the causes of social conflict and contradictions, of the underlying nature of society, and thence of the factors necessary for change.

During much of his social and political life, roughly from the late 1920s through the 1940s, Ambedkar accepted most of the economic analyses of Marxism and even attempted to organise along these lines, creating a radical movement of Mahar and Kunbi peasants against landlords, allying with communists in the working class struggle. These were years in which the pages of *Janata,* Ambedkar's weekly, were filled with reports of the struggles of workers and peasants against 'capitalists and landlords' as well as the fights of Dalits against atrocities. Ambedkar did not have much time for theoretical writing in this period of tumultuous organising, but his programmes and speeches indicate that he accepted broadly the Marxist analysis of class struggle so far as economic issues were concerned. What this led to, though, was a kind of dual systems theory which saw capitalism and Brahman-ism (casteism) as separate systems of exploitation, one to be fought by class struggle and the other by caste struggle. As he put it in his famous address to the Mahar railway workers at Mahad:

> There are in my view two enemies which the workers of this country have to deal with. The two enemies are Brahminism and Capitalism .... By Brahminism I do not mean the power, privileges and interests of the Brahmins as a community. By Brahminism I mean the negation ofthe spirit of Liberty, Equality and Fraternity. In that sense, it is

> rampant in all classes and is not confined to the Brahmins alone though they have been the originators of it.

The climax of this approach, in many ways, came with the writing of *States and Minorities,* proposed to be a draft of sections of the Constitution. Here, Ambedkar gave a severe critique of capital-ism and called for the nationalisation of land and basic industries, explicitly calling this 'state socialism'. In a sense, the term 'state socialism' indicated his difference with the communists in that in contrast to a revolution under 'working class leadership', the state ownership was to be written into a democratic constitution. At another level, the phrase simply made the assumption of a mechanical Marxism that 'socialism' or collective ownership of the means of production was equivalent to state ownership. There were, however, many problems with the 'dual systems' of Brahmanism and capitalism. These became clear in *State and Minorities* itself which seemed to contain two rather disparate sections, one advocating land nationalisation and state socialism and the other calling for separate village settlements for Dalits. The connection between the two was not clear. The problems of any 'dual systems theory' remained: seeing separate systems of class and caste exploitation left unchallenged the mechanical Marxist assumptions of a class analysis and accepted the idea that 'class' system of exploitation of dalits was an economic issue while the 'caste' system of exploitation was a cultural and ideological (superstructural) issue. The dual systems of'capitalism' and 'Brahmanism' provided useful rhetoric and a rule-of-thumb for analysis, but it left the question of the connection between the two systems completely unresolved. And if the other systems of oppression (for instance, 'patriarchy' and 'national oppression') were also included, then such an approach simply would yield to an unwieldy amalgam of many disparate 'systems' of exploitation. In other words, the dual systems theory could not give an integrated and holistic explanation. It reflected Ambedkar's initial grappling with Marxism when he insisted that 'caste' be added to a class approach (and even in that it should have priority) but did not develop an overall alternative theory.

As a result of this and some disillusionment with communism after the end of the Second World War, Ambedkar moved away from this analysis at the end of his life. As he moved closer to Buddhism, he reinterpreted it and sought to use it. In *The Buddha and His Dharma,* he gave it a modernistic, 'liberation theology' interpretation that interpreted *dukkha* as exploitation and called for a Sangha oriented to social welfare (Ambedkar), while in a draft essay on 'Buddha and Karl Marx' he tried to give a broad outline of what might be called 'Buddhist economics' seen as a conscious alternative to Marxist socialism. As he summed up his position at the conclusion of this essay:

> Society has been aiming to lay a new foundation as was summarised by the French revolution in three words, fraternity, liberty and equality. The French revolution was welcomed because of this slogan. It failed to produce equality. We welcomed the Russian revolution because it aims to produce equality. But it cannot be too much emphasised that in producing equality society cannot afford to sacrifice fraternity or liberty.

Finally, in a long historical essay such as 'Revolution and Counter-Revolution in Ancient India', he offered broadranging analyses that linked Buddhism, Brahmanic Hinduism and cultural exploitation to large-scale political changes in India. All of this implied the creation of a theory that sought to be a totalistic and all-encompassing alternative to Marxism, wedding the ideals expressed in the French Revolution, 'liberty, equality and fraternity', with his analysis of the role of Buddhism and Brahmanism in Indian history and with an economic approach that groped towards a social market economy.

This embryonic theory had the following characteristics:

(1) Ambedkar took as his basic goals the ending of exploitation and oppression and the achievement of equality, liberty and community. He was flexible about what he called it, insisting that it represented all that Marx had wanted to achieve with 'communism' but frequently describing it as 'social democracy'.

(2) He had a vision of development that emphasised the cre-ation of a modern society of abundance; though by the end of his life he rejected the economics of Marxism, his positive approach to economic growth, his insistence on creating a society free from suffering and his readiness to take the best of the global heritage was radically different from a Gandhian orientation to the traditional village and limitation of needs.

(3) The path to achieving this was backed up both by an understanding of the nature of human society and an interpretation of Indian history. Human society, as he saw it, was characterised by conflict and contradiction but also by reason and will. Not simply 'economic factors' were the motivating force in history, but also efforts to achieve power and efforts at liberation. Similarly, along with class caste (and by implication patriarchy) were stratification-defined sections of society which represented decisive factors in contradiction and processes of social change.'

Within India, Brahmanism/Hinduism was the historical basis of the stratification system of the social inequality which was constituted in the caste system. Hinduism meant the lack of liberty, the negation of equality for all groups especially for women and untouchables, and the destruction of community. Historically speaking, where a Buddhist upsurge had been revolutionary, Hinduism was the 'counter-revolution of ancient India'.

Dalits or the exuntouchables had a crucial role to play in defeating Brahmanic Hinduism and opening the road to a society of equality and liberation. Whereas Ambedkar had originally emphasised the destruction of caste as a prerequisite to economic equality (socialism), now he began to argue that untouchables were the carriers of Buddhism, the liberatory message of Indian tradition.

The process of change involved internal (spiritual) change, the 'slave's rejection of slavery', and also a process of social struggle, political dialogue and political organising. Ambed kar's rejection of violence was not a matter of absolute principle, like the Gandhians, but simply because he saw it as normally ineffective as a main method of change. Ambedkar's philosophy was an enlightenment philosophy that could be described as 'social liberation'combined with an emphasis on caste as a social reality; and it distinguished Ambedkar both from Marxists who saw the proletariat as revolutionary and neglected cultural and social factors, and from both the dominant Congress trends (not to men tion the Hindu right) which refused to see elements of exploitation and oppression in Indian tradition.

In the last years of his life, Dr Ambedkar gave a beginning to two institutions he saw as necessary for the liberation of his people and the welfare of the country: Buddhism and the Republican Party, a spiritual force and a political platform. Both were seen as more than the vehicles of the ex-untouchables. For religious and cultural change, he hoped that all of India would become *'Prabuddha BharaC* and experience a cultural renaissance. For political struggle, he hoped that the Republican Party would be a vehicle for all who sought to achieve the great goals, surpassing the narrow confines of the Scheduled Caste Federation. But this was not to happen.

Ambedkar himself could not really establish either the RPI or the organisational form of Buddhism. The RPI itself was formed with a constitution that emphasised its broad approach, projecting itself as a party of all the oppressed sections. Yet, it was little more than a change of name for the already-existing Scheduled Caste Federation. The dilemma of how Ambedkarite Buddhism (now referred to by many as *'navayana Buddhism')* would be carried on was, in many ways, even greater since there was not even any existing institution. The main Buddhist organisation in India, the Mahabodhi Society, was mainly staffed by Sinhalese Buddhist monks but was headed in India by (of all people) Shyam Prasad Mookerji (thus giving credence to the Hindutva position that Buddhism was only a form of Hinduism and Buddha was the ninth avatar of Vishnu). Ambedkar could not but reject this, and in the vacuum it was Englishbased Buddhist converts who took up the task of consolidating Buddhism among Dalits immediately following Ambedkar's death and formed the Trailokya Bauddh Mahasangh. Both, Buddhism in India and the Republican Party of India remained not simply 'Dalit' institutions, but institutions limited to specific*jatis* among Dalits: Mahars in Maharashtra and scattered groups of Chamars (known asjatavas in the 20th century) in UP Buddhist conversion allowed for a tremendous change in the consciousness of. ex-untouchables but it did not produce much of a change in their social identity. Almost no caste Hindus followed them in converting, and the result was that Buddhism itself became rather 'untouchable' in India.

In the case of the RPI, though it had enough of a base in UP and elsewhere to achieve the status of an 'all-India party' (its elephant symbol today, though, has been taken over by the BSP), in Maharashtra it not *onlf* remained a party of Mahars, but factions within it were based upon sub-castes. The RPI had genuine radical moments, under the leadership of Dadasaheb Gaikwad, when it joined socialists and communists (under the leadership of Nana Patil) in land satyagrahas in

1956 and 1965, aimed at gaining access to forest land and 'common' lands for cultivation by Dalits and other landless. But by the late 1960s, it had subsided into a co-opted and stagnant party, with some alliance with the Congress in exchange for patronage, and with membership and leadership drawn only from exMahars. Thus, even in Maharashtra, the centre of Ambedkar's efforts, the Dalit movement remained confined within the boundaries of *jati.*

The creative and transformatory potential of the Dalit movement, however, was shown by the fact that it took only a little over 10 years after Dr Ambedkar's death for the stalemate to be shattered. Following the stagnation in the first decades of independence, about the same time as the upsurge of Naxalism in the 1960s, came the beginnings of a powerful poetry of protest in Maharashtra, the Dalit Sahitya Movement, It was sacrilegious ('One day I cursed that motherfucker god ...'), defying cheap patriotism ('Shout victory to the revolution, but burn, burn those who strike a blow at tradition'), renouncing fundamentalism and expressing the raw urge of the rebellious youth.

4.3. Movement Lead by Dadasaheb Gaikwad

After the death of Babasaheb Ambedkar, the mantle of leadership fell upon the shoulders of Dadasaheb Gaikwad. He appeared to be the natural choice, by virtue of his stature in the movement as well as his age. He had grown up to be Ambedkar's trusted lieutenant through frontline participation in all the battles, right from the days of Mahad. He represented a typical activist of the Ambedkarian movement and had a mass identity. He seemed to know the exact pulse of dalit masses. It is interesting to note that the question of land that by and large constitutes the crux of the dalit problem was and could only be taken up by Gaikwad. It was the biggest and by far the most glorious event in the post–Ambedkar dalit movement. Even during the days of Babasaheb Ambedkar, the mass struggle for land had never materialised in direct terms and at such a scale. At any rate, as a mass struggle for land at the national level, it did not have any parallel in Indian history. It was the first time that the economic dimension of the dalit problem was effectively integrated with their social oppression. It had gained an overwhelming support from the masses all over the country.

However, although it had caught the fancy of dalit masses, the rest of the dalit leadership thought otherwise. They disproved Gaikwad's struggle as being communist and declared that it had no place in Ambedkarian agenda. They highlighted Ambedkar's statement that mass struggles were the grammar of anarchy in the constitutional regime and should not have any place in a parliamentary democracy. They argued that if the land question was at all important, it could have been taken up judicially in the Supreme Court of India. Fortunately, none suggested parliamentary solution. In tacit terms, the other leaders were accusing Gaikwad of being intellectually incapable of comprehending the subtleties of Ambedkar's ideology and hence unsuitable to step into his shoes.

Gaikwad, a rustic in the common man's Dhoti Kurta attire, and not embellished with university degrees, could not be accepted by these people. They considered themselves the true heirs to the leadership after Ambedkar on the sole criterion that they fitted the Ambedkarian mould better than Gaikwad. This mould was based on the contemporary middle class cultural norms that Ambedkar displayed in his attire and general demeanour. They would conveniently forget that his western attire was basically a counter to Gandhi's belaboured austerity and a representation of modernity as against Gandhi's anti-modern views. Instead, they aped him in all appearances. They would exhibit their law books as the key to the treasure left behind by Ambedkar. They could thus project themselves as better clones of Ambedkar to the gullible dalit masses. Gaikwad and the people of his ilk could be activists but not the leaders!

The first attempt to iconise Babasaheb Ambedkar and considerably successfully so, as the later times proved, is apparent in this early post-Ambedkar episode. That was the icon of a '*saheb*' the epitaph used for an Englishman but later used as an honorific for natives, who were educated, westernised and placed in bureaucratic authority. It denoted someone far above the masses, one who was endowed with authority and power. It was the icon of a saviour. It projected leader as the saviour incarnate who would liberate them from their bondage and lead them to prosperity. All that masses had to do was to stand solidly behind him. They did not have any specific role in the project of their own emancipation other than being meek followers of the leader. This particular icon distanced the dalit leadership from the masses in every way in terms of physical attributes like appearance, clothes, language and lifestyle. It promoted blind following and servile notions. The leaders were to be treated as their quasi-monarch. They could not be questioned on equal terms. They bestowed favours by their very existence. Without leaders the masses could not exist. Moreover, in so far as this syndrome reflected middle class aspirations and value associations, this icon helped petty-bourgeoisize the entire dalit movement.

Although, later the Dalit Panthers brought in a change in this leadership model, certainly in its physical attributes and so made it more people friendly, it approximately recoiled back to the old RPI model with the demise of the spirit behind Panthers. This leadership model was certainly regressive as it reproduced the decadent feudal structure that dalits were so familiar with in real life; perhaps it was both, its cause as well as its effect. Paradoxically, its protagonists and promoters were the very people who seemed to claim a larger share of modernity. Thus, this early icon of Ambedkar certainly blocked the emerging mass orientation of the dalit movement.

4.4. Dalits in Post-1947 Politics

The importance of dalits in the scheme of post-1947 politics was duly recognised by the ruling classes, then predominantly represented by the Congress party. It was vital for them to tie dalits to the parliamentary alternative. Hypothetically speaking, if the latent alienation and the proletarian consciousness of dalits were allowed to grow in an unhindered manner, revolutionary prospects for India would have been closer than in any other conceivable place in the world. However, no ruling class would allow this to happen, much less the Indian one, which had impeccable credentials in its adeptness at keeping its victims within the institutional bondage for millenniums with mere soft strategies. Whatever the other motivation, there was certainly this element of strategy at work in making Ambedkar the chairman of the drafting committee for the Indian Constitution. It is said that it was done at the instance of none other than Mahatma Gandhi. Could there be a better method to achieve this than getting Ambedkar- the undisputed leader of dalits, who had come to regard him as their Messiah, to author the Constitution! It is a tribute to

Gandhi's farsightedness and cunning that he prompted Nehru to make it happen. Gandhi and Nehru knew that the composition of the Constituent Assembly, surfeit with representation of the propertied classes by design, provided enough fortification not to let Ambedkar's ideology penetrate the Constitutional draft. But, at the same time, Ambedkar could be eulogised as its maker. Thus, although the content of the Constitution was decided by the ruling classes, the ruled ones were made to own it up. It was a feat of strategy certainly comparable in its import to that behind the caste institution. Behind its generosity and progressive veneer was hidden the trap which would effectively incapacitate the dalits for a long time to come. Once trapped they would stay in perpetual fragmentation in the turbulence of electoral game played by various sections of the ruling classes. Dalits constituting over 15 per cent of the total population are a significant factor in the number game of electoral politics. Every ruling class political party would vie with each other to get them as a vote block on its side and still collectively prevent their coalescence into a class.

The mass struggle that materialised under the leadership of Gaikwad certainly shook the ruling classes. They had to devise special strategies to contain the threat of the emerging dalit challenge. It was a challenge indeed, although inadequately articulated, that had exactly touched the most sensitive nerve of the feudal structure, which still lay at the base of everything that mattered to dalits. It culminated in the first alliance between the RPI and the Congress, which helped Gaikwad, and a few others reach the Parliament and Legislative Assemblies. The inauguration of the era of unprincipled alliances could be discerned right here. The Congress was undisputedly a representative party of the Indian ruling classes comprising the high caste capitalists and landlords.

In the face of it, it appears difficult to associate this phenomenon with Ambedkar who for the best part of his life had fought the Congress tooth and nail, criticised it ruthlessly and ultimately warned his followers to be away from it as it was the 'burning house'. It is interesting to note him standing out among his contemporaries, including the communists and socialists of all hues, in unambiguously characterising the Congress party as the representative of the capitalists and landlords and unmask its fake anti-imperialist facade. However, as it always happened, in this case too his life-saga left enough strands to be picked up by the vested interests in support of the seemingly contrary act. Whatever the situational contexts and strategic compulsions, but it could be cited that the same Ambedkar had joined the Congress government at the centre under Nehru's Prime Ministership, had accepted the chairmanship of the drafting committee for the Indian Constitution on the basis of support from the Congress majority, and had accepted the Congress support for getting re-elected to the Constituent Assembly after the partition of the country.

Whenever the oppressed masses organised their resistance against the oppression, repression and co-option have been the age-old twin strategic tools in the repertoire of the ruling classes. Contrary to the general feeling that the latter is the recent phenomenon, associated with the spread of liberalism, these strategies have been iteratively used by the rulers from time immemorial, depending upon their perception of the intensity of peoples' struggles. More often than not, co-option being the low cost option is preferred by the ruling classes. What Congress had done in allying with RPI was precisely implementation of this strategy. On the side of RPI, the motivation to ally with any party flowed from, as it seems, the clarion call given by Ambedkar to dalits to become 'the ruling race'. It was supposed to mean the rule of the dalits, the have-nots—the rule of the working classes. It was however conveniently taken to mean being part of the ruling team, the ruling class, by the dalit leaders. Any pursuit of power, regardless of means, thus became a quasi-sacred obsession for the dalit leaders.

In absence of any explanation of the strategic contexts in which Ambedkar had accepted support from the Congress, it provided good enough grounds to sustain the de-shaped icon of Ambedkar in the minds of gullible masses. This icon froze the alternative of parliamentary structure as the only alternative for dalits and consequently impelled them to rely on electoral methods to gain power. The Poona Pact had already eliminated the possibility of shaping up their truly representative leadership through the electoral means and in corollary laid foundation for the proliferation of irresponsible leaders. This icon thus fortified the emasculation of dalits in the political sphere. It approved the in-camera parleys of the leaders for their tailist pursuit of power shorn of the mass line and established the bourgeois model of politicking. Dalit movement thus became permanently an adjunct of the ruling class.

4.5. Movement during the Era of Disintegration

Then came the era of disintegration. The RPI split and further split till people lost count of its factions. Three predominant reasons could be discerned for this disintegration:

i) The ruling class strategy of 'divide and rule',

ii) The lack of ideological coherence in the dalit movement and

iii) The petty-bourgeoisie aspirations of its leadership. Apparently, these reasons reinforced each other and in that sense were not exclusive.

'Divide and Rule' is the well-known strategy of the ruling classes world over to basically weaken the ruled people. Indians generally attributed it to the colonial British policy but the fact is that more than any one else, it is ingrained in the blood of their own ruling class. It underlay their caste system in the form of a continuum of hierarchies that kept the people perpetually divided. This caste continuum has certainly played its obnoxious role even in avowedly 'caste annihilating' dalit movement in terms of providing potential fissures to crack along. As explained above, the post-independence reality, comprising mainly the 'Poona Pact' and enslavement of dalits within the framework of parliamentary democracy exposed dalits to ruling class enticements and resultantly led to their perpetual division. It had to be simultaneously weakened to perpetuate their political subordination.

The petty-bourgeoisie aspirations of dalit leaders made operationalisation of this strategy easy. Its feasibility was further enhanced by the ambivalence reflected in Ambedkar's sayings and doings from time to time, which provided scope for any one to interpret him the way one liked. It was his icon as the demigod of dalits that was used up by the competing commanders of his army to do whatever they liked. This deification that he himself severally warned against and abhorred but which paradoxically had started well during his life time and grew after his death with an accelerated pace particularly because he himself became an essential icon in the neo-Buddhist rituals after his embracement of Buddhism less than two months ago. The mass *Dharmantar* unprecedented in modern times and considered by many as the culmination of his life mission, released the flood of dalit religiosity that overwhelmed every other thing. It imparted him a quasi-spiritual aura as *Bodhisatva*. Many enthusiastically added a *sarana* in his name (*Bhimam saranam gachhami*) to the original *trisarana* of Buddhism. Thereafter the display of devotion towards Ambedkar became a surrogate for one's ideological allegiance to him. Everyone vied with another to display his kind of devotion and in turn to emphasise superiority of his ideological ware for justifying his separate shop. The process of establishing the shop invariably relied upon the collection of clientele from one's own sub-caste and building up subordinate political nexus with some section of the ruling class.

The ruling classes of course played their cards well in catalysing this divide in their pursuit of buying the dalit support. This electoral commerce paid off handsomely and created its own rationale and motivation for the permanent division of dalit leaders. Through this process, some of the leaders of the wretched, while serving their cause, amassed wealth worth crores of rupees, became industrialists, maintained fleets of cars, roamed around by air and taxis, without any evidence of the basic source of their prosperity. It is a tribute to the political consciousness of dalits that while they starved and bled themselves over the issue of unity of these leaders, it never occurred to them to ask, even in a whisper, a question about the source of their material well being! Many blatantly indulged in the acts contrary to their profession for amassing wealth- some set up liquor factories and still remained the front rank leaders of the Buddhists, some allied with the rank castiest and communalist and still claimed to be ardent Ambedkarites. Apart from the naked might of money in the electoral politics that tended to situate the moneyed men at the pedestal of power, the leadership model outlined above certainly contributed to their sustenance. With the money power they could invest into cultivation of their cronies and in turn command a better return in the wake of electoral parleys.

The splits were in a way a corollary of the leadership model and the over-reliance on the electoral politics sanctioned by the above-indicated icons. The leaders were always seen endowed with an uncommon wisdom that was really beyond the reach of masses. Leaders thus could do whatever they wanted without any scruples and they did it even breaking away from the party. As a result, the so-called giants who claimed the legacy of Ambedkar became contented with the identity of the parenthesised alphabets of their names after the RPI. They did not even worry about the fact that the formations represented by these parenthesised identities were basically a mere coagulation of their own subcastes, in their respective geographical areas. Every one claimed to be a better follower of Ambedkar than the other is, and in the process, proliferated his icons by projecting one's proprietary models.

4.6. Dalit Panthers

The degeneration that set in continued unabated till the birth of Dalit Panthers in early 1970s. There could be varied explanations for the paradigm shift in dalit politics (movement) marked by Dalit Panthers. Remarkably, they spoke the language of defiance and militancy, which created waves. These waves had shaken the foundations of the established order in the country and in essence demonstrated what the wrath of the wretched could be! It provided a valuable insight that was pathetically missing in the dalit politics. They imparted the proletarian—radical class identity to dalits and linked their struggles to the struggles of all oppressed people over the globe.

It reflected a historical dilemma characteristic of the Indian situation. The pathos of casteism integral with the dalit experience essentially brought in Ambedkar, as his was the only articulate framework that took cognisance of it. But, for the other contemporary problems of depravations Marxism provided a scientific framework to bring about a revolutionary change. Although, have-nots from both dalits and non-dalits craved for a fundamental change, the former adhered to what appeared to be Ambedkarian methods of socio-political change and the latter to what came to be the Marxian method which tended to see every social process as the reflection of the material reality. Both caused erroneous interpretations. Neither, there was theoretical effort to integrate these two ideologies, nor was there any practice combining social aspects of caste with say, the land question in the village setting. Essentially, it remained an emotional and a poetic negation of the status quo, craving for the broad revolutionary change and on ideological plane inevitably reflected an amalgam of Ambedkar and Marx.

The possibility of the radical shift in the paradigm of dalit politics indicated by the manifesto was totally submerged by the reactionary upsurge of the new version of orthodox Ambedkarism. The reactionaries objected to the radical content of the programme alleging that the manifesto was doctored by the radicals—the Naxalites. There is no denying the fact that the Naxalite movement which had erupted quite like the Dalit Panther, as a disenchantment with and negation of the established politics, saw a potential ally in the Panthers and tried to forge a bond right at the level of formulation of policies and programme of the latter. But even if the Panthers had chosen to pattern their programme on the ten-point programme of the Black Panther Party (BPP) in the USA, which had been the basic inspiration for their formation, it would not have been any less radical. The amount of emphasis on the material aspects of life that one finds in the party programme of the BPP could still have been inimical to the established icon of Ambedkar. The fact that for the first time the Dalit Panther exposed dalits to a radical Ambedkar and brought a section of dalit youth nearer to accepting it certainly marks its positive contribution to the dalit movement.

There were material reasons for the emergence of Dalit Panthers, as there are for any episode or event. Children of the Ambedkarian movement had started coming out of universities in large numbers in the later part of 1960s, just to face the blank future staring at them. The much-publicised Constitutional provisions for them turned out to be a mirage. Their political vehicle was getting deeper and deeper into the marsh of parliamentarism. Unfortunately, quite like the BPP, they lacked the suitable ideology to channel this anger for achieving their goal. Interestingly, as they reflected the positive aspects of the BPP's contributions in terms of self-defence, mass organising techniques, propaganda techniques and radical orientation, they did so in the case of BPP's negative aspects too. Like Black Panthers they also reflected 'TV mentality', dogmatism, neglect of economic foundation needed for the organisation, lumpen tendencies, rhetoric outstripping capabilities, lack of clarity about the form of struggle and eventually corruptibility of the leadership. One of the reasons for its stagnation was certainly its incapability to escape the petit bourgeois ideological trap built up with the icons of Ambedkar. It would not get over the ideological ambivalence represented by them. Eventually, the petit-bourgeoise 'icon' of Ambedkar prevailed and extinguished the sparklet of new revolutionary challenge. It was completely sapped of its rebellious image and its vitality and soon got corrupted with a ridiculous prefix 'Bharatiya' to it. It survived as another living monument to the ideological bankruptcy and the degeneration of the dalit leadership.

The Dalit Panther phase represented the clash of two icons: one, that of a radical 'Ambedkar', as a committed rationalist, perpetually striving for the deliverance of the most oppressed people in the world. He granted all the freedom to his followers to search out the truth using the rationalist methodology as he did. He abhorred all kinds of humbug and hated to be bound by any dogma. He desired his followers to do the same. Like his mentor, the Buddha, he would exhort his followers not to take any thing for granted until their own experience corroborated it or their intellect supported it. As it turned out, the radical icon of Ambedkar was projected without adequate conviction. It was implanted in an alien soil. There was no one committed to propagating such an image of Ambedkar, neither communists nor dalits. Eventually it remained as a veritable hodgepodge compared to the familiar set of icons coming from the other camp.

4.7. Movement Lead by Kanshiram

The movement of Kanshiram markedly reflected a different strategy, which coined the 'Bahujan' identity encompassing all the SCs, STs, BCs, OBCs and religious minorities than 'dalit', which practically represented only the scheduled castes. Kanshiram started off with an avowedly apolitical organisation of government employees belonging to Bahujana, identifying them to be the main resource of these communities.

Purely, in terms of electoral politics, which has some how become a major obsession with all the dalit parties, Kanshiram's strategy has proved quite effective, though in only certain parts of the country. He has given a qualitative impetus to the moribund dalit politics, locating itself into a wider space peopled by all the downtrodden of India. But he identified these people only in terms of their castes and communities. It may be said to his credit that he reflected the culmination of what common place icon of Ambedkar stood for. The religious minorities which potentially rears the sense of suffering marginalisation from the majority community could be easily added to it to make a formidable constituency in parliamentary parlance. Every one knew it but none did how to implement. Kanshiram has seemingly succeeded in this task at least in certain pockets. The careful analysis will show that the combination of certain historical developments and situational factors has been behind this success. If not, one will have to constantly exert to recreate the compulsions for their togetherness and allegiance. In absence of any class-agenda, which is certainly the case of BSP, these compulsions could only be created through manipulative politics for which political power is an essential resource. BSP's unprincipled pursuit of power is basically driven by this exigency. It is futile to see in this game a process of empowerment of the subject people as could be seen from the statistical evidence of the cases of atrocities, and of overall situation of the poor people under its rule. There should be no lament over this as essentially it is where any kind of political acrobatics is destined to end in the prevailing system. The imperatives of this kind of strategy necessarily catapult the movement into the camp of the ruling classes as has exactly happened with BSP.

It seems to have sustaining support from the icon that BSP itself created, where Ambedkar was painted as the intelligent strategist who could turn any situation to his advantage, who used every opportunity to grab political power to achieve his objective. He is the person who saw in political power, a key to the woes of dalits and therefore exhorted them to grab it at any cost. He did not think highly of mass struggles except for tactical reasons to demonstrate the might of the leaders. For him, there existed only means not the values for securing one's goals. He is seen as the person endowed with State authority the sole source of his power to benefit his people. He was the sole arbiter of the interests of his people. Of course, he had disdain for all shades of communism.

Kanshiram's reading of Ambedkar ignores the fact that Ambedkar had to carve out space for his movement in the crevices left by the contradictions between various Indian political parties and groups on one side and the colonial power on the other. For most of his time, he sought maximisation of this space from the contending Muslim League and Congress, to name the predominant players, and eventually brought dalit issue to the national political agenda. Kanshiram stuffs his Ambedkar icon entirely with such kind of superfluity that it would look credible to the gullible dalit masses. This icon approves of his sole ideology that political power to his party could solve all dalit problems. His strategy till then has been to be in vantage position to decide who would be the king and thereby leverage his bargaining power. He did not care for democracy. To some extent this non-democratic stance spells his compulsions to have unitary command over his party structure as without it, his adversaries would gobble it up. He did not have any utility for any programme or manifesto, no concern for any issue howsoever burning, no qualms about policy or principles because, his sole obsession is to maximise his power by whatever means. He never even spelt out what precisely ails his Bahujans except for highlighting their prejudiced social identities in worn-out casteist phraseology. That explains his entries into and exits from political alliances with any one with the same alacrity.

The underlying value of the movement of Ambedkar was represented by liberty, equality and fraternity. Kanshiram does not seem to respect any value than the political and money power. In Ambedkar, one cannot miss an overflowing concern for the oppressed and wrath against the perpetrators of oppression. Kanshiram's concern scarcely transcended his speeches in his electoral rallies. It was with this concern and commitment that Ambedkar kept on referring to Marx and Marxism till his end, something as a touchstone to test his alternatives. Kanshiram simply abhorred it. Ambedkar struggled to formulate the dalit problem. Kanshiram either took it for granted or did not care for it at all. For Ambedkar certain values, moral code etc. were paramount, Kanshiram never seemed to be bothered by these issues. Ambedkar always foresaw plans and programmes; visualised appropriate structures for the downtrodden. Kanshiram expressed clear disdain for such things. For Ambedkar political power was a means, to Kanshiram it appears to be the end.

The crux of Kanshiram can be traced to his superfluous attempt to replicate Ambedkar's movement of 1920s as if the times had stood still for the bygone five decades. Ambedkar's mobilisation of dalit masses through struggles is vulgarised by him as the 'agit-prop' tool to collect people behind him. When Ambedkar realised the potency of political power, he launched his Indian Labour Party that reflected his urge to bring together the working class, transcending the caste lines. It is only when the political polarisation took communal turn that he abandoned his ILP project and launched the Scheduled Caste Federation. Although, he accepted the Congress support and offered to work in their government, he never tied up his political outfit to the Congress. It always appeared a politically expedient step for him as an individual without any organisational implication. Declaredly he would avoid the leftists of all hues and accept the friendship of the rank reactionaries of every kind. Ambedkar pointed at the capitalism and Brahminism as the twin enemy for his movement but Kanshiram enthusiastically embraced them without any pinch to his conscience. Ambedkar, in his own way, has been in search of suitable ideological carrier for the dalit movement. Kanshiram has no utility for such a thing.

Apart from these broad political trends, there are many regional outfits like Dalit Mahasabha in Andhra Pradesh, Mass Movement in Maharashtra, Dalit Sena in Bihar and elsewhere, etc., some of which dabble directly into electoral politics and some of them do not. They offer some proprietary ware claiming to be a shade better than that of others.

4.8. Hinduised Buddhism

Another trend in the dalit movement emphasises the spread of Buddhism as its goal. As in politics, there are numerous organisations devoted to this task. According to them, Buddhism was the culmination of Ambedkar's mission and hence, the true Ambedkarite not only had to be a Buddhist but also had to work for the spread of Buddhism. Ambedakr's declared vision of making India a Buddhist country spells a mission statement to them. Their activities revolve around building Buddhist viharas, becoming *Shramners and Bhikkus*; imbibing religious mode of living and engaging in quasi-studious pursuits like learning Pali, reading Buddhist scriptures, rewriting the episodes in history. One of the underlying motives in this enterprise was to project superiority of Buddhism and in turn their own as they believed that they were the original Buddhists. Paradoxically, all of them quibble over the distinction between 'Dharma' and 'Dhamma', claiming that Buddhism is Dhamma whereas others are the Dharmas. Unlike other religions, Buddhism does not have any place for rituals, gods or any permanent entity like soul, and is just a practicable moral code for living. However, in practice, all kinds of mumbo jumbo that some times appears to be exceeding the familiar but on-the-wane rituals of Hinduism, are followed, so much so that not only Buddha but even Ambedkar is not spared from the godhood (*Bhim Bhagawan*). Of late, the relatively upwardly mobile among dalits are increasingly getting attracted towards 'Vipasyana'—a kind of meditation that is said to have been practised by Buddha himself to get his enlightenment and so is 'prescribed' in Buddhism to be a good Buddhist. It is amusing to see this mind-centric trend growing among dalits. In all this, Ambedkar's attempts at rationalisation and redefinition of Buddhism are completely forgotten.

The icon they follow is that of a man incarnate of Buddha who analysed the problem of humanity and ultimately prescribed *nirvana*–a indescribable State marked by the extinction of all kind of craving. One who after Ashoka made greatest contributions to the revival and spread of Buddhism. It shows Ambedkar as a spiritual person who ultimately finds the roots of all the problems in the world within oneself and therefore preaches the virtue of moral rearmament and inner purity. It lay rather in extinguishing their own craving. It tended to internalise all their problems to themselves and stressed the need to cleanse their minds. Inevitably, it envisaged typical religious conduct from the followers with the highly pitched religious benchmarks available anywhere.

The sphere of religions abounds in such paradoxes. Its idiom basically promotes them. Buddhism could very well be conceived as the rebellion against the predominant creed of the establishment that prevailed more than 25 centuries ago, quite like Marxism in our times. Buddha was the first philosopher who forsook the futility of sterile philosophising and stressed the need to change the world. It is interesting to see in him as the first dialectician, some one in the same lineage as Hegel and Marx. His conclusions are not important, as they are essentially constrained by the State of knowledge and overall development of the physical sciences during his times. What is important is to see the expanse of positive things that he could postulate at that time. Significantly, Buddha discarded the concept of God and soul and spoke against all kinds of rituals; he asked people to accept things only if it corresponded with their own experience or passed the test of their own intellect. But, it could not escape the pressures of institutionalisation, which transformed it into a religion. They made him a God, wove stories that well competed with any mythology, built elaborate rituals to be followed and sapped it of its essential zeal of changing the world.

The paradox would be better illustrated by the responses of ardent Ambedkarites to the recent news about one Islamic Taliban commander threatening to dynamite two fourth-century monuments 1500-years-old statues of Buddha in central Afghanistan. The response came from highly educated non-resident Indian Ambedkarites. It was interesting inasmuch as they reveal what havoc the religious mindset that owes allegiance to Buddhism can play with even its human-centric tenets. They said that the dalits in India should immediately take out a massive procession to the consulate of Afghanistan and threaten them that no Afghan would be spared in India if they carried out destruction of the Buddha statues in Afghanistan. It was a burst of anger at the first hearing of the news and was not to be meant but nonetheless it revealed the consciousness, the consciousness of Khomini or of any Hindu fundamentalist at work. It is important to realise the fact that even the Buddha's *Dhamma* whose roots are firmly in the soil of rationality and whose sole raison de etre' is the human suffering, could be mutilated to be its exact opposite by the very followers of Ambedkar who consciously cleansed it of the dust of irrationality and mysticism gathered over millennia.

4.9. SC/ST Associations

One more significant trend in the dalit movement has its source in the policy of reservations in services of the State. Apart from the central and State governments, the large number of public sector undertakings that were floated by them, and other institutions established and promoted with public money, also came to be the State, attracting the constitutional provisions regarding reservations for the SCs and STs in services. The dalits in these sectors represented the collective investment and achievements of the dalit community, as reservations were the only hope for them to secure material well being. The dalits had to conform their behaviour to this code for their survival. It reflected all the familiar prejudices against them. Their experience of the blatant violations of these provisions generally manifested in terms of backlogs in filling reservation posts, denial of promotions and general discriminatory treatment meted out in postings, transfers and other aspects of organisational life. The trade unions and management associations would not address their woes because they involved a contradiction between the interests of dalits and non-dalits.

It is a sad commentary on the functioning of the Constitution that over the last four decades it has driven these collectives to a State of hopelessness. The constitutional provisions regarding the reservations flow in the form of various circulars issued by the Government of India that are supposed to be implemented by its executive machinery. Over the years there has been a plethora of these circulars each written in such a convoluted language that even the highest court of law also felt it an arduous task to interpret them. One of the deliberate lacunae that exist in this scheme is that there is no effective onus on any one for the implementation of these provisions. The executive can blatantly refuse to implement them under the plea of variant interpretation and drive the SC/ST employee or his association to the courts of law. Even if the poor employee or the SC/ST association could last the long winding court process over the years and succeed in getting the favourable verdict the employer can still persist with his negative attitude. There are scores of cases of this kind where the petitioner employee or his association had to launch contempt proceeding against the employers and end up being bankrupt in the process. The helplessness of dalit employees in the services, in a way is the reflection of the sorry State of dalit politics.

The typical activities of these associations comprise celebration of the birth anniversaries of Ambedkar, representing dalit employees to the management or administration, and doing certain philanthropic and community service, depending upon the degree of their own organisation and resources. The icon that they seem to be following is that of a saviour, emancipator, to whom they need to pay their obeisance, to obey his commandments. Their community service for instance could be easily traced to Ambedkar's call to dalits to contribute 20 % of their earnings to the cause of the community. Although, rarely any dalit goes so far as to sacrifice one fifth of his income over the cause of the community, none seem to refuse some symbolic contribution.

They see in Ambedkar as the one who struggled to get them so many facilities and it is their bounden duty to take fullest advantage of the same. It was their sacred duty to occupy positions of power in bureaucracy. It is assumed, as Ambedkar appears to have assumed himself, that the educated dalits with bureaucratic authorities will serve the cause of their community in direct proportion to their relative position. Ambedkar's exhortation to 'agitate' is reduced down to making appeals to various authorities, having meetings with managements submitting memoranda and at the maximum, to filing the writ petitions in the courts in short all that in the feasible range of the public service rules. Ambedkar is reduced to a deity that imparts an identity. It is therefore that one curiously finds dalits celebrating the joint birth anniversaries of Babasaheb Ambedkar and Shivaji along with the Shiv Sena in the so-called den of Ambedkarism—the State of Maharashtra.

4.10. Gender Equality Movement

It is expected of the people who avowedly fought against their unequal status, to have a congenial attitude towards the victims of other inequalities. Women are one social group who despite constituting half of the human population and contributing equally to the sustenance of human society are being discriminated against all over the world in varying degrees of severity. Gender inequality should have been the foremost issue in the dalit movement. At least this problem could have been approached with the demonstration of a paradigm shift towards a radical culture. But unfortunately, with the rise of petty- bourgeoisie consciousness in dalits, they have adopted the more regressive culture of the forward castes. But now the cultural preference of relegating them to the background to do the household chores and / or to look after children is increasingly evident in dalit homes. It is a matter of pride that right from the days of Ambedkar, women have played a major role in the dalit movement.

In the din of what Ambedkar did for women, the icon that guides action is of the exponent of legal and coded equality of women, something like equality on the statutes. Culturally, dalits have not transcended the boundaries of sanskritisation, in the sense that their women folk have been given the worn out role model of a Brahmin woman; just because Ambedkar had once exhorted them to emulate her in the manner of donning their saris and other ornaments. Thus, it may be said that the approach towards women even in the glorious days of the struggle also had not gone beyond the men-centric traditional role women donned. Similar observation can be made against Buddhism, that its meta-ideals also could not so much as grant them the absolute equality with men. It is a well known fact that Buddha had granted his tacit approval for the ladies to enter the Buddhist order as the '*Bhikkunies*', at the instance of Anand -one of his close and favourite disciples, but had prescribed that they will always bow in reverence to a *Bhikku* irrespective of their relative seniority in the order. It is not to be forgotten that Ambedkar had to communicate with dalits in their familiar idiom. The cultural change, moreover is an invisible process. What Ambedkar said or did had the limitation of historical possibilities; he would not say anything for the sake of postulating. He craved for change and strove to bring it about with a practicable approach. Unfortunately, dalits seem to have frozen it into an icon and raised fences around themselves from the concept of radical gender equality.

4.11. Anti-Materialism

It is a sad paradox of history that the movement of dalits, who are undisputedly the biggest sufferer of material depravation, should show an utter disregard for things material in an era characterised by stark materialism. It smacks of its distaste for the real issues of life while displaying excessive enthusiasm for the emotional issues. After the massive movement of landless labourers led by Dadasaheb Gaikwad, incidence of the material questions that afflict most of the people, could be seen as just notional. Even the Panthers could not escape this trend. There have been massive displays of strength of dalit unity but it all has been for emotional issues. The examples abound. The glorious movements for 'Namantar', against the ban on the Riddles of Rama and Krishna, and many others representing the dalit-anger towards the attempts of castiest elements to denigrate and desecrate the statues of Babasaheb Ambedkar, certainly demonstrated potential force of dalits. In the Namantar case, in response to the Long March by dalits, the local dalit hamlets were burnt down, many people got lynched, many women were raped, and all were ostracised and boycotted. Every time this heinous episode recurs and dalits bear the brunt!

With regard to the neglect of material aspects of living in the dalit movement, the inspiring icon is made up of Ambedkar's much publicised opposition to the vulgar materialism propagated by the then communists. It is stuffed with his thoughts that reflect not necessarily disdain for the material things but a leaning towards a belief that the societal phenomena could well be shaped by the non-material things or processes.

It is coloured by the fact that the tone of the struggles he launched has always been in the realm of codes, norms, traditions, and institutional practices that he aimed his struggle against for bringing about the socio-cultural change, a social revolution. The culmination of his mission, as it is seen by dalits, in Buddhism, that predominantly taught the virtue of extinguishing the thirst for material things and reaching indefinable State of mental peace called *Nirvana*, has certainly lent strength to this icon. Dalits always defined their struggle to be for prestige—for '*Asmita*', for self-respect. In the history of four decades at no time any of their leaders or any intellectual cared to look at how the government policies or international happenings influenced the lives of average dalits in villages.Even in the face of atrocities that dalits suffer day in and day out, never does the realisation dawn on them that much of it could be traced to their State of material depravation. The fact that they cannot organise defence is also related with their material wherewithal. It does not seem to be a question of violence or non-violence. Fortunately, Ambedkar's own stand on violence, as he often declared it in order to expose the futility of Gandhi's obsession with non-violence in the long polemics is well known to dalits. But the icon of Ambedkar that came before people was conveniently shorn of this practical attribute. This icon seems to obfuscate even Buddha as the impracticable proponent of unqualified compassion and non-violence. It emphasises constitutionalism even in the wake of perpetration of heinous atrocities.

4.12. Dalits and Election Politics

Barring emotional issues, the dalit movement has been hijacked by the petty warring factions of incompetent leaders whose sole obsession appears to be elections of whatever kind. As roosters wake up crowing at the dawn or frogs surface out of nowhere around water pools formed with the first showers of monsoon, they all surface out of their slumber with any election announcement. Then follow the talks for alliances, allegations and counter allegations of money transactions, threats of splits and actual splits. This process could be preceded by the talks of unification of various factions, if they were not together, essentially engineered by the electoral strategies of some ruling class party. This cycle is seen repeated a number of times at least in Maharashtra, which has historically been assumed as the hub of dalit politics even after losing its provincial relevance. They would not have any manifesto, no strategy, no agenda or plan; no realistic assessment of their strength and weakness. Participating in elections however was their sacred duty. The Ambedkar-icon that appears to back this strange phenomenon derives its material from the fact that Ambedkar himself relied upon elections for securing power despite his own bitter experiences, that he tended to think of the popular mandate gained through periodical elections as the only legitimate political process in the Constitutional regime and denounce other modes of mass struggle. It is additionally imbued with a hope that despite several defeats Ambedkar rose to occupy seats of power through the electoral process.

Now the people are increasingly getting dejected with the games of dalit leaders and are found to be straying over to other parliamentary parties, even of Brahminical hues. Many of the latter have already co-opted Ambedkar. Some have lent him their veneration by including his name into their list of the *'Pratah smaraniya'*- the memorables at the dawn. They have launched the class assimilative drives like Rashtriya Samarasata Manch. Today, there is a sort of clamour for claiming Ambedkar's legacy among all the parliamentary parties. In the face of disintegration of the dalit block and increasing political crises faced by these parties, they all need Ambedkar for their survival. The icon they project is that of a staunch nationalist, of one who was proud of 'Indian' culture and tradition minus evils like untouchability and of one who was against communism.

The election mania is so deep entrenched in the minds of dalits that they ceased to think of any other alternative. There is no appreciation of the fact that they have been squarely cheated in this intoxicating game. At the first place, the resource sensitive game does not gel with the starkly resourceless players. Second, so far they do not transcend their caste confines, their constituency remains acutely constrained by the numbers of their own caste. Third, even if one succeeded overcoming these odds in the election, there may essentially lie series of compromises ahead for basic survival in the houses. The system ensures that a true representative of dalits does not reach the portals of power, and if reached, he or she is soon neutralised. It is amazing that the simple empirical evidence of the systemic failure does not get across dalits. Electoral dalit politics presupposes alliances and compromises invariably with the ruling class parties who may satisfy the thirst for power of its leaders but certainly not support the dalit empowerment.

4.13. Values of Ambedkar's Principles

Various icons that the post-Ambedkar movement of dalits appear to have built up, characterise Ambedkar as the maker of the Indian Constitution, provider of the present order, a Bodhisatva, a constitutionalist, a messiah, a saviour, an SC leader, a liberal democrat, a staunch anti-Communist, a social engineer who believed in the reform process and disliked revolutions.

Many students of the dalit movement are influenced by these post-Ambedkar reflections in characterising Ambedkar as the bourgeoisie liberal democrat. Does it really project what Ambedkar stood for? Does it capture the full essence of his movement? More importantly, is that the Ambedkar whom we are going to use as the weapon in the emancipatory struggle of dalits?

Dalits as a social group, are still the poorest of poor. A negligible minority has managed to escape poverty limits and to locate itself on to a continuum ranging up to a reasonable level of prosperity with the help of certain State policies like reservation and political patronage. In social terms however, all dalits, irrespective of their economic standing, still suffer oppression. This social oppression varies from the crudest variety of untouchability, still being practised in rural areas, to the sophisticated forms of discrimination encountered even in the modern sectors of urban life. More than 75 per cent of the dalit workers are still connected with land; 25 per cent being the marginal and small farmers and the balance 50 per cent being landless labourers. The proportion of dalits landless labourers to the total labourers has shown a steady rising trend. In urban areas, they work mainly in the unorganised sector where the exploitation compares well with that of a feudal rural setting. Out of the total dalit population of 138 million, the number of dalits in services falling in the domain of reservations does not exceed 1.3 million including sweepers; less than even a percent. And this too would be grossly misleading, as out of this 1.3 million the relatively well-off group A and B officers count only 72,212 as against 131,841sweepers.

With the new politico-economic order emerging in the world, the grammar of the dalit liberation struggle is going to be totally different from that familiar to dalits. The onslaught of the adversarial forces is being felt world over by all the oppressed people and it would be folly for dalits not to feel a part of the latter. Their objective situation as a social block is not represented by the minuscule minority that managed to find themselves in the organised sectors of economy, but by the vast majority who are left behind in the villages or the numbers who toil in the unorganised sectors in towns and cities. They need the weaponry for battling out their salvation. This battle is to be waged simultaneously on two fronts, marked by the caste and class. These terms under segmented and sectarian usage came to bear an erroneous exclusivity. Since, Ambedkar still provides a better framework for their problems than any other, and since he commands an unchangeable place in their hearts, the weapons in his armoury needs dusting and sharpening. Ambedkar, quite similar to Buddha in his own hands, needs redefinition.

The folklore 'Ambedkar' needs to be replaced by the radical 'Ambedkar', who would inspire people to claim the whole world as theirs and not to beg for petty favours from the robbers. It is the responsibility of all those who are capable of seeing the reality, to contribute to this task. For, without such a redefinition, Ambedkar could be fossilised as god but would fail in the emancipation project; he might be raised to the highest pedestal by the vested interests but then he would be unable to reach out to where he is most needed; he would lose out to the parody of history.

Ambedkar's thoughts are variously presented by scholars. Some tend to put them in familiar academic slots, viz.: social, political, economic, religious etc. The other method may be bracketed as biographical. The problem with the former is that it tends to discretise his thoughts within the artificial compartments of academic disciplines. Both of them are likely to miss out the underscoring vision and more so the futuristic dimension, which are essentially the attributes of the holistic conception.

Every great person has a vision that impels all her/his works. Its discernibility may vary from case to case, generally being the function of the degree of turbulence around her/him, her/his relative position within the power structure in the given environment, her/his own equipment and conception of self-role. Marx, for instance, offers an articulate vision in clearest terms as he assumed the primary role of a philosopher to bring about revolutionary change, whereas Ambedkar had donned the mantle of mass-leadership in his primary role to spearhead the change; the degree of turbulence in the work domain of Marx had been minimal as he basically struggled in the realm of thought spanning complete human history whereas Ambedkar situated himself in the political turbulence that obtained in India as his strategy; Ambedkar's position in the power structure that bounded his work domain was certainly weak relative to Marx's. With regard to personal equipment, both Ambedkar as well as Marx, could be taken to be equally equipped to undertake their respective tasks that they had undertaken. Marx had started off with philosophy and adopted the class-consciousness of the proletariat quite unlike Ambedkar, in whose case it was his own consciousness—the consciousness of an untouchable built up through concrete experience that had propelled his philosophical search. But, Ambedkar was always loaded with anxiety as he had to strategize his way through the political maze around him, winning for dalits the maximum he could in a short span of time. In process, his role also underwent transformation with the expanse of the battleground. Inevitably, his thoughts and action always remained context-laden, polemical and pragmatically purposeful. It is therefore a relatively difficult task to discern a coherent vision underscoring the life work of Babsaheb Ambedkar.

It is a moot point as to what extent a great person, who is essentially anchored in her/his space and time, could transcend these barriers and be equally effective in a different situation. A great person basically is the product of prevailing social relations. It is a particular moment in history that reflects an acute demand for such a person. Depending upon her/his location in the social setting, s/he imparts her/his individual feature to the historical moments and movements in terms of working out specific means for resolving contradictions that engender them and releasing the forces of history in a specific direction. The masses whose cause she / he espouses throng around her/him in this process, depending upon the level of their collective consciousness. The longevity of the ideas a great person propounds in a historical setting depends upon the nature of contradictions, the size and expanse of problems and the time domain in which they are situated. In this process, they would de-contextise some of the ideas and proffer them as universal theorems, if they perceive a pay-off for themselves in the sphere hegemonised by them. This phenomenon becomes clear only over a long time horizon. For instance, the religious principles that were sprouted in the soil of certain specific social relations have basically blossomed in an alien soil with the help of the nutrients of class interests.

In the case of Babasaheb Ambedkar, iconisation was inevitable. The combination of factors like his high stature, his devotion to the cause of his people; the historical setting in which he lived, the low level of literacy and political consciousness in masses; and the vested interests of internal as well as external people have been its cause. The problem is not with iconisation as it is with its multiplicity. A question may be pertinently asked can Ambedkar be uniquely represented by a single icon? As Prof. Upendra Bakshi had outlined in one of his articles during the centenary year of his birth anniversary that there were many Ambedkars and had questioned as to which Ambedkar do we commemorate? When he said so, Prof. Bakshi was referring to different facets of Ambedkar's personality that could be virtually segregated.

What comes clearly however, from this is that the changes in his outlook and role were essentially driven by his unstilted commitment to the cause of emancipation of oppressed humanity in general and dalits in particular. He might not have had appropriate methodological tools to deal with the problem at hand. With the equipment that basically belonged to a school of social engineers, he tried to dissect history. By training he did not have the facility to look at history as the continuum of human struggle with a certain inherent logic. He did use history as a repertoire of human episodes and attributed even logic to it but its source was externalised.

It appears that Babasaheb Ambedkar had really internalised the doctrine of momentariness (*Anityatawad* and later *Kshanikwad*) of Buddha and therefore even refused to care for consistency in his views and opinions. This doctrine states that every thing changes every moment, that things are constantly becoming. It follows that in this situation of flux not even mental processes could be static, they had essentially to match the dynamicity of the material world. He thus never hesitated in changing his thoughts or strategy as per the unfolding situation. Viewed another way, these changes can be understood in relation to foci of control. The degree of consistency in thought and action is generally inversely proportional to the distance of the subject from the foci of control of its surrounding. Ambedkar had nil or little control over his situation. He had to consistently create space for himself and strategize to influence the situation to his advantage. The framework within which he conceived his struggle had exposed him to his lot to respond to this dynamics. The hallmark of Ambedkar's thoughts is the dynamic rationale, which he has consistently employed to comprehend situations and to strategize his response thereto. 'Ambedkar' therefore cannot be captured in static terms.

The concept of *Anityawad* in Buddhism essentially belongs to dialectics that has made Buddha an early dialectician philosopher. The dichotomy that creeps in can only be resolved by dialectical method. It may be questioned whether Ambedkar's method was dialectical. It appears that while he accepts constant becoming of things as the principle underscoring the universe, he faces a dilemma with respect to the conception of order in this State. It could be resolved dialectically in terms of systemic attribute of self-regulation—a characteristic of internal control. But the conventional conception of order, essentially a non-dialectical conception, leads to externalisation of control. Ambedkar, having experienced the brutal aspects of history and unbridled exploitation of man by man, appears in need of a control mechanism operating at two levels, viz., internal and external, so as to maintain the societal order in the desired State. His internal control mechanism is the moral code provided by the religion and the one for external control is the State. If this moral code is internalised by all individuals and in turn by society as the summation of the latter, society is expected to have an internal order. If however the baser instincts of some people or group of people defy this order, either as a result of conflicting codes they follow or for any other reason, then in such case the State will step in and restore the order. It is therefore that Ambedkar has reservation in agreeing with Marx that 'religion was the opium of masses' or the 'State shall eventually wither away'. Ambedkar certainly did not know that the order could be the attribute of the system itself. It is only in the sixties that Cybernetics principles came to lime light that the complex probabilistic systems, which the social systems certainly are, do have the inherent capability of self-regulating and self-organising control.

By upbringing and training Ambedkar was influenced by western liberalism. The openness and liberal values of the western society had struck him with pleasant surprise by his own admission. There is a reason to believe that he had studied Marxism. His first essay on caste reflects some amount of analytical orientation of Marxism. One of the subjects in his curriculum also happened to be related to Marxian socialism and his guide Prof. Seligman was well versed with the economic interpretation of history. However, as his later work reveals, Ambedkar reflected more closeness with the liberal tradition than Marxism. Being aware of its pitfalls, he needed to declare that he was not a liberal reformist, although while having reservations with the postulations of Marxism he could never hide his attraction towards it.

The pitfall of his thinking emanates from his conception of the moral force of religion divorced from the material reality. He therefore hopes that without any bloodshed, the society based on liberty, equality and fraternity could be created. Of course as hypothesized above, he conceptualizes the constitutional State based on these principles. With this wishful thinking, he tends to ignore the fact that regardless of the pretensions of ruling classes, the impact of liberal governance in the multicentric iniquitous society is bound to result in sustaining multicentricity and inequality. It was a kind of contradiction in terms to assume that liberal democracy, which is actually the manifestation of the political power of the bourgeois, will do justice to the paupers. It might appear to extend certain concessions to the weaker sections, but its real motive is to maintain the existing rule of the ruling classes. Liberal democracy might appear better than the decadent Hindu caste system but it is incapable of bringing any real change in favour of dalits. It muffles the tension of the exploitative system and kills the revolutionary motivation of its victims.

Many of the constructs employed by Babasaheb Ambedkar in his working have a qualified meaning. Firstly, they are not absolute as they appear. They are the derivatives of his thought process, the source of which could be traced to his basic objective of annihilation of castes and creating a society based on equality, liberty and fraternity. Even these three principles that he held so dear to his heart, bear very different meaning from the familiar ones associated with the French Revolution. He said he had them from Buddha. What Buddha said also is to be understood from his interpretation, which could be as different from the accepted version as to be disproved by the Buddhist church. Understanding Ambedkar thus essentially demands extra consideration and care about the specific meanings of the constructs and concepts he uses. The lack of it has already caused much misunderstanding among many people. It is one thing to have a clear understanding of what he said or meant but quite another to extrapolate it to something congruent to his basic objective or vision that may be useable in shaping the future movement. Quite like Marx had said of philosophy, it could be said that the issue is not to understand Ambedkar as he is but to possibly think of him as a weapon in the struggle to which he devoted his life. The redefinition referred to here will have to essentially address both these issues. From the viewpoint of one seeking a revolutionary change, there are indeed many dimensions on which Ambedkar calls for critical interpretation. Paradoxically, he brings them to work for his emancipatory project, which potentially is no less than a revolution. Predominant among these concepts are identified as State, religion, liberal democracy, constitutionalism, revolution, socialism, violence and Marxism, that some way or the other have been the cause of misunderstandings about him.

It is important to appreciate that Ambedkar employed the search process that is essentially rational and the underlying objective undoubtedly radical. There could be flaws in the specific design or the application of the search process, depending upon the State of his knowledge and complexity of the situation to which it is applied. Besides this, the end result depends upon the repertoire of alternatives used for the search. What it means is that the specific method, thought or action of Ambedkar may constitute the historical facts but they cannot be taken in their face value if one wants to comprehend the ideological aspects of Ambedkar. In his usage of the above concepts for instance he does not always exercise the academic rigour. Besides the reason that much of his usage was addressed to the un-academic lot, most of the times he tended to impart his own meanings to the terms he used. For, hypothetically speaking, if Ambedkar had lived longer he would have certainly changed his views, looking at more information available or experiencing the undesired aftermath of some of his own beliefs and opinions. Had he not disowned the Constitution, which he had so laboriously written and so forcefully defended, saying that he was used as the hack to write it? Whatever he had done had several limitations. The redefinition project proposed here, in a way, is something, which he has done himself, all his life and would have continued doing if he had been alive. It is essentially something in the nature of continuing his unfinished task.

The methodological aspects of this exercise consists in the process of conceptualisation of the core vision and ideological proclivities of Ambedkar through the analytical study of his life within its contextual parameters, oriented towards capturing its intransient content. This process may not be free from bias. The bias could be in favour of the change craved for by the have-nots, not of the ruling classes that has necessarily been colouring the history so far. It cannot escape the viewpoint of the latter. The viewpoint is rather embodied in the basic intention to forge Ambedkar as the weapon for the future struggles of dalits. The process of conceptualisation may be formalised by drawing out multiple ideological patterns based upon the constituent parameters of the hypothesised vision and testing them with the facts in their macro and micro settings. The test results could be used to refine the definition of the parameters and repeating the exercise until they can no more be improved. The radicalisation consists in derivation of the programme from these dimensions with any scientific methodology.

The following discussion therefore directly deals with the salient dimensions of Ambedkar's life in order to capture its intransient essence.

4.14. Ambedkar against Exploitation

The underscoring vision in Ambedkar's thought and action is to be found in his yearning for the end of all kinds of exploitation. Whenever and wherever he smelt exploitation, he raised his voice against it. The caste system that subjugated more than one fifth of the population to levels worse than animals' for more than two millennia and which represented institutionalisation of the most heinous inequality by the Hindu religion as ordained by its gods, became the prime target of his life. He did not let this objective out of sight even for a moment and worked incessantly for its achievement. This Herculean task almost completely overshadows the fact that his struggles extend well beyond the caste struggles and rather encompass all other forms of exploitation.

Even the credit for struggling against untouchability was reluctantly granted to him by the establishment which had belittled him initially as merely a leader of his own caste–Mahar. This prejudicial treatment of Ambedkar could itself be taken as a measure of the severity of the problematic of caste. The facts are clear today that not only was his struggle directed towards the emancipation of all the untouchables but also towards annihilation of the entire caste system. It was basically against the systemic exploitation that ran unabated for centuries. He did not theorise the struggle on a hypothetical plane. He built it on the basis of real problems in a concrete situation. Unlike many cases, the motive force for his life mission was provided by his experience itself. The Bahishkrit Hitkarini Sabha that was the launch vehicle of his movement had majority from the forward caste people in its executive body. Even later, this intention of having a non-caste base for the organisation could be consistently seen in his movement, be it the Mahad struggle or the Indian Labour Party.

Although, he considered the magnitude of the problem of emancipation of dalits is such as to warrant his sole attention, he did take cudgels for other oppressed entities like workers, peasants and women. At one occasion in response to the accusation that he did not care for the tribals, he had to squarely admit the fact that he considered the problem at hand big enough to outlast his life and provokedly put that he never claimed to fight for whole humanity. While dealing with the socio-economic depravation of dalits, he comprehensively exposed certain systemic dimensions that help perpetuate exploitation. For instance, he was well aware of the capitalist and imperialist oppression besides the decadent feudalism within which domain his problem lay.

4.14.1. Capitalism

During the colonial British regime, capitalism started taking root in India with the collaboration of Indian mercantile capital and British capital. Unlike Europe, it did not have to battle against feudalism; rather it was implanted on the trunk of the latter in India. As a result, even in the capitalist institutions in the cities, caste discrimination simultaneously existed. Ambedkar was quite aware of the exploitative potential of capital and hence he had declared capitalism and Brahminism as the twin enemy of his movement. Moreover, he noted the reactionary compradore character of rising capitalism in the contemporary sectors of the economy and the inhuman exploitation of workers that it unleashed. His, Indian Labour Party (ILP) was an attempt to take up the question of capitalist exploitation, as well as to combine the struggle on both caste and class basis. Various workers' problems were taken up by the ILP, the leadership of combined strike of the mill workers, parliamentary fight for the workers' interest in relation to the Industrial Disputes Act, and various legal reforms that were brought about while he was in the Executive Council of the Viceroy, can be the examples of his concern for workers' exploitation. But, it was a model adopted out of familiarity and pragmatism, a matter of strategy, never thought out on an ideological plane to be a theoretical plank. Although, there cannot be any doubt that he stood against capitalism, he could not articulate a sound theoretical basis for doing so. Resultantly, his efforts remained constricted with a short view of workers' welfare but could not provide them a vision of their liberation.

4.14.2. Imperialism

Ambedkar's attitude towards imperialism has been projected in a distorted manner right from the beginning, mainly because he refused to take part in the freedom struggle or opposed Gandhi who for certain category of ignoramuses was the anti-imperialism personified. He strategically sought to maintain neutrality vis-à-vis the colonial State. He did not want to dissipate and squander his extremely limited resources on several fronts. He however knew the basic exploitative character of the colonial regime. At several occasions, he burst out saying that British imperialism and Indian feudalism were the two leaches that clung to Indian people. However, there was a fundamental difference between his and others' viewpoint. For instance, he did not approve equating opposition to imperialism with opposing the British. He noted that the opposition to imperialism couldn't be effective until its supporters within the country are left untouched. The then leader of the Communist Party of India—Manabendranath Roy once met him at his residence and during discussions insisted that destruction of imperialism had to be the first and foremost objective of Indian politics. Ambedkar's response to him summarised his outlook towards this problem.

The validation of his stand comes from an entirely unrelated corner and nearly half a century later. Suniti Kumar Ghosh, in his books has shown in great detail how the Congress representing landlords and capitalists had played a compradore role to serve the interest of imperialism during the so-called freedom struggle and how even after the transfer of power in 1947 the grip of imperialism instead of weakening became stronger. Does it not indicate that he was more correct than any of his contemporary politicians? The ones who biasedly wish to pronounce their half baked verdict that Ambedkar was a stooge of British merely on the basis of his acceptance of membership of Viceroy's Executive Council or talking to the Simon Commission, not only display their ignorance of history but also their casteist fangs.

In relation to British rule, Ambedkar basically makes two points. The first is that he questions the so-called freedom struggle launched under the leadership of Congress as an anti-imperialist struggle. He contended that the Congress basically represented the class of feudal lords and the urban capitalists the twosome exploiters of Indian masses. Although, it succeeded through the charismatic leadership of Gandhi in galvanising masses in its support, it essentially relied on bargaining with the colonial rulers for securing itself more share of power. It always throttled the mass spontaneity as in the case of 1942-uprisings and actively opposed the genuine anti-imperialist struggles of the revolutionaries like Bhagat Singh. The rhetoric of such statement apart, for he never appears to even take a note of other truly anti-imperialist struggles like the one referred to above, it is enough to reveal his attitude towards imperialism and understanding of the class character of the Congress. He knew that the class character of the Congress would not permit it to don this role in reality. Ambedkar could see through the anti-imperialist masks the real fangs of an exploiter of masses. He thus not only saw no point in siding with this more real exploiter of people than perhaps the colonial rulers, but also did not hesitate to openly oppose it when it came in the way of dalit liberation. He smelt rot in all such struggles that refused to notice existence of inhuman exploitation of some of their own people within their precincts and tended to over-externalise their woes. It may be pertinent to ask of those who raise the issue of Ambedkar's attitude and conduct towards imperialism, to answer as to why the problem of untouchability or caste system that reduced its one -fifth of the population to sub-human levels did not find a mere mention in the lofty discussions of freedom struggle that predated Ambedkar's raising it. The anti-imperialist aspiration also could be seen in the context of the class/caste division in the society. The battle for the lost kingdom waged by the vanquished lords also could be camouflaged as an anti-imperialist struggle and at the same time the genuine peoples' anti-imperialist aspiration manifested in the form of say anti-feudal struggle could be condemned as the pro-imperialism, merely because it directed its gun towards the props of the imperialism. The real anti-imperialist aspirations belong to the masses of people the manifestation of which is possible only through the peoples' war. While the scenes of anti-British struggles were being enacted for the 'mother' India of exploiters, Ambedkar busied himself to liberate the other India- the India of the exploited and oppressed.

4.14.3. Oppression of Women

Besides these mainstream forms of exploitation even the subaltern forms like women's exploitation, could not escape his agenda. He viewed them as the most oppressed of all. His approach to the problems was typically that of a liberal democrat constitutionalist. This certainly constrained his articulation of this problem as in many others. This issue will have to be seriously rethought by dalits under the redefinition project. But suffice here to say that at any opportunity, he raised his voice against women's discriminatory situation in the society. Right from the days of Mook Nayak and Bahiskrit Bharat, he appears to take cudgels for women. He always involved women in his struggles and tended to give them vanguard positions. For example, about 500 women had marched at the head of the historical procession at Mahad to assert the untouchables' right to drink water from the public tank. He was immensely pained to see the permanent denial of education and religious rights to women ordained in the Shastras of the Hinduism. His democratic consciousness never reconciled with any thing lesser than the equality of men and women though its expression was acutely constrained perhaps by his anxieties about the possibilities, so much so that it might even be mistaken as the male centric tactic. He described sacramental marriages as polygamy for men and perpetual slavery for women because under no circumstances within that system the latter would get liberty from their husbands, however bad or undesirable they may be. He insisted that women should have the freedom to break this contract.

Although, Ambedkar was conscious of the limitations of liberal democracy in the emancipatory project he had undertaken and at times had even declared that he was not a liberal democrat, for many reasons he could not escape its clutches completely. He could not be unaware that liberal democracy basically was born as the ruling class ideology in 19th century Europe. It takes individuals and their groups as basically selfish units as its premise. It holds that individuals and social groups progress only through competition. The French Revolution had demonstrated this potential in ample measure. As the Whigs in the English Liberal party had thought "the best way to ward off revolution was to adopt a liberal generous attitude toward the lower classes.

4.15. Challenges Ahead

The anticaste movement, a cultural revolutionary movement spearheaded by Mahatma Phule in the 19th century and Dr Ambedkar in the 20th century, and with all its aspects of being an alternative way of living, of working for reforms, of redeeming Indian society from the hold of Brahmanism, was basically a transformative social movement. It sought to deal with the problems of caste and Brahmanism, and went beyond this talk of issues of development in a way far different from either the Nehruvians or more dogmatic Marxists or the village-romantic Gandhians. Liberty, equality and fraternity, social transformation, political power, economic philosophy, and cultural transformation were all on its agenda.

The 'post-Ambedkar Dalit movement' was ironically only that in the end—a movement of Dalits, challenging some of the deepest aspects of oppression and exploitation, but failing to show the way to transformation. This failure of one of the potentially most powerful social forces in Indian society has left a gap. In terms of economic and political transformation, the only powerful ideological currents seem to be either an unadulterated acceptance of capitalist transformation or the new wave of swadeshi Hindutva. The latter while opposing 'Western commercialism' and globalisation in the name of the 'sacred Indian (Hindu) culture' seeks to maintain a closed economy to serve the needs of bureaucrats and big industrialists, Brahmans and Banias. The rejection of the modern world seen in Gandhian ecological fundamentalism, or the weak voices of left nostalgia for Nehruvian statism have proved no alternative; they have in fact only fed the flames of swadeshi. In spite of their promises, there is little room for a transformation in the interest of Dalits and low castes in this, and this has provided the gap for a rising Hindutva.

REFERENCES

Johannes Beltz, *Mahar, Buddhist. Religious Conversion and Socio-Political Emancipation*, New Delhi, Manohar, 2005.

Justice V.R. Krishna Iyer, *Ambedkar Centenary: Social Justice and the Undone Vast*, 1992.

Kadam K.N. (Editor), "Dr. B.R. Ambedkar: The Emancipator of the Oppressed", *A Centenary Commemoration Volume*, 1993.

., *Dr. Babasaheb Ambedkar and the Significance of His Movement: A Chronology*, 1991.

Kasare M.L., *Economic Philosophy of Dr. B.R. Ambedkar*, B.I. Publications Pvt. Ltd.,New Delhi, India.

Khairmode, C.B., *Dr. Bhimrao Ramji Ambedkar Charitra*, Vol. II, Bauddha Jan Panchayat, Parel, Bombay, Kshirsagar, 1958.

5

Ambedkar and Dalit Historiography

Ambedkar came to forefront in Indian academics from the decade of nineties with the intensified struggles of Dalits. The struggles of the ordinary people forced the centres of power and knowledge to consider the importance of Ambedkar and his ideas in social reconstruction of the nation. With Ambedkar as the source of inspiration, Dalits are struggling to write their own history by interrogating the dominant Brahminical traditions. The project of De- Brahiminisation of Indian history has appeal among the Dalit scholars in writing Indian history, culture and philosophy. The relevance of Ambedkar has to be read with the fifty years developments of post Ambedkar of post independent India. His approach to Indian society and its history are crucial in understanding contemporary India and the struggles of the oppressed.

Ambedkar's notion of history is identified with 'moral community' imbibed with the principles of equality, liberty and fraternity. His historical method borrows tools from Marxism in understanding the ancient history. Rather than mechanically applying Marxism, he had creatively used it in keeping the specific context of Indian society. He approached Indian society from the point of religion and finds the religion as source for the different ideological position. 'Rationality' is the guiding principle in evaluating the principles and practices of religion. For the claims of religion he applied rationalistic principle. He brings the religion as a focal point in reference to caste system. To construct the Indian history in proper, he avail all the convincing ideas of his times, from liberal to Marxist. This may go in tune of pragmatism. The pragmatism of Ambedkar differs from the context of western societies. In essence he made a serious attempt in constructing the Indian history in which one finds dignified place for 'sudras' and 'untouchable communities'. Ambedkar is a source of inspiration for contemporary dalit movement and so for constructing history from dalit point of view.

Historians have always tried to provide rationally justified knowledge about past, cause and effects of events. Philosophy of history can function as a conceptual enhancement for working historians and also it can function as a source of rational criticism of specific methods or approaches within contemporary historiography. Historically, there are various attempts to read history from diverse ideological and methodological positions. Many thinkers contributed to the philosophy of historical ideas. Broadly there are two streams identified in approaching the historical knowledge- idealistic and materialistic. In the realm of epistemological understanding of truth value of historical knowledge- rationalistic and empiricist methods were followed. The empiricist views past as an ordinary object of empirical investigation. The rationalist views past as an object of rational reconstruction and understanding. There raised a basic questions what is history about? Kant, Hegel and Marx have common strand and answered this question differently. For Hegel, history is unfolding of human freedom. Hegel's conception of history presupposes an abstract or absolute spirit. 'World history', in his words, 'exhibits the development of the consciousness of freedom on the part of spirit, and of the consequent realization of that freedom.'

Marx answered in another way that the underlying driver in historical change is the tension between the forces and relations of production or class struggle. For Marx, the first premise of all human history is, of course the existence of living human beings. All historiography must begin with these natural bases and their modification in the course of history by men's activity. Unlike the idealist view of history, it does not have to look for category in each period, but remains constantly on the real ground of history, it does not explain the practice from the idea but explains the formation of ideas from material practice. Consequently, history has always to be written in accordance with external standard, the real production of life appears to be a historical.

During the Nineteenth century the central concern is changed from metaphysical issues about 'direction of history' to epistemological issues about 'historical truth'. In twentieth century these concerns about truths in history focus on dispute between two views on question into what is history. A good part of the twentieth century was devoted to a debate sparked by the philosopher of science Carl Hempels claiming that historical explanations to be legitimately scientific ones have to be developed from the physical sciences. In contrast with Hempel's thesis, some, such as R. G. Collingwood and William Dray, have insisted that the historian is more concerned with understanding the motives of historical agents than with predicting events.

Philosophy of history-as-discipline has also addressed concerns about the justification and limitations of historical objectivity, the truth of historical claims, and the nature of historical explanations. Are there any proper methods in understanding history? Is it possible to find the historical method without any ideological and political positions? The discussion further continued that historians' ideological and political positions play a role either approaching the knowledge of past or constructing the ideas of past. The historians are selective in interpreting the knowledge of past. As the historian Croce said 'all history is contemporary'. As Carl Becker declares, 'the facts of history do not exist for any historian till he creates them.' As E H Carr explains, 'history is a continuous process of interaction between the historian and his facts and unending dialogue between the past and the present.' 'All history depends ultimately upon its social purpose.'

5.1. Historiographies in India

Keeping the above discussion as a background, it gives emphasis on the historical method of Ambedkar in countering the dominant social groups' construction of the Indian history. Both in construction of history of India and in having its historical method-Colonial, Orientalist, Nationalist, Marxists, Cambridge historians and Subaltern historians who played a vital role.

History writing in India as a conscious exercise began with scholars of Colonial and Orientalist persuasion and followed by nationalist elite and others. At present four dominant streams in Indian historiography are important Colonial, Nationalist, Marxist and Subaltern schools. Each school has its historical social context in emphasizing its method in writing Indian history. Each school argued its case in relation to other. The decade of eighties is turning point in Indian history in bringing new epistemological positions corresponding to the struggles of Dalits, Women, Adivasis.

When researches into India's past began in the late 18th century and early 19th centuries, Orientalist ideas structured historical representations. Inspired by the romanticism and classicism of the time, Orientalists like William Jones and H.T. Colebrooke returned to the ancient past, discovered its greatness and defined a specific notion of a glorious classical age. It was in this age, so the Orientalists told us, that the essence of Indian civilization embodied in its language, laws, institutions and religious texts came into being. Subsequent to this golden age there was a continuous or cyclical decline to a degenerate present before the British rule. The Orientalists saw themselves as the mediators who would define this relationship between the past and the present. As codifiers and translators they would be the ones to discover the ancient texts and ascribe to them their true meanings.

By the early 19th century, with liberalism gaining ground, Orientalist histories were questioned from within the fold of imperial thought. If Orientalists had glorified India's past, the liberals condemned it. From a veneration of classicality we moved to a phase of arrogant deification of modernity. Liberal histories idealized the modern West and the assumed principles of its order individualism, freedom and democracy. Other societies of the past and present were understood and characterized only in terms of the presence and non-presence of liberal values. While Orientalists had discovered in India's past a succession of golden ages, liberals like James Mill and Thomas Macaulay could see only shades of darkness. Modernity had emerged from the age of darkness, through the Renaissance and Enlightenment into the modern age. In India and other 'dark continents', as the liberals saw it, this transition never took place. India had remained unchanged, constrained by the social institutions that defined it – caste, village community and Oriental despotism.

The colonial historians were tried to construct the Indian history that suits their political interests. The colonial historians tried to show that Indian nationalism was nothing more than an unprincipled, selfish, amoral bid for power by a few Indian elites. The colonial assumptions of historical thought was enshrined by Hegel and expounded by Macaulay, Mill, Seeley, and many others. In the historical literature, colonial powers escaped serious interrogation outside of the specific contestations of the nationalist struggle until new critical inquiries were initiated by figures as various as Bernard Cohn, Edward Said, and Ranjit Guha. Nicholas Dirks argues that British colonialism played a critical role in both the identification and production of Indian 'tradition'. The tendency to read Indian history in terms of a lack, an absence, or incompleteness that translates into 'inadequacy' is obvious in these excerpts. The British conquered and represented the diversity of 'Indian' pasts through a homogenizing narrative of transition from a 'medieval' period to 'modernity'. The terms have changed with time. The 'medieval' was once called 'despotic' and the 'modern', the 'rule of law'. 'Feudal/capitalist' has been a later variant.

While the nationalists mounted a critique of colonial ideas, they continued to accept many of the key categories through which imperial representations of Indian society were fashioned. But in their critiques, nationalists still borrowed from the Orientalists, transforming the founding Orientalist notions of India's past the idea of classical golden ages and the corollary myth of a subsequent civilizational decline – into accepted orthodoxies of Indian history. But most nationalist histories continued to periodize pre-colonial history through religious categories.

By the 1980s history writing in India saw a new phase of dramatic change. Influenced by the new social history in England and the cultural turn in social sciences, *Subaltern Studies* challenged the elitism of earlier histories that attributed historical agency to the elites and looked at the world from above. Subaltern histories emphasized the need to understand the experiences and lives of the dominated – peasants and workers, tribals and lower castes, women and dalits – people who leave few written records, whose voices are difficult to hear, whose actions appear inconsequential. Power and domination, economy and society, experience of work and leisure, identities and interests, were all seen as culturally constituted.

The real break came with the rise of a much more sophisticated historiography from the 1950s and '60s pioneered by scholars, to name few of the most important, like D.D. Kosambi, R.S. Sharma and Irfan Habib. There was a veritable paradigm shift, particularly in ancient and medieval Indian history.

The historiography of the Hindu Right necessarily sticks to periodization by religion: in effect, the religion of rulers, for that is the only way through which the premise of medieval 'Muslim domination' or 'tyranny' can be made credible. The only real evil for it is religious, cultural or political domination coming from sources it considers external and alien, because non-Hindu. The failure to go beyond the single evaluative standard set by the colonial/anti-colonial binary produces similar problems for histories of subordinate caste and Dalit protest. Its many virtues include a valid stress on the complicities between colonialism and continued or refurbished high caste domination as well as on the numerous overlaps between 'mainstream' nationalism and Hindutva. Even Nehru's *Discovery of India* is revealed as being not entirely immune from such contamination.

In the decade of eighties, a group of scholars identifying with subaltern historiography got prominence by differing with earlier nationalist and Marxist historiography. This rise coincided with that of the Dalit movement which was taking aspiration from the philosophy of Ambedkar. The scholars influenced by the Dalit movement are even critical about the subaltern studies especially their treatment of the issue of caste.

Subaltern studies came into prominence from the decade of eighties in projecting a new method of historiography by countering the earlier ones. This approach came along the line of 'history from below' approach of European history writing in 1970 and 1980s. It came in opposition to both colonialist and nationalist historiography. It is skeptical about the established orthodoxies of both liberal nationalist and Marxist historiographies. Writing history from subaltern point of view was to show that neither nationalist nor left progressive historiography had a place for autonomous historical actions of the subaltern classes. As mentioned by Rajit Guha in an introductory note to Subaltern studies Vol.1: 'The historiography of Indian nationalism has for a long time been dominated by elitism-colonialist elitism and bourgeois-nationalist elitism.' The thrust of the argument is subaltern consciousness is distinct and autonomous. The histories of class divided societies have been written and preserved in accordance with interests of dominant classes. Subaltern consciousness evolved out of the experience of subordination, out of struggle, despite the daily routine of servitude, exploitation and deprivation. The subaltern consciousness can not be found in archival material conventionally used by historians, since it is prepared and preserved by dominant groups. It is only the moment of rebellion that subaltern appears as the bearer of independent personality.

The subaltern studies are criticized by scholars on different grounds. The criticism is on the agency involved in this project and on the method. Many complained that subaltern history was becoming bhadralok history, the history of elites. Sumit Sarkar in an article, 'The decline of the subaltern in subaltern studies' argued that in the name of theory, a tendency emerged towards essentializing the categories of 'subaltern' and 'autonomy', in the sense of assigning to them more or less absolute, fixed, de-contextualized meanings and qualities. What is conveniently forgotten is that the problems do not disappear through a simple substitution of 'class' by 'subaltern' or 'community'. Reifying tendencies can be actually strengthened by the associated detachment from socio-economic contexts and determinants out of a mortal fear of economic reductionism. The handling of the new concepts, further, may remain equally naivest subaltern studies, symptomatically has ignored histories of the left and of organized anti-caste movements throughout, and the line between past and present-day neglect can be fairly porous.

There is another criticism by branding the subaltern school as idealistic. 'Guha masks his idealism by formulating a critique of official, liberal and left historiography. Guha's idealism can be seen most clearly in his attempt to criticize the analysis of the social and economic conditions which generate rebellion. It is at a par with the Hegelian 'geist' which is not determined by history, while the development of history is march towards the self realization of this spirit. Guha's idealism consists not in emphasizing the importance of consciousness, but in placing consciousness beyond the pale of historical determination or mediation.

Definitely there is a breakthrough in methodology in constructing the history with much authenticity. Subaltern Studies becomes a blanket term for all subaltern communities like dalits, women, peasants, adivasis etc. in countering the hegemony of the dominance. Within the subaltern studies, if each community had its own logic and approach to history, then the project of subaltern studies is in trouble. Immediately, it even dismisses the so called subaltern by dismissing them as elite/ or non dalits.

Dalit historiography throws a challenge to colonial, nationalist, Marxist and right wing and even to the so called historians of subaltern studies. In this context, Ambedkar's method of constructing the history from dalit perspective is path breaking, and provides insights for contemporary historians of all shades. Infact, very few historians worked out in the field of ancient history with sound ideological commitment and with a purpose of liberating the oppressed masses from dominant social and philosophical systems.

5.2. Dalit Historiography

One may derive Ambedkar's 'historical method' in all his major writings on Indian history, culture and philosophy. The writings on this kind of issues not only provoked the scholars, political leaders of nationalist movement and orthodox Hindus of his times but helped deconstruct the dominant construction of ideas of Indian society. He made a systematic attempt to construct the histories and genealogies of the submerged social groups of Indian society by questioning the elite and dominant established Brahminical positions. He seems confident of his position by declaring it as 'fresh insights and new visions' in looking at Indian history and philosophy. In the year 1946, Ambedkar identified five streams of thoughts among the Hindus of Indian society in his writing on 'who are Shudras'- Orthodox, Aryasamajists, respecters of law Political minded and Rationalists. Among these five classes of Hindus, Ambedkar would like to identify his position with rationalist Hindus who were arguing for social reform as immediate agenda rather than any other.

In the words of Ambedkar; "I claim that in my research I have been guided by the best tradition of the historian who treats all literature as vulgar I am using the word in its original sense of belonging to the people to be *examined* and *tested by accepted rules of evidence* without recognizing any distinction between the sacred and profane and with the *sole object of finding the truth*."

As has been well said, an historian ought to be exact, sincere, and impartial; free from passion, unbiased by interest, fear, resentment or affection; and faithful to the truth, which is the mother of history, the preserver of great actions, the enemy of oblivion, the witness of the past, the director of the future. In short he must have an open mind, though it may not be an empty mind, and readiness to examine all evidence even though it be spurious. The non-brahmin scholar may find it difficult to remain true to this spirit of historian.

Respect and reverence for the sacred literature cannot be made to order. They are results of social factors which make such sentiments natural in one case and quite unnatural in another. Respect and reverence for sacred literature of the hindus is natural to a Brahmin scholar. But it is quite unnatural in a non-Brahmin scholar.

In the historical method of Ambedkar; man is the maker of history: Ambedkar evaluates the three different views on the causes of historical changes, Augustine, Buckle and Marx. According to Augustinian, history is only an unfolding of divine plan in which mankind is to continue through war and suffering until that divine plan is completed at the day of judgment. Ambedkar pointed out that this is not acceptable to many except theologians. Ambedkar finds the limitations of these three arguments by holding the opinion that none of these would admit that history is the biography of great men. Indeed they deny man any place in making of history. He considers there is a truth in Buckle and Marx, but their views do not represent the whole truth. They are quite wrong in holding that impersonal forces are everything and that man is no factor in the making of history. That these impersonal forces are a determining factor can not be denied, however, the effect of impersonal forces depends on man must also be admitted.'

The methods employed by Ambedkar in reconstructing the history are unique and convincing. In developing an historical method he followed Goethe, as he said 'the historian's duty is to separate the truth from false, the certain from the uncertain...' Ambedkar agrees with Goethe in bringing out the relevant and necessary facts to forefront. Ambedkar proceeds further and points out into what the duty of historian in reconstructing the authentic history in situations, where he confronts with many missing links. He himself faced this kind of situation in explaining the origin of sudras and untouchable as in both cases no documentary evidences were available or its antiquity.

Ambedkar appears very much aware of the role of *historian's social affinity* in dealing the material in relation to the problems of social history. In an introduction to 'who are the Shudras', he made this point more clear. He finds the difference between the non-Brahmin scholar and Brahmin scholar in treating the same source material of sacred literature of Hindus. The Brahmin scholar's attitude is identified as uncritical commendation, and where as the Non-Brahmins attitude in dealing this is unsparing condemnation. Ambedkar finds both the attitudes are harmful to historical research.

It is often argued by many Brahmins that sacred literature has to be treated with reverence and respect. Ambedkar staunchly believes that in pursuit of historical truth, there is nothing wrong in exposure of these very sacred texts which are responsible for the decline and fall of nation and society. It is the duty of a scholar to treat the literature without having any distinction of sacred or profane in pursuing truth. It is quite natural for Brahmin scholar to treat it as sacred with lot of respect and reverence. More over its object is to sustain the superiority and privileges of Brahmins as against the non-brahmins.

Ambedkar had more focus on philosophy of religion in understanding the socio-historical phenomenon and the moral basis of Indian society, than exclusively depending on either religion or philosophy. He developed it as a method. It seems in evolving this method, he got influenced by John Dewey. In the west, religion is identified with faith, and philosophy is with reason/science/rationality, in the age of enlightenment. It is also understood as tradition and modernity dichotomy. Religion and science started considering adverse to each other.

Religion is an institution or an influence and like all social influences and institutions, it may help or harm a society which is in its grip. Religion not only crossed everywhere the wrap of Indian history it forms the wrap and woof of Hindu mind. The life of the Hindu is regulated by religion at every moment of his life. Besides religion acts as a social force, and it stands for a scheme of divine governance. The scheme becomes an ideal for society to follow. 'The power of religious ideal depends upon its power to confer material benefit'. Ambedkar favours for religion that stand for reason rather negating religion. He felt that Hindu religion need to undergo a reform. To abolish the sanctity and sacredness of caste, one has to destroy the authority of the shastras and Vedas. One has to destroy the religion of sruti and smriti. Ambedkar not only proposed the religion that should stand for reason, but also tries to link it up with the governing principle of politics. In simple terms, he thought *reason* and *critical analysis* as a method used for the study of religion.

5.3. Role of Caste in Ancient India

Ambedkar identified caste as an important institution, in understanding the Indian society. In evolving his political theory, one could not ignore the role of caste system in India. No political theory is possible without some understanding of the caste. Ambedkar is the first thinker who systematized the conception of caste in analytical way. Earlier discussions on caste are ethnographic and descriptive in nature. His approach is more political rather etnographical. He understood that whole Indian social system was founded on the caste and the beliefs, customs, knowledge all are centred around caste system. All the human activities are determined by the caste. Caste has social, political and economical implications.

Most of his writing occupied the discussions on caste. It is generally understood that Indo-Aryan society of ancient India was based upon varna system, where the society was divided into Brahmins, kshtriyas, vaishyas and sudras based on the principle of labour and heredity. Some of the scholars would like to argue that chaturvarna system based on economic theory of division of labour and that the varna system is scientific. In later days where the people deprived of this varna system contesting it is argued that the individuals are defined as their innate qualities (guna) but not by birth. Further, this chaturvarna is opposed to natural law and spirit of human development.

Ambedkar argued that initially there were only three varnas in indo Aryan society. The shudras were not a separate varna but were part of kshatriya varna. There was a constant fued between sudra kings and Brahmins. Brahmins were insulted and tortured by these kshtriya kings. Ambedkar believes that Brahmins began to take revenge upon kshtriyas through 'divinity' and 'infinity' ideas which later on came to be attached to religious laws continued in course of time as sacred laws.

Brahmins hatred towards sudras culminated into a situation where Brahmins refused to invest the sudras with sacred thread. Owing to the loss of sacred thread, the sudras were socially degraded and demoted to the rank of the fourth varna. Amedkar illustrates this point through the examples from hindu mythology.

5.4. Marxism in Indian Context

Ambedkar made an attempt to interpret Indian society by using Marxian methodology for his own convenience. Contrary to the opinion that ancient India doesn't have any history, Ambedkar tried to dig out its history with the help of Buddhist literature. The rise of Budhism considered by him as a revolutionary against Aryan Brahminism in the history of India. More than religious revolution, it is social and political. The Brahmins were the custodians of religion by monopolizing the priestly profession and guided the people in all its moral and spiritual matters. They set the standards to be followed by all others. The Aryan community at the time of Budha was steeped in the worst kind of debauchery: social, religious and spiritual.

The phenomena of the decline of Budhism, followed by the triumph of Brahminism—was considered by him as counter revolution and attempted to situate the sudras, women in relation to this counter revolution. In understanding this phenomenon, Ambedkar made an attempt to understand the Brahminic literature and mythology from historical point of view. He finds the riddles of Hinduism in its sacred literature. He questioned the very authority of vedic literature and its privilege of *apaurusheya.*

'Present day hindus are probably the strongest opponents of Marxism. They are horrified at its doctrine of class- struggle. But they forget that India has been not merely the land of class struggle but she has been the land of class wars'.The bitterest class war took place between Brahmins and kshatriyas. The classical literature of hindus abounds in reference to class wars between these two varnas.

Conceptual structures will grow only when they are used in everyday life and in the context of thought and when contemporary thinkers in India begin to articulate their experiences about man, society, and polity in terms of classical thought, a new direction will be given to concepts. Indian philosophy like Indian culture approached with either too much enthusiasm or total negation of it. To assess Indian Polity properly, one has to keep aside both positive and negative emotions. There are certain myths about IP and claimed as facts. The claim of spirituality was never put to the test. In fact it seems so self evident as to require any argument or evidence on its behalf. No body feels it to question the worthiness of this claim.

Amedkar's contributions are not only significant in writing Indian history but in evolving a method which is more relevant even for contemporary historians of different schools. On the one hand, he tried to prove that historian's social affiliation plays a role in interpreting the past. On the other, he argues for objectivity in case of non-brahminical scholars rather carried by the romanticism of non-brahmin struggles. He identifies the historical change with socio-economical, political and cultural struggles of the people. He observed that this historical phenomenon reflected as a whole in evolution of religion. He considers the religion on moral basis that stand for the reason. He borrowed the tools of Marxism in understanding Indian history in this fashion. Buddhism had been considered as revolutionary strand against Brahminism and against the triumph of Brahminism. Moreover, he made a systematic attempt to bring in view the history of victims of Indian society, where one finds no trace of any historical evidence in official records or narratives of dominant brahminical class.

5.5. Historiography and Dalit Struggles

There is a significant scholarship coming up from Dalits in writing their own history. Their intervention is crucial in many ways. The history writing came along with the dalit struggles. In search of their identity, they dig the past in all possible ways. In writing of dalit history or interrogating dominant history from Dalit point of view, Dalit scholars/ activists/ writers may not be systematic, argumentative but are striking in their attack and provide an alternative forcefully. One may find many missing links in the construction of the dalit history or questioning the dominance from Dalit point of view. They are in vernacular languages. These writings are often reproduction of oral narratives. Some of them are in the form of autobiographies.

In this connection it presents historical claims of dalits of Telugu society as a case study. The word 'Dalit' in telugu society become familiar with Dalit Mahasabha, which came into existence with Karamchedu massacre of 1985. Dalit movement had taken roots at popular level and oppressed Dalit masses started questioning the dominance and hegemony of the upper caste people. The newly emerged dalit middle class, however small, played a role in production of knowledge systems in the fields of literature, culture, politics, philosophy and history. Dalit movement provided the spectacle through which they could uphold the culture, history and politics of the lower caste. The literature coming in the name of Dalit, shattered the existing canons of Telugu society. As a Telugu Dalit writer G. Kalyana Rao felt, 'We have to dig a lot and simultaneously bury a lot.' The Dalit intelligentsia is active in this mission to strengthen the on going Dalit struggles. However, caste becomes a reference point in understanding history, philosophy, culture and politics, with active Dalit struggles.

From the trained historians, though negligible, there exists significant number of historical writings. Kancha Ilaih's *Why I'm Not a Hindu* (*Nenu Hindunetlaitha* in telugu) is a prominent intervention from Dalit-Bahujan perspective against Brahmanism. It is a critique on hindutva, culture, politics and economics from a sudra perspective. He reflected on these issues from his social experience. He argues that dalit-bahujans have different food habits, culture, customs, and religious practices, which are unique, democratic and different from brahminical Hinduism. Dalit bahujans culture emerged from their involvement in labour. They are productive classes and so their culture is real, natural and authentic. In his article, *The Dalitbahujan Understanding of Telugu culturtal and Literary History*, he argues that construction of history taking place from two opposite and conflicting views: the brahminical and dalit bahujan. He questions us to whether the brahminical writings should really be called history at all? 'For brahminical people, history is a march of god on earth; where as for dalit bahujans, history is the march of people on the earth.' Further, the dalit bahujans history mostly lies in folklore/oral tradition. The language of this folklore is far richer, humanitarian and democratic-perhaps that is the reason why it has been relegated to the margins by the brahminical historians. On the other hand, productive castes had their own Telugu language, but it never figured in the brahminical writings. A. Sayanarayana, Professor in History made an attempt to write history from dalit bahujan perspective in his book *Dalits and Upper Caste, Essays in Social History.* He tried to construct dalit history by using the alternative literary discourses of dalits which are marginalized in the mainstream literary discourses. Y. Chinna Rao's doctoral dissertation *Dalit Movement in Andhra, 1900-1950* captures the dalit struggles of colonial times. To focus on the specific nature of resistance and struggles of dalits against the dominance, he uses the framework of James Scott's 'Weapons of the Weak.' The major argument is that contemporary dalit struggles are in continuation of these struggles. In other words, charging the mainstream historians for not documenting the dalit struggles. 'Dalit movements have not become a part of Indian historiography yet, even though their study is of immense importance in view of their inherent radical democratic identity and their interrelation with contemporary movements. The available studies on dalit movement in India suffer from lack of historical and written documentation, leaving scope for ambiguity.' Moreover, there are attempts from the conscious Dalit activists also. From late nineties, there are considerable numbers of books on history. Katti Padma Rao, Sanskrit teacher and activist in rationalist movement turned to a leader of Dalit Mahasabha. His *Dalitula Charita* constructs the history of the dalits based on the sources of Sanskrit texts. His *Caste and Alternative Culture* makes an attempt to construct history and struggles of the untouchable and sudra castes against Aryan – Brahmin-Hindu culture. He explores this theme from ancient times to contemporary times. He is even critical of the communist movement of contemporary times led by the upper castes like Reddy and Kamma communities and their silence on the issue of annihilation of caste. He explains the philosophical background of dalit movement. The matriarchal culture, Carvakas materialism, Budhist sangha philosophy and humanism are the foundation of dalit movement. The Aryans after arriving in India established Hindu kingdom and tried the culture of the ancient indigenous Indians. They introduced casteism, patriarchal culture and politico-economic dictatorship. Suppressing all the indigenous castes, they propagated their own Hindu culture in Indian society, and forcefully implemented Hindu way of life. Dr. Vijaya Bharathi came out with three books on *Puranalu-Kulavyavastha.* She has critically evaluates the puranas and their role in protection of caste system. On analysing the story of Satya Harischandra, though this story seems to uphold the truth, but its purpose is essentially to consolidate the varna system and controlling the women in the name of pativratyam. She made her analysis based on Markandeya puranam, skandha puranam and Harischandropakyanam. 'If we observe the stories and the constructed ideology around the avataramurthi's of different yugas, the whole effort is to implement and intrcduce the sanctions of the varna systems in the lives of ordinary people. Dharmasamsthapanam means varna dharma samsthapanam. The stories of the *shatchakravarties* are made popular because they stand as the symbols in protection of varnadharma. In a similar fashion the mythological god *Rama* represents the dominant brahminical system. Bonigala Rama Rao made an attempt to trace out history of untouchables. In his *Antarani Jathula Charitra,* he tried to establish that untouchable communities are not only the sons of the soil but also earlier ruling communities. Though weakened economically, they are protecting their culture and social ideology. To construct the history of untouchable communities he relied mostly on historical texts, books of linguistics and inscription rather puranas and epics. He further wrote *Mala Kannamaneedu* and *Adiguruvu Acharya Chandala.* The writings of Kathi padma rao and Bonigala Ramarao have influenced the later writings on the history of dalits – this includes Dr.K.Lakshmi Narayana who tried to explore history of dalits in the *Aadibharatteyula Charitra* and Pilli Rambabu's *Adi Baratheeyulu.*

Apart from these, Dalit literature as a creative intervention of dalit intelligentsia played a significant role in constructing dalit history. The historical consciousness is very much internalized in the structure of their literary narratives. The importance of dalit writings lies in authentic representation of the community by questioning the existing brahminical and progressive writings. The protest against the caste and class dominance is central to the dalit writings. Mostly, Dalit literary writings are autobiographical reflections of the community. Dalit writings are conscious effort of bridging the oral and written cultures. Dalit writings often invoke social memory as the source of their knowledge system. This also helps in maintaining the historical continuity. There has been constant effort from dalit writers in translating the condemned life styles and practices of marginalized people into symbols of protest and pride. In the process of writing their own history, they thoroughly interrogated the existing histories of dominant caste/class groups in their literary writings. As Dalit writer, Sivasagar marking the assertion of dalits in writing their own history against the brahminical history centred around advaita of Sankara.

References

Dhananjay Keer, *Dr. Ambedkar: Life and Mission*, published by Popular Prakashan, Bombay, India.

Gautam C., *Life of Babasaheb Ambedkar,* Ambedkar Memorial Trust, London, Milan House, 8 Kingsland Road, London E2 8DA Second Edition, May 2000.

Gore M. S., *The Social Context of an Ideology: Ambedkar's Political and Social Thought,* 1993.

Jaffrelot, Christophe, *Dr. Ambedkar and Untouchability: Fighting the Indian Caste System*, New York: Columbia University Press, 2005.

6

The Mahar Movement

Dr. Bhimrao Ramji Ambedkar, is famous for being "the most highly educated Untouchable in India." His education, encouraged and financed largely by the Gaikwad of Baroda, led to his role as the Untouchable's chief spokesman, the founder of a political party for Untouchables, and the moving spirit behind organizations, schools, and colleges established for their uplift. This part of Ambedkar's story is well-known. However, his family's military service in the British Raj is not widely acknowledged for creating an environment that laid the foundation for his later success. The Mahars benefited from their participation in the British Army in a number of ways. First, military service became "a significant part of caste élan and mythology." The first section provides the historical evidence they use to establish their credentials as a caste with martial traditions.

The Mahar movement under the leadership of Ambedkar abandons Hinduism altogether and embraced Buddhism. The Mahars formed an important section of the scheduled castes of Maharashtra (10%) of the population. They served as village watchmen, messengers and removers of cattle carcasses. These services were hereditary and were paid for in kind. They occupied a low position in the caste and occupational hierarchy and as such suffered from many religious, economic, educational and political disabilities. Thus the ideology of the Mahar movement reflects a total rejection of the religion of the caste Hindus, which was identified with hierarchy and inequality. Mahars now belong to a religion that stands for egalitarian values and hence they are superior to the caste Hindus. This is another strategy to gain self-respect and esteem on the one hand and to protest against the religion of the upper castes on the other. The civil rights ideology based on democracy, motivated the Backward Classes to evolve campaigns to fight for equality in educational, economic and political opportunities. Thus the leaders of the SNDP and the Mahar movement agitated for their basic civil rights. They also incorporated the religious-cultural ideology in this approach in seeking to gain self-respect and honor.

The Dalit Panther movement emerged among the Mahars of Bombay and Pune in 1972.Its spokesmen were Namdeo Dhasal, Raja Dhale and J.V Pawar all eminent literary men. It cashed in on the frustration that the urban youth were experiencing when faced with diverse forms of discrimination against the untouchables and the oppressed. In its ideology class struggle cannot be separated from an anticaste Hindu attitude. Thus the protest ideologies of the Backward Classes movements reveal four organizing principals:

— Reinterpretation of myths of origin or of one's own religion.

— Rejection of Hinduism and Aryan religion and culture

— Civil rights

— Class conflict

Among the Backward classes the Dalit panthers adopted the ideology of class conflict and anti caste Hindu feeling. The new identity that emerged based on these two principles enabled the young urban Mahars to attack the upper caste Hindu capitalists. Thus both secular class conflict and religious-cultural principles can be seen as transformations. All these movements arose due to the extreme exploitation of the lower castes by the upper castes and the lower castes were subjected to frequent oppression and exploitation over a period of time.

6.1. History of Mahar Movement

Eleanor Zelliot explains that the British gave Mahars the opportunity to seek different occupations from their traditional role as a village servant. Military service provided Mahars with the opportunity to move beyond their traditional social position in the village. In fact, the Mahar tradition of being in armies precedes the British Raj.

The recorded history of the Mahars' military achievements dates back to Shivaji's Army in the 1600s. The Mahars met this condition according to descriptions of their loyalty. This sense of loyalty and trustworthiness led Shivaji to include Mahars as a vital component of his army.Shivaji, leader of the Maratha nation, fought for a Hindu empire, but using Untouchables did not bother him. He "found the Mahars useful, for the wily Maratha chief realized that the best way of obtaining the maximum results was to mix up various castes in his garrison forces." This was the first exposure of the Mahars to an organized army that provided its soldiers with steady pay and benefits. After Shivaji's death, Mahar units continued to serve his descendants throughout the 1700s. Their experience with Shivaji and others encouraged them to seek similar employment as sepoys of the British East India Company.

Ardythe Basham, in her detailed examination of the Mahars and the military, found the perceived early martial history to be an important part of Mahar identity.

Mahars began their service with the British in the 1750s. Stephen P. Cohen, an expert on the Indian Army, discusses the importance of Mahars in the Bombay Army in his seminal work, *The Indian Army: Contribution to the Development of a Nation*. In addition to the size of the Mahar contingent, they were also praised for their conduct as soldiers. The Mahars rewarded the British with the same loyalty that Shivaji had enjoyed.The Bombay Army fought in several battles, and in most, the Mahars were recognized for their skills.

The recorded history of their exploits, especially prior to the mutiny of 1857, supports this effusive adoration. Basham located evidence of Mahar participation in the Second and "Third Anglo-Maratha War, the Second Anglo-Sikh War and the Second Afghan War." The Mahars' exploits in these conflicts form an important part of their military lore.

The Mahar participation in the battle of Koregaon on 1 January 1818 is the most famous, and also the best documented, action involving Mahar soldiers. This battle gave the British the advantage in the Third Anglo-Maratha War.

Mahars dominated Staunton's unit. The Peshwa's troops inexplicably withdrew that evening, despite their overwhelming numbers, giving the British an important victory. The men of the 2/1st Regiment Bombay Native Infantry, including many Mahars, who fought in this battle, were honoured for their bravery. The official report to the British Resident at Poona recalls the "heroic valour and enduring fortitude" of the soldiers, the "disciplined intrepidity" and "devoted courage and admirable consistency" of their actions. Further, the action is commemorated by a monument, with the names of twenty-two Mahars killed there, erected at the site of the battle and by a medal issued in 1851. Similar anecdotes are recorded in the written histories of the Mahar Regiment and Bombay Army. All demonstrate that most Mahars soldiers were dedicated and courageous.

In addition to Army units on land, the Mahars formed a vital component of the Bombay Army's Marine Battalion. This unit's history is well documented and provides numerous examples of Mahar actions, including several acts of bravery by Mahars in the battalion. In September 1810, during the Second Maratha War, several Mahars proved their loyalty when captured by the French Navy. On this occasion, the Bombay sepoys [soldiers] were shown the captured Bengal and Madras Sepoys dressed in French uniforms and enjoying considerable privileges and luxuries, whereupon the Bombay Detachment started abusing them as being dead to all shame that they could forget the oath and desert their colours.

The upshot was that they were very roughly treated and some were severely wounded. To the seventeen survivors who reached Bombay a special medal was given and of this number twelve were Mahars.This is just one of many cases where Mahars distinguished themselves as a part of the Marine Battalion and is another part of the martial history that the Mahars used to legitimize their important role in the British Indian Army. But, in the wake of the 1857 mutiny and threats from Russia, the British re-examined their recruitment policies. The Mahars were a casualty of this new thinking.

6.2. The Mahars Delistment

Despite the Mahars' long martial history, the British ceased recruiting them in 1893. The Bombay and the other Presidency Armies were re-evaluated following the 1857 mutiny. The Peel Commission first examined class composition of the armies in 1858. This led to the discrimination against the Mahars and other low-caste groups as well as some Brahman castes which were considered unreliable.

General Lord Roberts, while not originating the concept of martial races, was instrumental in implementing a strategy of building "class regiments." Recruiting policies were rewritten, and the Bombay Army "was notified that the Mahars, together with a number of other classes of the Bombay Army, would no longer be recruited to the Army."

The Mahars believed that their martial history demonstrated their abilities as warriors, but the British had made their decision. Mahars could only enlist as bandsmen or clerks. This would not provide the same opportunities for promotion, and allow little change in their social status. As expected, the Mahars felt the British had betrayed them after over 100 years of loyal service to the British Raj.

Throughout India, there was controversy about which groups should remain in the Army. The Mahars had support from some British soldiers, including three commanders who recommended their continued service.

The Mahars would continue to fight for the right to re-enlist in the Indian Army. They were loath to lose the benefits that the military provided. Furthermore, the education provided to the soldiers had created an educated cadre that would transfer their skills into political action. However, there were few Mahars left in the Army by the beginning of World War I.

6.3. Benefits of Military Service

Eleanor Zelliot notes that the "emergence of Mahar leaders and a new spirit of militancy in the 19th century was due in large measure to the influence of education acquired in the military."

The Mahars' ability to work among the British exposed them to Western ways, and helped them to realize that their status as Untouchables did not keep them from working in successful and satisfying occupations. They aggressively used the advantages provided by their relationship with the British.

Military service provided important benefits to its soldiers. The benefits include "pay and pensions, access to education and/or specialized training, preferential access to employment, enhanced social status, and personal satisfaction." For the Mahars, the access to education and increased social status was the most important benefits.

In fact, Ambedkar extends much of the credit for the start of the movement to improve the Untouchables' place in society to contact with the British Army. It is indisputable that this access to education was helpful to Ambedkar, and therefore, to all of India's Untouchable communities.

Ambedkar's family had extensive links to the military. Additionally, his mother's "father and her six uncles were all Subedar Majors in the Army," the highest rank that Indians could hold. Ambedkar's father also was a Subhedar Major and a full-fledged teacher trained at the Normal School then established by Government for turning out teachers to impart education that was then compulsory for the children as well as both male and female relations of the military servants.

Undoubtedly, the accomplishments of this family were exceptional. Nonetheless, the availability of education had a positive effect on all members of Mahars in the military, including women. Consequently, Basham concludes, "The loss of this education option with the loss of their right of enlistment was therefore a real blow, not merely the loss of a theoretical benefit which few actually received." The quality of life for soldiers and their families suffered because of the loss of educational opportunities available through participation in the military.

Mahars joined the military with the intent of improving their social status. They were successful in this regard. After growing up in this environment of equality it was a shock for the Untouchables to travel and live in situations away from the military cantonments. The important point is, even after retirement, Mahars with a military background still had access to the British government. The retired military officers were an effective lobby for Mahar rights.

Retired officers also created a group of political leaders with access to the Indian government. This was especially true near military cantonments in Poona, Satara and Ahmednagar. Basham relates an incident where Mahar children were not being offered equal educational opportunities. Local caste Hindus and low-level British education officials refused the Mahar demands for Mahar boys to be integrated into classes with caste-Hindu boys. The dispute was resolved in favour of the Mahars. Basham argues that this demonstrates they were seeking not just education for their sons, although this was obviously important, but also an improvement in their social status. The fact that many of these parents were retired officers, and therefore could legitimately make a claim on the attention to government officials, indicates the value of military service in this respect.

Clearly, the type of access available to the soldiers, active or retired, was unavailable to most Untouchables. All the benefits the Mahars received were the result of their ability to develop a link with the British. This helped them overcome the obstacles erected by the Hindu social system. Such an exposure socialized them sufficiently early to the new political order so that when new opportunities and alternatives became available, they were found prepared to use them more effectively than those groups which did not have this opportunity. Following the delistment of 1893, the Mahars would need all the access and knowledge they had gained to overcome the impact of being refused service in the Army.

6.4. Fight for Re-enlistment

The Mahars did not give up their positions in the Army easily. The British decision of Mahar. The Mahars used two different strategies to influence the government; with both they tried to regain enlistment privileges in the army and an improved social status. Zelliot maintains that these efforts "illustrate the importance of army service to the Mahars. This was clearly the beginning of their efforts to induce government to intervene on their behalf, and their questioning of their traditional inferior status." In both instances, the movement was led by educat ', former military officers.

The first organized attempt was in April 1895. Some of the details of the petition drive presented by Zelliot and Basham are speculative. Basham, who has completed the most recent study, states it was originally presented to the Viceroy, but was later returned for resubmission through the Bombay Government. It appears that the petition was submitted by Gopal Baba Walangkar, a retired military officer, on behalf of the Anarya Doshpariharak Mandali, the non-Aryan committee for the rightings of wrongs, an Untouchable organization.

The petition's pleas were simple. The Mahars believed that, in 1859, the Government had declared that the castes who fought loyally for the British were to be given due preference for military enlistment. The case they presented for reinstatement was more complicated than their demands. Much of their argument attempts to demonstrate that their identification as Untouchables was a mistake.

The 1895 petition argues that the Mahars as a group who are actually of the Kshatriya caste. This represents the Mahars attempt to change their position in the caste structure by "Sanskritization."It continues by attacking the legitimacy of the higher castes. It claims, "The so called high caste and pure people's ancestors were as degraded as our people and were used [sic] to eat flesh of cow and beef. They wrote their own religious scriptures." Finally, the petition provides a "creation myth" about the high castes. The document's tenor shows the importance of military service to the Mahars and the use of Sanskritization tactics to show they were at least equal to the alleged high castes. This campaign was unsuccessful. The Mahars were unaware of the debate "over recruitment policy or the acceptance of Lord Roberts views on martial races" which was the prime component in the British decision. Shortly after the turn of the century, a second attempt was organized.

The second major petition was submitted to the government three times between 1904 and 1910. The document's "signatories included forty-two military pensioners" including Dr. Ambedkar's father. This petition had a broader base of support than the one in 1895. This campaign was more sophisticated than the first. The spokesman, Shivram Janba Kamble, spoke English. More importantly, the petition's "appeal for consideration was not on the basis of the Mahars' having been demoted from Kshatriyahood, but on the grounds of former service, English justice and human worth." This pragmatic approach attracted greater support than the earlier petition, and used arguments that were later refined by Dr. Ambedkar. In fact, Ambedkar took over leadership of the Mahars from Kamble. The 1910 petition was more polite and less argumentative than the 1895 petition.

Despite the reasoned arguments, this petition demands, like the first, were denied. The manpower demands of World War I had a greater effect, and beginning in 1914 Mahars, again, were recruited into the Army and given their own Regiment, the 111 Mahars. The Regiment's three battalions "were formed the toward the end of the war, but they did not see action and their martial qualities were untested." More important, however, is that the petition drives provided an organization for Dr. Ambedkar to use after the war to improve the social status of Untouchables. The long association with the military gave Mahars an issue to organize around and the movement then worked to achieve more substantial achievements than just military service.

References

Bakshi S.R., Ambedkar B.R., "Statesman and Constitutionalist", *Indian Freedom Fighters Series*, 1992.

Chanchreek K.L., *Dr. B.R Ambedkar: A Rebel Dalit Leader,* New Delhi, Shree Pub., 2006.

Christophe Jaffrelot, *Dr. Ambedkar and Untouchability: Analyzing and Fighting Caste,* 2005.

David Pandyan K., *Dr. B.R. Ambedkar and the Dynamics of Neo-Buddhism,* 1996.

7

Ambedkar and Reservation Policy

Hindu society is divided into four *varna*, or classes, a convention which had its origins in the *Rig Veda*, the first and most important set of hymns in Hindu scripture which dates back to 1500-1000 B.C. At the top of the hierarchy are the *Brahmins*, or priests, followed by the *Kshatriyas*, or warriors. The *Vaisyas*, the farmers and artisans, constitute the third class. At the bottom are the *Shudras*, the class responsible for serving the three higher groups. Finally, the *Untouchables* fall completely outside of this system. It is for this reason that the untouchables have also been termed *avarna*.

Jati, or caste, is a second factor specifying rank in the Hindu social hierarchy. Jatis are roughly determined by occupation. Often region-specific, they are more precise than the sweeping varna system which is common across India and can be divided further into subcastes and sub-subcastes. This is also the case among untouchables.

Jatis in the three highest varnas in the hierarchy—Brahmins, Kshatriyas, and Vaisyas—are considered "twice-born" according to Hindu scripture, meaning they are allowed to participate in Hindu ceremonies and are considered more "pure" than the Sudras and "polluting" untouchables. This concept of pollution versus purity governs the interaction between members of different castes. The touch of an untouchable is considered defiling to an upper-caste Hindu. In southern India, where caste prejudice has been historically most severe, even the sight of an untouchable was considered polluting. Untouchables usually handled "impure" tasks such as work involving human waste and dead animals. As a result, until reforms began in the 19th century, untouchables were barred from entering temples, drawing water from upper-caste wells, and all social interaction with upper-caste Hindus. These social rules were strictly imposed and violators were severely punished; some were even killed.

Despite constitutional prohibitions and laws, most recently the Scheduled Castes and Scheduled Tribes Act of 1989, violence and injustices against untouchables continue today, particularly in rural areas of India. Accounts of caste-driven abuses continually appear in Western media and surely affect foreigners' perceptions of India. More recent examples include Dalit students at a government school in Rajasthan who were punished for asking to drink water from a pitcher used by higher caste students and a Dalit in.

For India in 2001, the Department commented, inter alia, that:

i) Dalits are among the poorest of citizens, generally do not own land, and often are illiterate. They face significant discrimination despite the laws that exist to protect them, and often are prohibited from using the same wells and from attending the same temples as higher caste Hindus, and from marrying persons from higher castes. Dalits tend to be malnourished, lack access to health care, work in poor conditions, and face continuing and severe social ostracism.

ii) The Scheduled Castes and Scheduled Tribes Act lists offences against disadvantaged persons and provides for stiff penalties for offenders. However, this act has had only a modest effect in curbing abuse. Under the Act, 996 cases were filed in Tamil Nadu and 1,254 cases in Karnataka in 2000. Human rights NGO's allege that caste violence is on the increase.

iii) Intercaste violence claims hundreds of lives annually; it was especially pronounced in Uttar Pradesh, Bihar, Rajasthan, Madhya Pradesh, Tamil Nadu, and Andhra Pradesh.

In addition to specifying an economic and social role, caste is also accompanied by certain popularly held generalizations. Brahmins, for instance, are often believed to be fair skinned, sharp-nosed, and having more "refined" features, consistent with their Aryan roots. Untouchables, on the other hand, are commonly held to be dark-skinned and possessing coarse features. A dark-skinned Brahmin girl, for example, is a source of anxiety for her parents since the task of finding a husband is made harder. Matrimonial advertisements, a staple in Indian newspapers, are full of families seeking "wheatish" brides for their sons.

Nevertheless, there is increasing social mobility, especially in India's urban areas. Some untouchables and sudras have tried to move up in the hierarchy by adopting customs of upper castes, a process labelled *sanskritization*. Others have attempted to escape the system entirely by converting to Buddhism or Christianity. Over time, significant numbers, although only a tiny portion of India's Dalits, have followed his example; in November 2001, thousands of untouchables participated in a mass conversion to Buddhism in Delhi.

7.1. Pre-Independence Initiatives

Christian missionaries took the lead in adopting the cause of the Depressed Classes seeking to provide welfare for them. By the 1850s, either inspired or shamed into action by the missionaries' example, Hindu reformers emerged. Jyotiba Phule was one such activist, and in 1860 he called attention to the plight of victims of caste discrimination in Maharashtra.

British and other Indian leaders soon followed suit, spurred on in part by reports of discrimination against Indians in South Africa. Thus, in the 1880s, British officials set up scholarships, special schools, and other programs to benefit the Depressed Classes. Forward-thinking maharajas (princes) in "native" states like Baroda, Kolhapur, and Travancore, which were not under direct British administration, established similar initiatives. Ambedkar, from the Mahar caste of Maharashtra, was one beneficiary. One result was that Ambedkar was able to attend government primary and secondary schools. The Maharaja of Baroda, recognizing Ambedkar's gifts for scholarship, sponsored his study abroad, first at Columbia University in New York, where Ambedkar obtained a Ph.D. in Economics, and later at London University, where he earned a DSc. and entrance to the Bar from Grey's Inn.

As early as 1858, the government of Bombay Presidency, which included today's Maharashtra, declared that "all schools maintained at the sole cost of Government shall be open to all classes of its subjects without discrimination." Although a 1915 press note revealed that this policy was not being enforced—in one case, a Mahar boy was not allowed to enter the school room, but was relegated to the veranda—the Bombay government maintained its position on the issue, and, in 1923, announced a resolution cutting off aid to educational institutions that refused admission to members of the Depressed Classes. Other initiatives followed including the 1943 Bombay Harijan Temple Entry Act and the 1947 Bombay Harijan Act. In the United Provinces, now Uttar Pradesh, the 1947 United Provinces Removal of Social Disabilities Act was put in force. In what is now Kerala, the Maharaja of Travancore announced the "Temple Entry Proclamation" in 1936, in what has been called a "pioneer [effort] in the field of reforms relating to the eradication of untouchability before independence." Other measures affecting what would become the present state of Kerala included the 1938 Madras Removal of Civil Disabilities Act and the 1950 Travancore-Cochin Temple Entry (Removal of Disabilities) Act.

7.2. The Government of India Act of 1919

Caught in the turmoil of World War I, Britain focused its attention on Europe, not on India. Nevertheless, the British passed important legislation during this turbulent period that would have a significant impact on the development of Indian governmental institutions: The Government of India Act of 1919.

The Act had its immediate origins on August 20, 1917. With Britain in a war for survival in Europe, in need of continued support from India and the Empire, and desiring to avoid confrontation with the Indian independence movement, Secretary of State for India Edwin Montagu, in an announcement in Parliament, defined Britain's India policy as:

> Increasing [the] association of Indians in every branch of the administration and the gradual development of self-governing institutions with a view to the progressive realization of responsible government in India as an integral part of the British Empire.

Montagu and Lord Chelmsford, then Viceroy, embarked on an analysis of the Indian situation, eventually laying out proposals forming the basis for the 1919 Government of India Act.

The reforms included devolution of more authority to provincial governments and dyarchy, a system in which elected Indian ministers, responsible to the legislatures, were to share power with appointed British governors and ministers. The Act also addressed minority safeguards, including the particularly vexing issue of communal electorates.

Montagu and Chelmsford firmly rejected communal electorates, characterizing the system as a "perpetuat[or] of class division" and a "very serious hindrance to the development of the self-governing principle."

Despite their repudiation of communal electorates, Montagu and Chelmsford realized it would be unfeasible to take away communal representation already granted to Muslims by the 1909 Morley-Minto reforms. At Lucknow in 1916 the Indian National Congress and the All India Muslim League had agreed to separate electorates for Muslims. Britain for political reasons was not willing to risk the combined ire of these Indian groups. Other, including Sikhs, Anglo-Indians, Europeans, Indian Christians, and non-Brahmins, also clamoured for special representation, but Montagu and Chelmsford largely resisted their demands—they did grant the Sikhs communal representation—proposing instead a system of nomination. If nomination proved ineffective, they proposed reserving seats for communities in plural constituencies, but with a general electoral roll.

In Britain, the decision against communal electorates was controversial. Indian moderates and some British members of Parliament (MPs) supported the Montagu-Chelmsford position. However, most feared an "oligarchy of Brahmins" if communal electorates were not set up for non-Brahmin Hindus. Several factors contributed to such "Brahminophobia," a fear that had been developing even before the Montagu-Chelmsford Report.

Some Britons perceived Brahmins as "untrustworthy," oppressive towards the lower castes, and subversive regarding British governmental and social reforms. Valentine Chirol, a prominent *Times* correspondent, published *Indian Unrest*, in which he asserted that Brahminism was the biggest threat to the British. The Rowlatt Report of 1918, the product of a study on the causes of political violence in India, described Brahmins as "revolutionaries." Annie Besant,

English-born leader of the "Home Rule" movement for Indian independence, accused Brahmins of repressing the lower castes.

7.3. The Simon Commission

In keeping with the 1919 Government of India Act, the British government in 1927 appointed a commission to assess the Montagu-Chelmsford reforms and "whether, and to what extent it [was] desirable to establish the principle of responsible government, or to extend, modify, or restrict the degree of responsible government existing therein." The seven-member commission was headed by John Simon, MP, and included MP Clement Attlee.

This "all-white" panel proved controversial. The competence of the nominees was not at issue, but rather the lack of any Indian representatives.

The Simon Commission toured every Indian province. Its findings were based largely on memoranda from the Government of India, from committees appointed by the provincial legislative councils, and from non-official sources. The final report contained recommendations for reform.

One area the Commission identified was the need to safeguard minorities and other disadvantaged members of Indian society. Noting that "the spirit of toleration has made little progress in India," the Simon report detailed the plight of the Depressed Classes in particular, which it saw not only as a problem of caste, but as an issue with distinct political overtones.

Based on its assumption that the "true cause of communal conflict...is the struggle for political power and for the opportunities which political power confers," the committee saw the improvement of the Depressed Classes' situation as hinging on increased political influence.

In its consultations, the Simon Commission found that most provincial governments supported a nominating system. The Government of Bihar and Orissa, for example, asserted that a nomination was best since the Depressed Classes were too backward to choose their own representatives. Despite these arguments, the Commission discarded the idea, arguing that the Depressed Classes needed opportunities for training in self-government. Support for separate electorates was strong among the Depressed Classes. Their representatives proposed combining separate electorates and reserved seats. The Bengal Depressed Classes Association, for instance, lobbied for separate electorates with seats reserved according to the proportion of Depressed Class members to the total population as well as for adult franchise. The All-India Depressed Classes Association proposed separate electorates for each of what it termed the four major groups in India: the Brahmins, Muslims, Depressed Classes, and Non-Brahmins. The governments of Assam and Bombay supported similar concepts.

Seats were to be reserved for the Depressed Classes in general constituencies and these seats would be filled by election, based on a broadened franchise. The Commission also recommended drawing up rules to ensure the competency of candidates for reserved positions. In addition, provincial governors would have the power to nominate or allow non-Depressed Class members to run for election. Competency was of particular concern to the Commission. As a result, the Commission suggested, "the proportion of the number of such reserved seats to the total number of seats in all the Indian general constituencies should be three-quarters of the proportion of the Depressed Classes to the total population of the electoral area of the province." Again, these measures were regarded as strictly temporary, with the goal that an improvement in the Depressed Classes' condition would eventually make reservations unnecessary.

7.4. The Round Table Conferences

In 1931, sixth months after the Simon Commission's report was published, a Round Table Conference convened in London to review the Commission's proposals and how they might be incorporated into a new constitution. This time, there were Indian delegates from various interest groups. Gandhi and his Indian National Congress were conspicuously absent, refusing to participate on the grounds that Congress alone represented Indian opinion.

How to treat minorities was a major topic at the conference. Prime Minister Ramsay MacDonald chaired a subcommittee to focus on this problem. Ambedkar and Srinivasan appealed for separate electorates and adult suffrage. Separate electorates were designed to be temporary. In the end, the subcommittee could not reach an agreement, a general reflection of the entire conference, which was inconclusive.

A second Roundtable Conference convened eight months later. Ambedkar and Srinivasan again attended. Gandhi also joined, representing the Congress. Having taken up the cause of the *Harijans* Gandhi adamantly opposed separate electorates, especially for the Depressed Classes. Arguing that untouchability was inseparable from Hinduism, he linked creation of separate electorates for the Depressed Classes to alleged British "divide and rule" strategy and asserted that the group should be included in the main body of Hindus. As a result of staunch opposition from Gandhi and the Congress on separate electorates, the second conference was inconclusive and the minority issue remained unresolved.

Ambedkar originally had misgivings about separate electorates as well, but was compelled to ask for them at the second Roundtable conference when he felt the Depressed Classes were in danger of not gaining any concessions. Earlier in the conference, Ambedkar had attempted to compromise with Gandhi on reserved seats in a common electorate, but Gandhi, who had declared himself spokesman for India's oppressed, rejected Ambedkar's proposal, and denounced the other delegates, including Ambedkar, as unrepresentative. It is apparent that political considerations might have also motivated Gandhi to adopt this position.

Given the failure of the conference to settle minority representation, Prime Minister Ramsay MacDonald, who had chaired the committee on minorities, offered to mediate on the condition that the other members of the committee supported his decision. The product of this mediation was the Communal Award of 1932.

7.5. THE POONA PACT

MacDonald announced the Communal Award on August 16, 1932. Based on the findings of the Indian Franchise Committee, called the Lothian Committee, the Communal Award established separate electorates and reserved seats for minorities, including the Depressed Classes which were granted seventy-eight, reserved seats. Unlike previous communal electorates set up for Muslims and other communities, the Award provided for the Depressed Classes to vote in both general and special constituencies, essentially granting a "double vote."

Gandhi, who was in the Yeravada Prison in the city of Poona at the time because of his civil disobedience campaign, reacted by declaring a hunger strike "unto death." In his opposition to the Award, he compared the creation of separate electorates for the Depressed Classes to the "injection of a poison that is calculated to destroy Hinduism and do no good whatever." Rajah, another leader of the Depressed Classes, opposed the separation of the community from the Hindu fold.

As a result of widespread disapproval of the Award and Gandhi's hunger-strike, a new agreement, the Poona Pact, was reached on September 24, 1932. The Pact called for a single general electorate for each of the provinces of British India and for seats in the Central Legislature. At the same time, specified numbers of seats, totalling 148 for the provincial legislatures and to be taken from seats allotted to the general electorate, were reserved for the Depressed Classes. Voting members of the Depressed Classes in each reserved seat constituency were to form an "electoral college" to select four candidates from among their number. The Pact also called for "every endeavour" to give the Depressed Classes "fair representation" in the public services "subject to such educational qualifications as may be laid down."

7.6. Gandhi v. Ambedkar

The Poona Pact set in motion what one student of caste in India has termed "Ambedkar's qualified victory over Gandhi and the Congress." Although Ambedkar had given in on the common voting roll, he had ensured that specified numbers of Depressed Classes legislators, nominated by members of those Classes, would be included in Indian provincial and national legislative bodies. The number of reserved seats was higher than in the Award. Gandhi and the Congress had little choice.

The Poona Pact is significant in that it initiated a pattern of political compromise between "caste" Hindus and the Depressed Classes in the allocation of legislative representation and government jobs. Although much has changed in India, seventy years after the Pact 81 of the 543 members of the Lok Sabha, the lower house of Parliament, are from what were formerly known as the Depressed Classes and 79 of them hold reserved seats.

A by-product of the Pact was the highlighting of the underlying problems between "caste" Hindus and "outcastes." Gandhi initiated a national campaign to eliminate the evils of untouchability. Six days after the Pact, with help from wealthy industrialists like the Birlas, he started the Harijan Sevak Sangh and its weekly journal *Harijan*. The serious gulf in Hindu society that continues until now along with the reservations system is evident in an exchange between Gandhi and Ambedkar in the February 11, 1933, issue of *Harijan*.

In his rejoinder, Gandhi noted: "Dr. Ambedkar is bitter. He has every reason to feel so." Gandhi continued, commenting that Ambedkar's "exterior is as clean as that of the cleanest and proudest Brahmin. Of his interior, the world knows as little as that of any of us." Affecting humility, Gandhi announced that *Harijan* "is not *my* weekly" but belonged to the Servants of Untouchables Society and that Ambedkar should feel "it is as much his as of any other Hindu."

Therefore, according to Gandhi, the "joint fight is restricted to the removal of untouchability," a fight into which he invited Ambedkar "and those who think with him to throw themselves, heart and soul..." Ambedkar preferred to carry on the fight through legal and constitutional measures. His legacy is the existing system of reservations. Gandhi, a Hindu traditionalist, sought to inspire Hindus to cleanse the caste system of the evil of untouchability. Judging from his writings, he saw this as an achievable goal.

Gandhi's Harijan Sevak Sangh continues his work throughout India. While the sincerity of the Society's efforts cannot be doubted, some Dalits see the organization as paternalistic and condescending. At the Society's start, Gandhi opposed having a harijan on the board of directors. Some sense of caste attitude comes from a report in *Harijan* of some early activities.

7.7. The Government of India Act of 1935

The reservation of seats for the Depressed Classes was incorporated into the Government of India Act of 1935, legislation by the British designed to give Indian provinces greater self-rule and set up a national federal structure that would incorporate the princely states. The Act went into force in 1937. The Act brought the term "scheduled castes," now the Indian Government's official designation, into use, defining the group as including "such castes, races or tribes or parts of or groups within castes, races or tribes, being castes, races, tribes, parts of groups which appear to His Majesty in Council to correspond to the classes of persons formerly known as "the Depressed Classes," as His Majesty in Council may specify." This vague classification was later clarified in "The Government of India Order, 1936 which contained a list, or "schedule," of scheduled castes throughout the British provinces.

7.8. All-India Depressed Classes Conference at Nagpur, 1942

Efforts by both Indians and British officials encouraged untouchables and the lower castes to form their own organizations to call for more equitable treatment and to demand economic assistance. Ambedkar was at the centre of these activities. Changing tactics, he used a July 1942 All India Depressed Classes Conference in Nagpur to establish an All India Depressed Classes Federation.

Among the group's demands were those for a new constitution with provisions in provincial budgets, specifically in the form of money for education, to support the advancement of the scheduled castes; representation by statute in all legislatures and local bodies; separate electorates; representation on public service commissions; the creation of separate villages for scheduled castes, "away from and independent of the Hindu villages," as well as a government-sponsored "Settlement Commission" to administer the new villages; and the establishment of an All-India Scheduled Castes Federation. Ambedkar, by contrast, supported the war effort and became a member of the Viceroy's Executive Council. He used his new position to advance the interests of the Scheduled Castes.

He had played the situation perfectly. With independence in sight, Congress leaders locked up, and Britain desiring to keep India quiet Ambedkar had successfully expanded the scope of reservations from legislative seats to government jobs and education.

7.9. Altruism or Political Interest

Were these pre-independence efforts to uplift the Depressed Classes driven by simple altruism and the desire to correct past injustices? Or were political interests what motivated British and Indians to act? While one cannot deny that leaders such as Gandhi certainly were sincere in seeking to improve the plight of the "Harijans" and weaker elements of Indian society, scholars have argued that politics influenced and continues today to drive the advocacy of reservations and special provisions for Depressed Classes. Suma Chitnis, for example, has argued that the British saw this issue as useful against Indian independence seekers. The Congress Party, the dominant Indian party at the time, sought to keep the Depressed Classes in its fold to prevent political fragmentation of the independence movement and to counterbalance the Muslim League, especially in "mixed" provinces like Bengal and the Punjab. Nevertheless, Congress' interest was relatively late in coming. Chitnis points out that the Congress Party's interest in the welfare of the Depressed Classes did not emerge until 1917, when Gandhi made it one of the main planks of the party.

7.10. Framing Reservations Policy

On May 16, 1946, the British government released the Cabinet Mission Statement, a set of proposals to guide the framing of a new Indian constitution. By this time, the wheels for India's independence had already been set in motion by Clement Atlee's Labour Party government in London. Among other recommendations, the Cabinet Mission laid out a detailed plan for the Constituent Assembly's composition, such that the body be "as broad-based and accurate a representation of the whole population as possible." In addition to divisions for Muslims and Sikhs, the Cabinet Mission suggested a "general" category which would include all others groups—Hindus, Anglo-Indians, Parsis, Indian Christians, the Scheduled Castes and Tribes, and women, among others.

In March 1947, Britain sent Lord Louis Mountbatten, war hero and royal relative, to New Delhi as the King-Emperor's last Viceroy. His mission was to transfer power to an independent Indian government. In the end, power was transferred to two successor entities, Pakistan on August 14, 1947, and India on August 15, 1947.

Under the Cabinet Mission plan the Constituent Assembly was to consist of 389 seats, 296 of which were filled by delegates elected from the directly-administered provinces of British India and 93 of which were allotted to the princely states. The total number of seats was based on an undivided India, and, overall, represented a cross-section of the population of the country. With the 1947 partition, many Muslim delegates left for Pakistan, terminating their membership in the Assembly. As a result, the body was reorganized. By November 26, 1949, it consisted of 324 seats, divided among the provinces and the princely states and representative of all major minority groups.

The make-up of the Constituent Assembly reflected the reality of what groups wield power in India, then and now. An analysis of membership in the most important advisory committees of the Constituent Assembly found that 6.5 percent were SCs. Brahmins made up 45.7 percent. Dr. H.C. Mookherjee, an Indian Christian, was Vice-President of the Constituent Assembly as well as Chairman of the Sub-Committee on Minorities. However, by far the most important was Dr. Ambedkar.

Jawaharlal Nehru (1889-1964), India's first Prime Minister and dominant political figure until his death, had already selected Ambedkar, an accomplished lawyer, as his Law Minister. A Brahmin himself, Nehru sought to build a secular India free from caste discrimination. He was among the "many educated Hindus" opposed to the caste system as noted by Gandhi in his 1933 *Harijan* exchange with Ambedkar. Given Nehru's views and Ambedkar's talents, it is not surprising that Ambedkar became chairman of the drafting committee for India's new constitution. For Nehru, it kept the independently minded Ambedkar "on board" with the government at a critical time; for Ambedkar, it was an opportunity to influence preparation of the new constitution and protect Scheduled Caste interests.

From the outset, the Constituent Assembly laid out clearly its objectives and philosophy for the new constitution. Several of the framers' main goals, articulated in the "Objectives Resolution," included guarantees of equality, basic freedom of expression, as well as "adequate safeguards...for minorities, backward and tribal areas, and depressed and other backward classes." These principles guided the delegates throughout the Constitution-making process.

The Assembly set up a special Advisory Committee to tackle minority rights issues. This committee was further divided into several subcommittees. The Subcommittee on Minorities focused on representation in legislatures, reservation of seats for minorities in cabinets, reservation for minorities in the public services, and administrative machinery to ensure the protection of minority rights.

Vallabhbhai Patel (1875-1950), Chairman of the Advisory Committee and the most powerful member of the governing Congress party after Nehru, submitted the Report on Minority Rights to Rajendra Prasad, President of the Assembly, and on August 27, 1947, the Assembly convened to discuss the Report. Rejecting separate electorates—Congress wanted no repeat of the separate electorates granted to the Muslims by the British—and a "weightage" system, the Report endorsed the creation of joint electorates and proportional representation. Reservations were approved for minorities, as long as the reservations were in proportion to the population of the targeted groups. Some minorities, like the Parsis, voluntarily gave up this right.

Treatment of the Scheduled Castes was extensively debated. Efforts by Ambedkar and his allies to craft a provision requiring a "tripwire" 35 percent of Scheduled Caste votes in a constituency reserved for the Scheduled Castes failed. The principle of common voting and reserved seats in legislative bodies throughout the country was retained despite strong opposition from influential Constituent Assembly members like Nehru. However, the colonial-era system of having the Scheduled Castes choose candidates for reserved seats through local "electoral colleges" was dropped. Throughout the debate, caste Hindus permitted nothing that would suggest splitting off the Scheduled Castes in an electoral sense from the Hindu community.

7.11. Reservations under the Constitution

On January 26, 1950, India ended its "Dominion" status, became a republic, and put in effect its new constitution. With an entire section dedicated to "Fundamental Rights," the Indian Constitution prohibits any discrimination based on religion, race, caste, sex, and place of birth. This law extends to all public institutions, such as government-run educational facilities, to access to hotels and restaurants, public employment and public wells, tanks, and roads. The practice of untouchability is declared illegal.

Significantly, Article 15, which prohibits discrimination, also contains a clause allowing the union and state governments to make "any special provision for the advancement of any socially and educationally backward classes of citizens or for the Scheduled Castes and Scheduled Tribes." The speed of the amendment is indicative of the strong political support for reservations, Nehru's personal views notwithstanding.

Similarly, Article 16, calling for "equality of opportunity in matters of public employment," contains clauses permitting the "reservation of appointments or posts in favour of any backward class of citizens which, in the opinion of the State, is not adequately represented in the services under the State" and another allowing "reservation in matters of promotion" for Scheduled Castes and Scheduled Tribes.

A separate section of the Constitution, "Special Provisions Relating to Certain Classes," requires the reservation of seats in the "House of the People," or Lok Sabha, and the Legislative Assemblies of the states for the Scheduled Castes and Scheduled Tribes. The numbers of reserved seats are determined by the proportion Scheduled Caste and Scheduled Tribe members to the general population, based on population estimates from the most recent decennial census.

Several safeguards accompany these provisions for reservation. First, the Constitution originally required the reservation of seats in the Lokh Sabha and state legislatures to end after ten years. After five amendments, the policy is now set to expire on January 25, 2010. Secondly, regarding the reservation of jobs, Article 335 of the Constitution mandates that the "claims of the members of the Scheduled Castes and Scheduled Tribes shall be taken into consideration, consistently with the maintenance of efficiency of administration." Another Commission was also created to investigate the conditions of the socially and educationally backward classes.

It is interesting to note that the Constitution's reservations construct, which explicitly singles out certain castes for special preferential treatment, contradicts the document's prohibition on discrimination based on caste, race, and other such criteria. Furthermore, India's caste system itself, with its strict hierarchy dictated by birth, is at odds with the ideals of equality and social justice.

Despite the creation of centrally based commissions to monitor reservations and other schemes, the Constitution gives great liberties to the individual states to determine the quantity and limits of reservation and what, for example, qualifies as the "maintenance of the efficiency of administration." The clause giving states the authority to formulate and implement policy to facilitate "the advancement of any socially and educationally backward classes of citizens," is also decidedly vague. No concrete definition of "backward" is provided either.

To give teeth to the protections for the Scheduled Castes and Tribes mandated by the Constitution, India's Parliament has passed two major laws. The Untouchability (Offences) Act of 1955 (renamed the Protection of Civil Rights Act in 1976) was intended to provide enforcement of Article 17 of the Constitution, outlawing untouchability. It fell short of expectations. In 1989 a new law, the Scheduled Castes and Scheduled Tribes Act, came into force. Similar to an American hate crimes statute, it provides heavier penalties than under ordinary law for eighteen specified crimes including forcing the eating of obnoxious substances, bonded labour, and sexual exploitation.

7.12. Assessment of Reservations

As the reservations policy expands, involving more groups of people and continuing to generate debate, so too does the task of assessing this system. A review of the literature reveals entire books dedicated to the issue, and even these efforts cannot fully sort out the reservations puzzle. In addition, because consistent and complete state-specific data were unavailable, this assessment of reservations relies primarily on all-India statistics.

Though the scheduled tribes (STs) and the other backward classes are undoubtedly important players, covering them thoroughly would be beyond the scope of this study. The other backward classes (OBC), particularly since the release of the Mandal Report, have often been at the centre of the controversy surrounding reservations.

Nevertheless, Oliver Mendelsohn, for example, has attributed the relative lack of controversy over reservations for SCs and STs who are guaranteed seats in legislatures in addition to preferential treatment in education and public employment, to the reservation system's "failure." It is for this reason, Mendelsohn argues, that the policy has not generated the animus of a more successful program.

7.12.1. Government Services

As Marc Galanter has observed, government employment in India is widely considered prestigious and a guarantor of security and advancement. Government jobs still account for the majority of jobs in the economy's organized sector. Public sector jobs are divided into four levels, distinguished by income and selectivity: Class I (or Group A), Class II (or Group B), Class III (or Group C) and Class IV (or Group D).

Class I, the highest-paid level, includes members of the elite Indian Administrative Service (IAS), the Indian Foreign Service (IFS), the Indian Police Service (IPS) and connected Central Government services. In the next income bracket, Class II employees comprise officers of the state civil service cadre. Competitive exams and interviews are usually used to fill these top two tiers, which require highly skilled and well-qualified candidates.

In contrast, the bottom two job categories, Class III and Class IV, include low-skill, low-qualification posts such as primary school teachers, revenue inspectors, constables, peons, clerks, drivers, and sweepers. These are typically low-income jobs and are not subject to strict selection processes. This is particularly relevant given that Class III and Class IV jobs make up the bulk of public sector employment in the organized economy. According to estimates from 1994, 94 percent of public sector jobs in the Central Government fell into the Class III and Class IV levels.

It is clear that there has been a general rise in SC representation in all four categories of employment in central services across time. The SC presence in Class I, for instance, has increased by tenfold, from 1.18 percent in 1959 to 10.12 percent in 1995. The Class II figures show an upward trend from 2.38 percent in 1959 to 12.67 percent in 1995. The lowest class, which initially had more SC employees in 1959 than any of the other classes had in 1995, has had a slower rate of increase.

While these are all good indications that reservations are working, it is difficult to ignore certain realities that detract from this success. First, SC representation in the Classes I and II, after over 50 years, still fall short of the reservations quota of 15 percent for SCs, while the less-prestigious and lower-paid Class III and IV jobs are amply filled. Even prior to 1970, when quotas were set at 12.5 percent, only Class IV met the quota of places allotted to SCs. The steep increase in Class I and II positions since the 1960s suggests that the percentage of new SC recruits is nearing the SC reservations quota.

Secondly, certain posts are "exempt" from reservation. Under the current policy, reservations do not apply to cases of transfer or deputation; cases of promotion in grades or services in which the element of direct recruitment exceeds 75%; temporary appointments of less than 45 days; work-charged posts required for emergencies; certain scientific and technical posts; single post cadre; upgradation of posts due to cadre restructuring; and ad hoc appointments arising out of stop gap arrangements. As far as scientific and technical posts are concerned, reservations do not apply to positions above the lowest grade in Group I services.

Finally, another factor undercutting the positive trends is the prevalence of false caste certification. Non-SCs, whether out of opportunism or desperation, have been known to pose as SCs in order to take advantage of reserved government jobs, in addition to other benefits afforded to SCs, such as relaxation of maximum age limits and waiving of civil service exams and fees. However, the plan was shelved when the authorities realized how costly such a policy would be, given that around 90 percent of the state's population could be counted as SC, ST or OBC.

7.12.2. Legislatures

One of the most explicit constitutional provisions concerns the reservation of seats for SCs in the Union and state legislatures. An analysis of the composition of the current Lok Sabha indicates adherence to the Constitution's mandate. All seats reserved for SCs are filled, with two states, Maharashtra and Andhra Pradesh, each having an SC Member of Parliament (MP) from a non-reserved constituency.

While all seats reserved for SCs are filled, a look at the portfolios and posts held within the 13th Lok Sabha by SCs undercuts the degree of substantive SC representation.

Out of a total of 40 Lok Sabha committees, five are chaired by SCs. Ganti Balayogi, an MP from Andhra Pradesh who served as house Speaker until his death in a helicopter crash on March 3, 2002, headed three of these groups—Rules, General Purposes, and Business Advisory—*ex-officio* in addition to presiding over the Lok Sabha. Though the Speaker is mainly responsible for the maintenance of order and the conduct of business in the house, he also can wield considerable influence, especially in cases where a tie vote occurs, and his vote breaks the deadlock.

As a result of the need for governing parties to accommodate party factions with office and to secure representation for certain regions and groups, the Council of Ministers includes 73 ministers. Eight SC MPs currently serve in Union cabinet minister and minister of state positions. Portfolios such as Labour and Employment are not insignificant, but conspicuously absent from the list are such major ministries as Finance, External Affairs, Defence, and Home.

There have been other influential SC MPs in past cabinets. Ram Vilas Paswan, a Dalit from Bihar, has held a seat in Parliament since 1977. In addition to serving as Minister for Labour and Welfare in the V. P. Singh Government of 1989-90, Paswan was also Railway Minister, an office considered a "classic source of patronage," from 1996-1998.

Despite not always controlling "heavyweight" portfolios, SC MPs are generally well-qualified. 80.25 percent of SC MPs possess at least an undergraduate degree, compared to 87.5 percent for the entire Lok Sabha. Breaking down these figures by gender brings out some interesting contrasts. All female SC MPs have had, at the minimum, an undergraduate education and 66.67 percent have had postgraduate training. Among the general pool of female MPs, only 74.5 percent had at least an undergraduate degree.

Given the last available all-India literacy rate for SCs (37.41 percent according to 1991 estimates), the high educational attainment of the majority of SC MPs resonates with what has been dubbed the "creamy layer" effect. Critics of reservations have often asserted that the policy has had disproportionate effects, benefiting only the most forward of the SCs—those already in a better position to take advantage of reservations—and facilitating the emergence of an SC "elite."

In the case of the female SC MPs, their high educational qualifications might also be an indication of an inherent disadvantage in their ability to seek political influence. In order to obtain office, they need to be even more qualified than non-SC females.

Data to construct an educational profile for an earlier Lok Sabha were not available for the purpose of drawing comparisons. However, information showing the number of reserved constituencies and the distribution of SC MPs among political parties was obtainable. With the intention of finding as much difference in time as possible and avoiding the shuffling of state borders that occurred in the years after Independence, the third Lok Sabha was chosen for analysis.

In the years between the third Lok Sabha and the present one, the number of seats reserved for SCs has only decreased by one. Comparing the party affiliations of the SC MPs in each Lok Sabha group brings out more striking differences.

One of the major differences brought out in the table is the Congress' fall from dominance. This is not only reflected in the total number of seats controlled by the party (366 down to 112), but also in the number of its SC MPs, which has been reduced from 63 to 6. In contrast, the BJP, with 180 seats, has taken Congress' place. The BJP has 24 SC MPs, 17 more than the next highest party.

Another change over time has been the significant growth in the number of political parties to which SC MPs belong. SC MPs only represented 12 different parties in the third Lok Sabha. This number has doubled in the current Lok Sabha. Though the BJP has the most SC members of any party, it does not enjoy the same "monopoly" as the Congress party did in the third Lok Sabha.

Finally, an additional important development with the election of the current Lok Sabha has been the emergence of the Bahujan Samaj Party (BSP), the first major party formed to advocate Dalit rights that has achieved electoral success. Ýronically, the BSP's increasing prominence, mainly in northern India has depleted the Congress' traditional vote bank.

7.12.3. Education

Education has long been identified as key to achieving the advancement of the SCs. In line with Article 15(4) of the Constitution, which empowers the State to make special provisions for the educational development of SCs, the Indian government currently allows the reservation of 15 percent of seats for SCs in universities and colleges. Reservations can also extend to the allotment of places in dormitories. State governments observe different rates of reservation, based on the size of their SC population.

Along with these measures, Central and state governments have also instituted scholarship/stipend programs, as well as initiatives to furnish SCs with special tutoring, books, midday meals, stationery and uniforms. One such scheme, funded entirely by the Central government, provides four years of special and remedial tutoring to select secondary-school students to help SCs gain admission to universities and technical institutions.

Created in 1956 by an Act of Parliament, the University Grants Commission (UCG) oversees the implementation of these policies in institutes of higher education. There are currently 166 central/state universities, 37 "deemed" universities, and 9,278 colleges. The UCG has routinely published guidelines to encourage and aid state governments in filling reservations quotas entirely.

Despite these special concessions, enrolment statistics for undergraduate, postgraduate, technical and professional courses indicate that the SC are still under-represented, with only 13.30 percent enrolment. This falls short of both the instructed reservation of 15 percent of seats as well as the proportion of SCs to the total population. However, it should be noted that the percentage of SCs in courses of higher education has nearly doubled since 1978.

A survey of SC admission to central universities backs this finding. Among the institutions examined, only Visva Bharati in West Bengal clearly met the 15 percent quota, with 17.6 percent of those enrolled in the non-professional school from the scheduled castes.

Banaras Hindu University in Uttar Pradesh, reporting 14.78 percent SC representation, nearly filled reserved non-professional seats.

Out of eight categories of posts, the reservations quota is met in one, and, as is the case with all central government services, it is the bottom-ranked, lowest-paid group of positions. None of the remaining job groups has more than five percent SC employees. In all central universities, SCs held two out of a total of 1,155 professorships. The National Commission for Scheduled Castes and Scheduled Tribes attributed this low level of representation to the "lukewarm attitude of the authorities in the Union Department of Education" which failed to initiate legislation making the implementation of reservations in central universities mandatory. As a result, universities were not instituting reservations because the University Acts contained no legally binding provisions to do so.

Setting the context for the under-representation of SCs in all aspects of university life—learning, teaching, administrating has been an SC literacy rate lagging behind that of the rest of the Indian population.

In 1991, SCs were trailing the rest of the population by 14.8 percent in literacy, a larger margin of difference than in 1961 when the deficit was 13.75 percent. While SC males have gained some ground over the past decades, now only 14.22 percent versus 17.48 percent behind, SC women are not faring as well. The gap for women has widened from 9.66 percent in 1961 to 15.53 percent in 1991.

A state-wise breakdown shows that even in states like Kerala, where universal education has been, by and large, achieved, SCs still lag behind by 10 percent. However, compared to the disparity in 1961 between the total population and SCs in Kerala the gap seems to be narrowing. In "Hindi belt" states like Uttar Pradesh, literacy rates among SCs did not clear 30 percent in 1991. At 19.49 percent, SC literacy in Bihar was even lower.

As mentioned above, the process of collecting statistics on SCs was frequently complicated by the lack of sufficient information. In addition, when data could be obtained on the representation of SCs in services, legislatures, and educational institutions, there was no guarantee that the figures necessarily reflected whether such representation was due to reservations policy alone.

Further compounding the problem was the issue of reliability of the figures and tables obtained from government reports. Facing pressure from bodies like the UGC to reserve and fill adequate numbers of seats for SCs, universities have been known to inflate enrolment figures.

In addition, this study made extensive use of reports from the National Commission for Scheduled Castes and Scheduled Tribes. Like the Lok Sabha Committee for the Welfare of Scheduled Castes and Scheduled Tribes, the Commission is composed of SC politicians. As a result, the potential for bias in assessing the working of reservations should be taken into account.

Despite such uncertainties and possible distortions of data, the fact that SCs are still under-represented in government services and educational institutions undercuts the goals of the reservations policy. The evidence presented in this study also shows that even when all reserved seats are filled, as in the case of the Lok Sabha, there may not always be substance to the positions attained through reservations.

7.13. Accounting for Success

It has shown that the reservations policy has not been entirely successful in significantly improving the conditions of the SCs. As a perusal of any report from the National Commission for SCs and STs will reveal, the Indian government, from central to local levels, has often displayed a lackadaisical attitude in administering reservations policy. The reservations system has evolved into a bureaucratic structure with major inefficiencies.

There are two major reasons for these realities. First, with the fading of the Congress party's dominance, the Indian political scene has witnessed the flowering of many new parties and the intensification of party competition. As the population of SCs increases, faster than the rate of growth of the general population, political parties have realized the electoral potential of this group and have sought to use reservations as a way of garnering votes. However, once in office, politicians lose their incentive to see that reservations are implemented effectively.

A second reason is the fact that Dalits have failed to unite as an All-India political force. Though there have been Dalit political success stories, such as the rise to power of the Bahujan Samaj Party in Uttar Pradesh, these achievements have been restricted to certain regions. Dalits have been plagued by internal rivalries, including their own caste hierarchy.

A politically influential national Dalit movement has yet to emerge. Consequently, they have not been able to lobby effectively for the efficient implementation of the reservations policy. Dalit politicians who are elected to reserved seats in legislative bodies like the Lok Sabha have also been known to be servants of the party rather than representatives of their SC constituents.

This section will examine obstacles to the success of the reservations policy. It begins with an example of the administrative difficulties and inefficiencies of the system. Next, there is an analysis of the role of the government commission that oversees reservations policy. The current political setting is also an important component, including the views of the BJP-led coalition that governs India.

7.13.1. Administrative Deficiencies

7.13.1.1. Flawed and Cumbersome System

Any consideration of reservations as a form of social engineering to redress the grievances of a minority must touch on the mechanics of the system. It is a system that has grown enormously since its origins in the 1930s and reaches into all levels of Indian politics, education, and government employment, including the substantial number of public sector "undertakings," as government-owned industries are known.

The cornerstone of the system is the official list, or schedule, that gave the "Scheduled Castes" (SCs) their name. Originally compiled by civil servants in the 1930s, the current version shows 1,091 Scheduled Castes. States with the greatest numbers of SCs are Karnataka (101), Orissa (93), and Tamil Nadu (76).

Over time, a large body of administrative regulations, forms, and case law has come into being to guide the reservation process. There are, for example, a "Pro forma for sending proposals for dereservation of vacancies," an instruction for the "Grouping of isolated posts for purposes of orders regarding reservation," and "Descheduling of

Caste of Scheduled Caste person after his initial appointment." However, the most important form is the certificate every Scheduled Caste member must have to apply for reserved employment, educational benefits, holding reserved legislative seats at any level, or receiving "benefits under various developmental programmes meant for members of Scheduled Castes & Scheduled Tribes."

Any of *eighteen* specified local officials can issue a certificate, but the rules for issuing a certificate are complex. An applicant who moves to an area of his state in which his group is not "scheduled" can still get a certificate, but if he moves to another state where his group is not "scheduled" he will not. If he converts while holding a "reserved" job, he will be stripped of his SC promotion advantage. Should he reconvert, he can get a certificate only if he can show he is accepted back by his former group.

Inevitably, the issuing of certificates has become a source of corruption. Jobs, schooling, grant money, and even some share of political power—perhaps a seat on a village or municipal council—are at stake. On the receiving end, there is often a lack of Scheduled Caste candidates for mid- or higher-level positions. Given employer or school interest in filling SC positions, a "don't ask, don't tell" attitude may prevail. At all levels above traditional untouchable occupations like sweeper, the possibility exists that caste Hindus with bogus SC certificates are squeezing out real members of the Scheduled Castes.

Although the possibility that officials were selling certificates is not mentioned, it is implied by the threat to use the Indian Penal Code. By the mid-1990s, the problem had worsened and "False Certificates" has its own chapter in the two most recent reports of the National Commission for Scheduled Castes and Scheduled Tribes. Concerned about the "widespread incidence" of false certificates, the Commission in 1996 carried out pilot field studies in several states. The studies confirmed the irregularities and the trend. In the end, only six were dismissed after what the Commission termed "enormous delays." Nearly a quarter of the individuals thwarted removal by getting stay orders from cooperative local courts.

The Commission has repeatedly called on the government to crack down on fraudulent certifications. It has made detailed proposals for corrective measures, but none have been forthcoming. The appearance is that few in government really care. The Commission's 1998 report provides a final word:

i) ... certificates have been issued to ineligible persons, carelessly or deliberately... This has resulted in wrong persons availing of the benefits meant for the Scheduled Castes and Scheduled Tribes on a false pretext.

ii) ...the menace of false caste certificates is on the increase...

iii) A considerable number of seats in the educational institutions are also secured by these wrong persons.

iv) ...there have been instances of persons being elected to elective offices on the strength of false Community Certificates.

7.13.1.2. National Commission for SCs and STs

As mandated by Article 338 of the Constitution, a special officer was appointed in 1950 to monitor safeguards for the SCs. The post has since been altered several times. At one point, two government organizations existed concurrently—a Commissioner's office and the Directorate General of Backward Classes. A constitutional amendment in 1978 merged the two bodies to create the National Commission for Scheduled Castes and Scheduled Tribes.

In 1992, six of seventeen field-office directors posts were abolished. Offices in Patna, Bihar and Hyderabad, Andhra Pradesh, two states where atrocities against SCs are particularly prevalent, were among the posts sustaining cutbacks.

Another problem the Commission has encountered consistently is the difficulty of obtaining data from state and local governments in a timely and complete manner.

This is still an issue. The Tamil Nadu government, for example, which has been conducting censuses of its employees since 1978, did not collect any data on reservations until 1992. Such evidence is illustrative of the general lack of priority given to issues involving the welfare of SCs. The story at the central level is no better. Frequently, Commission reports are not reviewed by Parliament for months or even years after they are completed. In 1964, Commissioner Anil Chanda politely noted the "long gap between presentation of [the annual] Report to the President and its placing before Parliament." He attributed this to a delay in printing and in translating the text into Hindi. Commenting on the same problem thirty years later.

Sharma was not exaggerating. The most recent National Commission report available to the public is from 1998. Subsequent reports are still pending Parliament's review before they can be released.

7.13.1.3. Dalits and the Law

When SC legislators do not represent their interests, Dalits do not have many other options for protesting transgressions of the reservations policy or atrocities they sustain. The police, for example, are often indifferent to the SC's grievances and have frequently been known to be aggressors themselves. In October 2000 in Mataila village, Uttar Pradesh, upper caste men severely beat up and threw acid on six Dalits, blinding two.

Though the conduct of the police in this case showed more negligence than brutality, many cases of violence committed by the police against SCs have been documented. Of the 418 cases brought to the attention of the National Commission for Scheduled Castes and Scheduled Tribes in 1993-94, 52 involved the commission of atrocities by the police. Such cases included torture while in police custody, rape in police custody, and other harassment. In 1994 for instance, police in the Vaishali district of Bihar beat an SC youth to death. Another 23 cases involved lapses such as the failure of the police to arrest the accused and to provide protection to victims of caste-based atrocities. The local police wrote off the incident as a "fire accident" and did not press charges on the culprits. SCs also do not often have means for or access to legal resources to contest violations. Few have obtained judgeships and other positions in courts.

Between the eight states and one union territory surveyed, there were a total of five SCs with positions on high courts. Himachal Pradesh, where, according to the 1991 census, SCs make up 25.30 percent of the population, had no SCs in its high court. Punjab and Harayana, which share the same capital of Chandigarh, have SC population of 28.30 percent and 19.70 percent, respectively, but have no SC high court officials out of a total of 29. In contrast, it is estimated that Brahmins hold approximately 78 percent of judicial positions though this group accounts for only 3.5 percent of India's population.

Thus, part of the explanation for the reservations policy's problems stems from the system having become a political tool for political parties looking to expand their vote banks. Though they may jump to support reservations and even seek the policy's extension, such parties lack the political will to follow through with their promises once they have achieved election.

7.13.2. Reservation as an Electoral Tool

A survey of the manifestos of the major political parties in the late 1990s indicates that nearly all groups address the issue of reservations. Furthermore, adopting a pro-reservations stance is often the course of action, since, as the policy expands, opposing the reservations is considered "electoral suicide." In 1996, for example, four major parties— Congress I, BJP, Janata Dal, and CPI(M)—endorsed reservations. While the BJP, Janata Dal, and CPI(M) supported reservations for backward classes, the Congress party even proposed to extend reservation to women in the Lok Sabha.

This is not a new development on the Indian political scene. As Christophe Jaffrelot argues in his forthcoming book *India's Silent Revolution: The Rise of the Low Castes in North Indian Politics*, the Congress party had long been aware of the significance of the SC vote as well as of the electoral potential of the reservations system.

The Changing Face of the BJP Since the waning of Congress' dominance, the BJP has emerged as India's leading party. In addition to being characterized as a Hindu nationalist party fiercely opposed to Muslim culture, the BJP has also been described as perpetuating a "Brahminical Social Order" in which upper caste Hindus dominate and oppress the lower castes in Indian society. Since its political troubles after the 1996 elections, when the party could not find any coalition partners and was unsuccessful in forming a government, the BJP has attempted to alter its image to widen its appeal.

One major change has been the BJP's effort to tone down its traditionally militant Hindu nationalist rhetoric. Its manifesto features sections on "Commitment to the Welfare of the Scheduled Castes and

Scheduled Tribes" and "Untouchability: A Crime Against Humanity." Among its promises are those for a law to back up the reservations policy, special tribunals to deal with complaints of non-implementation of the policy, and efforts to see that preferential opportunities benefit the largest and widest cross-section of SCs. The most recent manifesto from 1999 for the BJP-led National Democratic Alliance contains pledges to protect existing reservations policy for SCs. Such statements are no doubt aimed at wooing SC voters.

Moderating its position has also facilitated the BJP's attempt to forge more widespread alliances with regional parties. In 1997, the BJP formed a coalition with the BSP in the Uttar Pradesh government. Most recently, with its success in the 1999 elections, it heads the National Democratic Alliance. The Alliance, which includes leftist parties like SC-politician Ram Vilas Paswan's Lok Jan Shakti Party, controls the Lok Sabha.

Within its party ranks, the BJP has also tried to advance members with non-traditional backgrounds, such as SCs. For example, it made Bangaru Laxman, an SC, its president. However, he was forced to resign when the Tehelka scandal involving bribery and defence contracts surfaced in 2001.

7.13.2.1. Spending on Scheduled Castes

Budget allocation and spending are often telling indicators of a government's policy interests and priorities. Since 1979, the Government of India has implemented a Special Component Plan (SCP) with the goal of boosting SCs above the poverty line. Based on the proportion of SC population, the umbrella program is designed to direct the flow of outlays and benefits from general sectors in State and Central Ministry plans into the development of SCs.

SCs in the population, SCs benefit from spending on general public infrastructure development, like roads.

The program has also been hampered by the tendency of state governments to divert funds to other sectors, away from the target group. In a village in Lucknow, Uttar Pradesh, it was discovered that the President of the *gram panchayat* had fraudulently tried to obtain grant money. He claimed that the request was at the behest of some SC residents in his village, but it was later found that the SCs had never applied for money and had not given the council president permission to do so on their behalf. Thus, despite the programs designed to extend economic aid to SCs, corruption and inefficiency have hindered their economic progress.

Indicates that even though a lower proportion of SCs are below the poverty line than in the 1970s, compared to the all-India estimates the SCs remain behind in the climb out of poverty. In 1989 the Planning Commission, which produced the poverty estimates above, decided to review its estimates based on a new methodology devised by a contractor "expert" group.

The group neglected to generate statistics on the SC population, but the National Commission for SCs and STs, using the new methodology, made such estimates, finding that for the year 1993-94 approximately 48.8 percent of the SC population was below the poverty line. This is much higher than the original estimate of 41.5 percent for the year 1987-88. Though the discrepancies could simply be accounted for by improvements in data collection and statistical analysis, the underestimates could be indicative of the desire to downplay the seriousness of the poverty problem, especially concerning the SCs. Whichever poverty estimates may be closer to the truth, the common denominator is that economic development programs have not had a significant impact.

7.14. Dalit Mobilization

With poverty widespread among the SC population, many SCs are still not able to take advantage of preferential policies. A large proportion live in rural areas far removed from many of the opportunities for job and educational reservations. According to the 1991 census, the ratio of rural to urban population was 81:19 for SCs, while that for all of India was 74:26. Over half of SCs are employed in the agricultural sector, primarily as landless agricultural labourers. Thus, benefits such as reserved seats in institutions of higher education are of little consequence when many SCs do not make it past the primary level of school.

In contrast, as noted by various commissioners for SC/STs, the "forward" among the SCs, who are better off economically and have political connections, are securing a disproportionate share of reservations benefits.

It is apparent that many of the SCs who made use of reservations, such as to obtain seats in legislatures, had such advantages as educational opportunities, better economic positions and political links. Mendelsohn, who conducted interviews with SC members of Parliament in the 1980s, found that "self-made" politicians, those who did not depend on earlier generations to break from the economic condition of the SC community, were the exception to the rule. The majority of SC politicians interviewed had also received higher education. The analysis in this study of the backgrounds of members of the current Lok Sabha also reflects a high level of education. Prominent SC politicians like Ambedkar, a Mahar from Maharashtra, came from comparatively more prosperous SC families. Ambedkar's father and grandfather were in the military, often a way of getting access to education and more stable pay.

The November 1993 elections in UP brought a coalition government of Mulayam Singh Yadav's Samajwadi Party (SP) and Mayawati's Bahujan Samaj Party to power. The event marked the "emergence and consolidation of a successful organizational and political focal point for the Dalits of UP for the first time in 20 years." The BSP's rise to power was also the first time a political party that depended on the Dalit support and advanced a Dalit-based agenda was voted into government office. The election resurrected the modern Dalit movement spearheaded by Ambedkar that had lost steam by the 1970s.

Demographics have been a deterrent to achieving unity. Because SCs, who constitute 16.4 percent of the population based on 1991 Census estimates, are distributed fairly evenly across India, they do not make up the majority of any Lok Sabha district. Given India's first-past-the-post electoral setup, candidates in these reserved constituencies do not always have to depend on the SC support for victory. As a result, Dalit representatives who are elected do not always derive their main support from the SCs, but from caste Hindu constituents.

Though the quotas for SC parliamentary representation have been filled, Dalit politicians do not appear to be gaining influence or support outside of these special constituencies. The situation has not changed. The success of only two SC MPs in non-reserved constituencies in the 1999 Lok Sabha elections supports this observation. As a result, SC MPs in reserved seats have less of an incentive to fight for SC interests than they would if separate electorates existed.

India's parliamentary system amplifies the problem. Unlike presidential-style governments, such as in the United States, the parliamentary set up requires a greater degree of party discipline. Therefore, especially when Dalits do not form a significant part of their contituencies, Dalit politicians may show more loyalty to their parties than to their Dalit constituents. This situation has been summed up by one former Indian state governor: "Unfortunately these members belonging to different political parties are more loyal to the parties than to the millions of Dalits whom they represent. They seem to have become silent and voiceless surrogates of the parties."

7.14.2. Intra-Dalit Rivalry

More significantly, the emergence of a powerful Dalit movement has been hindered by intragroup rivalry. Dalits, too, have there own caste hierarchy, with some groups clearly more dominant and influential. Such groups have enjoyed a disproportionate share of reservations. The ongoing conflict between the Mala and Madiga castes, both groups considered "untouchable," in Andhra Pradesh is a case in point. Of the 59 scheduled castes in Andhra Pradesh, the Mala and Madiga are the largest, constituting about 80 percent of the state's SC population. Between the two groups, the Madigas are considered to be lower than the Malas in the Andhra Pradesh SC hierarchy—they are "outcastes" who "eat beef, drink and loaf around" to the Malas. Since 1972, the numerically larger Madiga community, which cites the Malas' disproportionate share of reservations quotas, has demanded that the state's 15 percent SC quota be subdivided. In the meantime tensions between the communities continue, even though so far few violent incidents, like on in 1997 in which a Madiga youth was clubbed to death by Mala youth, have occurred.

In addition to the friction with the caste Hindus, the politicization of reservations has created tensions within the ranks of the SCs between "haves" and "have-nots." McMillan has hypothesized that the BJP has played upon these intragroup rivalries and tried to reach out to the most backward SCs. Last year, controversy arose over BJP Chief Minister of Uttar Pradesh Rajnath Singh's proposed policy to create quotas within the existing ones for this very group.

7.14.3. The Bhopal Conference

In January 2002, the Madhya Pradesh government sponsored an all-India meeting of Dalits in Bhopal. The conference, which took place four months after Dalit groups gained worldwide publicity for their cause at the United Nations meeting on racism in Durban, South Africa, marked the first time since independence that a state government had supported a forum focused on Dalit issues and entertained participation from critics of the state's policies for helping Scheduled Castes.

In organizing the Bhopal meeting, Madhya Pradesh Chief Minister Digvijay Singh publicly demonstrated a commitment to improving Dalits' status in Indian society, not simply the politician's habit of reaffirming reservations in order to garner votes. With the theme "On Charting a New Course for Dalits in the 21st century," the event culminated in the Madhya Pradesh government's release of the 21-point Bhopal Declaration. The declaration, which points out the lack of progress of Dalit movements in the past 50 years, calls for a series of economic reforms. These include policies to ensure Dalits a fair share in the appropriation and use of rural and urban common property resources and legislation to achieve diversity in both public and private sectors of the workforce. Dalits proposed an economic agenda to achieve socio-economic advancement. As the reservations-free private sector grows, the whole structure of compensatory discrimination, spearheaded by B.R. Ambedkar, is brought into question.

It is too early to conclude that the Bhopal conference is a precursor of major change for Dalits and the central and state governments. So far, governments have been reluctant to venture outside of the established reservations framework. At the same time, lack of a cohesive pan-India movement has slowed Dalit efforts for advancement. Though Ambedkar did serve as a figure around which

Dalits could unify, he never achieved a politically potent pan-Indian following. Unity has been elusive for Dalits. With a cohesive national Dalit movement yet to be established, what political consolidation of Dalits that has occurred has mostly been restricted to states such as Maharashtra and Uttar Pradesh.

References

Aggarwal, Patrap. *Caste and Social Stratification Among Muslims in India*. Manohar. 1978.

Ambedkar, Bhimrao. *Pakistan or the Partition of India*. Thackers Publishers.

Ansari, Ghaus. *Muslim Caste in Uttar Pradesh: A Study of Culture Contact*. Lucknow, 1960.

Bayly, Susan. *Caste, Society and Politics in India from the Eighteenth Century to the Modern Age*. Cambridge University Press. 1999.

Srinivas, M. N. *Religion and Society among the Coorgs of South India*. Oxford, 1952.

8

Dalits and Public Policy

India's powerful independence movement (1885-1947) produced perhaps the world's most extensive system of affirmative action for oppressed peoples like the Dalits. And, since the 1970s, Dalits like Ram Pyari have organized to use these assets to overturn the caste system, organize for power, and fight for their rights.

When national level discussions for the World Conference on Racism (WCAR) began in India in 2004, the problem of caste immediately stirred controversy. The Hindi-Right dominated government was chary to raise the issue of caste on the world stage, particularly at this juncture when it revels in the US-sponsored praises for being the world's largest democracy. The government seeks to avoid anything that makes India "look bad" on the world stage. Apart from these international political reasons, the Hindu-Right government has a commitment to the perpetuation of caste discrimination. Not only are its ranks filled with representatives of the dominant castes, but its public policy platforms frequently privilege the rights of those dominant castes who hold wealth over the rest of society. Furthermore, allied organizations of the Hindu-Right have even convened religious conclaves given to the topic of a formal "revival" of strict Brahmanical social organizations, such as *varnashramadharma* or the fourfold division of *varnas*.

Dalit rights activists have, naturally, been eager to raise the question of caste discrimination on the international stage, particularly since this government (in power since 1998) has been the first to block discussion of caste in international forums. Martin Macwan, national head of the National Campaign for Dalit Human Rights, reminds us that "in earlier international forums, notably the Committee on Elimination of Discrimination Against Women, the Government of India had successfully taken up the issue of caste-based discrimination. Why is it insisting that caste is an 'internal' matter?" The idea that caste is an "internal" matter is specious, mainly because "caste" as we know it today is decidedly fostered by a combination of Indian social relations, European-driven colonialism, and global capitalism. These three factors produce what we know as caste today, since the practice cannot claim to be an a historical reflection of what one reads in Sanskrit texts.

It should be said, however, that there are some that want to reduce caste to a form of race, and therefore make a strong connection between the anti-racist work and the anti-caste work. Afrocentrics and Dalitocentrics are particularly notable here, especially with the claim that Dalits are "negritos" and that they suffer oppression at the hands of their "Aryan" oppressors, just as black folk around the world are held down by white folk. That the evidence for race as biology has been discredited does not seem to bother the indigenistas, many of whom deploy old racist texts to make their claims. One reason many indigenistas use the language of race in an unreconstructed manner is because they get ideological sustenance from a simple-minded US race politics, where the black-white dyad drives the political landscape. Indeed, in an interview with me, a leading US-based Afrocentric scholar who was instrumental in the creation of the Afro-Dalit thesis conceded that "I feel bad about it. I gave the impression that Dalits are Black people." Nevertheless, he argued that "I think large sections of Dalits would be seen as Black people if they lived anywhere else." One of the dangers of US imperialist hegemony is that the global anti-imperialist agenda may also end up being set in US anti-imperialist terms.

That is, the anti-racist program for organizations and activists from across the global might replicate the terms of the US movement. The enthusiasm for epidermal determinism occurs despite the Dalitcentric editor V. T. Rajshekar's early warning that " in India, it is no longer easy to distinguish a touchable from an Untouchable, especially for foreigners." Whether it was ever possible to tell caste by skin color is a question for debate, but certainly to make such judgements now is rather impossible.

8.1. Apartheid by any Name

When the Portuguese first landed in the southwestern coast of India in 1498, they came upon a form of social organization to which they gave the name caste (from castus). What they referred to was not one system, but a series of social formations to which they gave one name. But there was never just one simple caste hierarchy in India. Even today there are some 4,635 ethnic communities, many with distinct land bases and systems of hierarchy. What the Portuguese called caste was probably a social form called jati. The Europeans saw jati as rigid and oppressive, perhaps forgetting their own rigid feudal social order. Jati hierarchies emerged from the ancient world in various forms: occupations, marriage bonds, dietary habits, and religious customs. Indeed, no one principle explains "the caste system." Different jatis attained dominance in different parts of southern Asia, but all commanded the fealty and labour of others based on their monopoly over land and force. Over time, these others would come to be branded as "Untouchables." There is no subcontinental-wide caste system, since each locality produced various forms of local oppression where those who came to dominance, in and around the fight against Buddhism adopted ideas of superiority. Many of these xenophobic and elitist ideas articulated with and drew from the Brahmanic texts of an earlier era, notably with the *varnashramadharma* of the *Puranas*. Endogamy, ritual ranking and class power are three of the most important forces that constitute, in varying degrees, the complex of social differentiation and power in South Asian pre-modernity. There was nothing polite about the way the dominant jatis made their demands. Dalits fought off routine violence from dominant jatis, who, in turn, tried to erect vicious mechanisms to control the will of Dalits. Dalit women worked in the homes of the dominant jatis, and they fell prey to the sexual violence of elite men. However, these men disdained from any other interactions with the women.

When the Europeans began to conquer and administer the landmass of South Asia in the 18 century, they began to pay careful attention to the social order that lay before them. The anthropologist Bernard Cohn has shown us that the British impact on South Asian social life was decisive, mainly through the classification regime set in place by the colonial rulers. Certainly, work on two oppressed castes shows us that the British intervention transformed their relations to production and power: the Balmikis, as Chuhras, and the Jatavs, as Chamars, lived with control over land, as well as shares of the commons, until the British land officials decided, mainly in the late 18 century, that these Dalits should work only as drudge labour and not toil on land that was their own. What was the reason for this British response and how was it put into place? The reason was the Haitian Revolution of 1791-92 and of the birth of raciology as a means to justify the brutal control over labour with dark skin. In 1793, Jeremy Bentham, otherwise quite clear about the importance of the "rights of man," asked "Would the declaration of rights translate into *Sanscrit*? Would *Bramin*, *Chetree*, *Bice*, *Sooder*, and *Hallochore* meet on equal ground?" Hegel, after the Thermidor in Paris and in Port au Prince, checked his enthusiasm for freedom, with the caveat that "universal freedom can produce no positive work or deed, only *negative action* remains to it; it is the *fury of destruction*." The East India Company, are the lords of the land [India]; for it is the necessary fate of Asiatic Empires to be subjected to Europeans," and to be ruled without even a qualified kind of freedom for the darker skins.

The East India Company disregarded, indeed squelched, the dynamic for freedom within South Asia, as they produced knowledge about India that was, in many ways, the template for their land revenue and other public policies. The Europeans liked the stereotypical order of the "caste system" and they did all they could to bolster the Brahmanical order. An early text was *Hindu Manner, Customs and Ceremonies* by the Abbé Dubois, who had fled the French Revolution with the Missions Étrangéres in 1792. "I believe caste division to be in many respects the *chef-d'oeuvre*, the happiest effort of Hindu legislation," he wrote in this book that was very influential for the East India Company officialdom. "I am persuaded that it is simply and solely due to the distribution of the people into castes that India did not lapse into a state of barbarism, and that she preserved and perfected the arts and sciences of civilization whilst most other nations of the earth remained in a state of barbarism." The point is taken further in his discussion of the Pariahs, the Parayars of the Tamil speaking regions. "I am persuaded that a nation of Pariahs left to themselves would speedily become worse than the hordes of cannibals who wander in the vast waste of Africa and would soon take to devouring each other." If

Africans can be ordered by the brutality of chattel slavery and by a reconstructed tribalism, then the dark skins of South Asia can be ordered and managed by the reconstruction of caste along imperial lines. The discourses of race and caste then, emerged simultaneously, as both terms enabled the Europeans to justify the expropriation of values from certain parts of the world to what was to become the centre of the world economy: Europe. In the aftermath of the French Revolution, European conservatives justified their ill-gotten gains on the basis of race/caste, now rendered in terms of biology, and they continued their reliance upon military force on the basis of their imputed racial superiority. This had labour effects: just as the labour power of the European worker was commodified, the labour power of the darker skins was animalized, treated as something that required physical coercion to extract the maximum effort. The notion of race, then, was at the foundation of the reconstruction of caste in modern times.

In an act of bad faith, the European powers blamed the oppressed for their own oppression and they exculpated themselves from the manufacture of biological ideas of inferiority. Take Dubois again. "The idea that the [Dalit] was born to be in subjection to the other castes is so ingrained in his mind that it never occurs to the Pariah to think that his fate is anything but irrevocable. Nothing will ever persuade him that men are all made of the same clay, or that he has the right to insist on better treatment than that which is meted out to him." But if Dubois and the early EIC officials asked the Parayars what they thought of their subjection, they would have got a different answer: when the colonial ethnographer, Thurston, did just this in 1909, the Parayars of the Tamil-speaking region told him that they suffered the social indignity because of an ancient betrayal due to a linguistic error.

In the transition to capitalism, Marx argued, labour is freed in a "double sense, free from the relations of clientage, bondage and servitude, and secondly free of all belongings and possessions, and of every objective, material form of being, *free of all property*, dependent on the sale of its labour capacity or on begging, vagabondage and robbery as its only source of income." The means of production are wrenched from the workers at the same time as they are free to sell their labour-power as a commodity on the market. At the periphery of capital, labour is made fre only to be damned to unfreedom through the Brahmano-colonial mythology of an ancient division of labour known as the caste system. Caste, as a form of social relations, certainly predates colonial rule. However, caste as we know it today was radically transformed during the colonial period. Colonial sociology and policy worked together to expropriate Dalits from the soil. In Punjab, for instance, the land laws in the late 19 and early 20 Centuries specifically noted that Dalits, as drudge labour, should not be allowed to own land, a marked departure from the facts of land holding at that time: these Dalits lost control over their resources and fell prey to the direct, and brutal exploitation of newly landed classes, as well as of the wiles of capitalism's economic cycles. Modern employment was segregated along a stereotyped version of "native tradition" despite the fact that these "traditional" modes had not previously existed. This process demonstrates how labour is freed in the Indian colonies — freed, that is, into caste.

In 1999, Human Rights Watch (New York) published a report entitled *Broken People: Caste Violence Against India's "Untouchables."* HRW found that the situation of Dalits was deplorable and called their condition "hidden apartheid." There is nothing *hidden* about the violence against Dalits, one that moved M. K. Gandhi (1869-1948) in the 1930s to bring their struggles to the centre of the Indian national movement. His was a liberal gesture, far from the radicalism of some sections of the politically active Dalit movement led by Dr. B. R. Ambedkar (1891-1956). Ambedkar, a Dalit from western India, felt that 'it is wrong to say that the problem of Untouchables is a social problem,' a reference here to Gandhi's attempt to create social reform. Rather, he argued, "the problem of the Untouchables is fundamentally a political problem." It is also, as we've seen above, an economic problem, one of land rights and control over capital.

Ambedkar tapped into a long history of resilience among Dalits, and one can get an intimation of these vibrant Dalit struggles from the songs of Dalit poets. Raidas (1414-1540), for instance, sang that "don't ask of jati, we are all equal in the eyes of divinity." Or Kabirdas (1440-1518) who asked his fellows to seek truth in themselves and in their acts. By the 18 Century, the region of Punjab was treated to the anticlerical songs of Bulleh Shah who sang that "God permeates each and every house, and he permeates every human soul." These songs against hierarchy based on a claim to religion remind us that few among the oppressed took their condition for granted. The tradition of protest does not exist only amongst the most oppressed castes, but the history of the Lingayats, Jains, and others, shows us that middle-castes too found the entire ensemble inhuman.

Over the past two hundred years, more self-conscious acts of anti-jati campaigns resulted in a further awareness of the outrageous of untouchability and anti-Dalit violence. Just as Frederick Douglass reminded the world that "power concedes nothing without a demand," Jyotibai Phule (1826-1890) declared that "we know perfectly well that the Brahmin will not descend from his self-raised pedestal and meet his low caste brethren on an equal footing without a struggle." Jyotibai and Savitribai Phule founded the Satya Shodhak Samaj in September 1873 to educate the oppressed jatis as well as to conduct cross-jati marriages, radical acts against hierarchy. Alongside the Phules, Dalit peasants rose in hundreds of revolts against the yoke of British colonialism, local landlords and moneylenders.

8.2. Dalits as Citizens

In 1947, the Indian national movement ejected British colonialism and inaugurated a period of national construction. These were heady days, as anti-colonial movements from Indonesia to Ghana took power of States to make freedom something tangible for the masses. India was no exception. The first Indian Prime Minister Jawaharlal Nehru (1889-1964) was impatient to rework the oppressive present, so the State in the 1950s took a few bold steps toward the emancipation of the Dalits. Ambedkar is known, in many Dalit circles, as the architect of the Indian Constitution. If there was no political movement of Dalits to backup Ambedkar, the judiciary provided that cover. When the government's protections of freedom for Dalits was challenged in the Courts, a Supreme Court justice argued that "advantages secured due to historical reasons cannot be considered a fundamental right guaranteed by the Constitution." When Martin Luther King, Jr., traveled to India in 1959 he was stunned by the State's monetary and legal commitment to Dalit emancipation.

While Article 14 of the 1950 Indian Constitution guaranteed equality before the Law, the Courts refused to interpret it to mean absolute and unequivocal equality. In order to produce equality, the courts developed a framework to prevent the notion of equality from suppressing active governmental intervention on behalf of certain groups. In order to produce social and economic equality, the Courts allowed the State to intervene on behalf of oppressed and exploited groups, to use equality as the means to freedom. The Courts identified women and backward classes as the two major groups towards whom the State was enjoined to act in a compensatory manner. The institutions that the Indian State created were a means to the politicization of 'equality' in order to produce a future moral, free community. Rather than bear the full implications of this courageous policy, the Indian administration settled for the 'reservations' policy that enabled a few Dalits to join what was once called the 'Harijan elite.' The actual benefits from the policy of compensation were not evenly distributed among the Dalits because certain caste groups benefited more than others and only a few individuals and their families were able to capitalize on State policy. The vast mass of the Dalits remained outside the purview of the 'reservations' packages. The Balmikis, for instance, were only able to take advantage of the reservations scheme as a collectivity in their monopoly over one particular occupation in the municipalities: Class IV employment, typically with the sanitation departments. Most of the reservations are in low-skilled, low-paying jobs that do little to move Dalits up the economic ladder.

By the mid-1960s, the limited compensation schemes began to suffer from the economic and political crisis that followed the Sino-Indian war of 1962, the Indo-Pakistan war of 1965 and the monsoon failures of 1965 and 1967. A serious crisis of political hegemony followed from the late 1960s, which developed into the ruling clique taking extraordinary powers into its own hands through centralization, whose most notable instance was the promulgation of the Emergency in 1975. Among Dalits, serious doubts were being raised about the commitment and ability of the State to provide the conditions of equality. In 1969, L. Elayaperumal's report on Dalits for the Department of Social Welfare pointed out that "to our utter dismay the Committee found that untouchability was still being practised in virulent form all over India." In the Lok Sabha on 19 August 1970, the Minister of State for Home announced that between 1967 and 1969,

1117 Dalits had been reported murdered. Of these, 63 cases were in Maharashtra, 332 in Uttar Pradesh and 76 in Punjab. The "Harijan Atrocity" of the 1970s was not part of an ancient story of the caste system, but must be embedded in the social relations of the caste struggle that intensified after Dalits felt emboldened by their constitutional protections. Pipra was in line with a host of such massacres whose aetiology may be in the revanchist attempt by dominant castes to hold onto power that seemed to be on the wane.

In response to the failure of India to resolve the contradictions of political democracy, young Dalits in the late 1960s took inspiration from worldwide student movements, from the Black Panther movement in the United States and from the resurgence of militant left-wing activity within India toescalate their own struggle for freedom. On 29 April 1968, Shyam Sunder launched the Bheem Senain Gulbanga to militarily confront caste Hindu atrocities against Dalits. In June 1972, the Dalit Panthers emerged as the major political formation of this new militancy. In a manifesto penned by one faction of the movement, the Panthers declared themselves in favour of "a complete revolution" as opposed to "partial change." This was, for the Panthers, insufficient. In their 18 point program, they called for land redistribution, an increase in wages, free education, and censorship of offensive literature, and an end to economic corruption and mostradically, "all means of production must belong to the Dalits." Calling for "people's democracy" the Panthers argued against the contradictions of the liberal state and put forward the slogan, "in our struggle we will become free."The Panthers' alert us to the manner in which the Indian State attempted to resolve the contradictions of "equality." The Untouchability Offences Act of 1955 and the workings of the Commission of Scheduled Castes understood untouchability to mean the social and cultural oppression of the Dalits by caste Hindus and by Muslims. To compensate for the lack of access to public buildings and lack of expression were the central tasks set by the state in its anti-untouchability campaign. Most of the recorded complaints by Dalits to the Commission were along these lines. By the late 1970s, however, most complaints to the Commission concerned issues such as land rights, housing and education. Harassment continued to be an important issue, but it was not the major issue. From the perspective of the Panthers, untouchability had to be seen both as status and class inequality, for that is the peculiarity of Dalithood. The Panther intervention dramatized the structural critique of 'untouchability and it alerts us to see caste not only as a political-cultural-ritual system, but also as the form of socio-economic exploitation. Colonialism recast caste in such a way as to provide for the various economic and political needs of a system ravenous for the wealth generated in India. No doubt the *Dharmashastras* continue to influence the doings and thinkings of caste Hindus, but the experience and structures of contemporary untouchability can hardly be interpreted on the basis of a text written sometime in the first two centuries B. C. E.

The Panthers were unable to craft wide enough solidarities to make a mark on the national political scene; further, infighting amongst the leaders and the cadres on the status of whom to ally with ended any hope of building a political opposition to the State's limited policy towards untouchability. In recent years, the most effective, but largely opportunistic, Dalit political bloc to emerge on the national scene has been the Bahujan Samaj Party (BSP). Since the government put restrictions on its employees from doing political work, Ram formed the Dalit Shoshit Samaj Sangharsh Samiti (DS-4) in December 1981, which, in April 1984, formed an electoral wing, the BSP. In 1987, Ram told the media that the Dalits "nurse a feeling that the government in spite of its best efforts has not been able to remove poverty. This is truly unfortunate. The bureaucracy, which we inherited from the British, is caste ridden and officers have yet to rise above caste. I have seen how they work half-heartedly towards implementing the government's programmes for the backward communities." The BSP is not the only organization to lay claim to the Social Democratic tradition of Dr. Ambedkar. They are joined in their commitment to Dalit politics by the historic Dalit parties, the Scheduled Castes Federation and the Republican Party of India and by various socialistic parties which draw from Rammanohar Lohia and from Jayaprakash Narayan. What these parties share is a commitment to protecting the Dalits from the harshness of capitalism. The brief alliance between the BSP and militant Hinduism in 1995 demonstrated the impoverishment of the defensive agenda which has been cultivated by the social democratic parties which draw inspiration from Dr. Ambedkar.

The contradictions of equality reappeared on the national political agenda in the 1980s through the second Backward Classes Commission that the government appointed on 1 January 1979 under the chairmanship of B. P. Mandal. The Janata Government (1977-80) responded to the grassroots mobilisation which characterized the 1970s in India by putting forth certain limited reforms of which the Mandal Commission was exemplary. The Commission offered its report on 31 December 1980.

The Mandal Commission warned Indian society in 1980 of the very contradictions identified by Ambedkar in 1949: the contradiction between the principle of equality before the Law and social and economic inequality. Unwilling to grapple with the contradictions at the foundation of Indian society, the unrest over Mandalization after 1990 revealed the reluctance of many Indians to even consider the project of producing equality. The attacks on the "protections" to "minorities" and to the "public sector" have made the struggle for freedom hard and yet imperative. The State is pledged to interpret untouchability as harassment and the anti-untouchability movement as a struggle for civil rights; once the question of structural disenfranchisement is put on the table and once the struggle is for human rights, the dominant classes and castes enjoin the state to undercut those political gestures. For the Balmikis, compensation has meant that a few of the community succeed and that they are allowed to control the sanitation departments in municipalities; there is little to defend in the system from their point of view. Democracy works in that the Dalits now have the possibility to effect change; that they have not been able to effectively gain power is a mark of the strength of the dominant classes and castes in India.

Dalits still fight forms of apartheid. The State failed the Dalits because it did not truly dismantle the "advantages secured for historical reasons," such as land relations and the control over capital. Attempts by the state to extend favour to Dalits draw an enormous resistance from the dominant jatis. Among Dalits, as a result, their rate of literacy is barely 22%, only 16% of Dalits live in cities, about 50% are agricultural labourers, and only 4% work in the industrial workforce. The extent of poverty, because of these factors, is about 50%. Of those who work in the fields, 71% are marginal farmers who must sell their labour at low rates to dominant jatis. The poverty of Dalits is matched by their lack of political power. Since the 1970s, militant Dalit groups emerged to fight landlords and to use the franchise. The exertions of the Dalits have, by all accounts, increased anti-Dalit violence. In this cauldron of struggle, many Dalit organizations emerged, such as the Dalit Panthers the Republican Party of India, and the Bahujan Samaj Party. Over the years, these groups have floundered on the rocks of either opportunism or of extreme nationalism. In recent years, liberal Dalit groups have made linkages with non-governmental organizations to create such platforms as the National Campaign on Dalit Human Rights. Their exertions, Smita Narula of HRW says, drew the attention of the Human Rights Watch to the atrocities against Dalits.

Part of the problem is the lack of focus on land relations, and this is what differentiates the fight for anti-racist justice in the advanced industrial North with the relatively rural South. The compensatory discrimination scheme created by the Indian government concentrates on public jobs but this occludes the fact that only 16% of the total Dalit population live in urban India. Most of the rest are marginal farmers, sharecroppers or landless labourers. For these Dalits land ownership is the cornerstone of liberation. The recent reportage of celebrated journalist P. Sainath confirms the centrality of land, as do news reports of anti-Dalit violence in rural Bihar and Haryana. Indeed, the failure to underscore the importance of the land question serves to undermine the centrality of the Left to Dalit liberation. For most Dalits, wealth is land. This is not the view of the so-called Dalit parties, such as the BSP: when Dalit landless workers forcibly occupied the land of the ex-Raja of Benares in Uttar Pradesh, the BSP Chief Minister Mayavati sent in the police to arrest them. Her actions once more subordinated the Dalits to poverty. The centrality of land to the Left, on the other hand, is made clear by the 20 December 1998 All India Democratic Women's Association Convention in support of Dalit women's rights against untouchability and oppression.

Meanwhile, on the ground, change is afoot. Narula of HRW reports that processes of emancipation can be gleaned in the fight to gain local political power. In 1996, the Dalits of Melavalavu won control of the local governmental body. As they tried to take office, local goons killed six of the leaders. Of the six, the man elected to lead the body was beheaded, a "brutal reminder," Brinda Karat of the Communist Party of India notes, "that, for the non-Dalits, Dalits are meant to serve, not rule." Karat points to the data from West Bengal where the Left has been in power since 1977. Only there, she says, the Dalits have benefited from land reforms and from the devolution of political power. West Bengal has only 3.58% of the cultivatable land in the Indian Republic and yet, it has contributed over 20% of the total surplus land that falls under the land ceiling laws. Apart from land reform, the Left Front-initiated Operation Barga in 1978 which registered 1.4 million tenant farmers and provided them with legal instruments to stave off eviction and to struggle for shares of the harvest. These land reforms are "the backbone of Dalit self-respect and dignity in the state."

In 1949, Ambedkar told the political leaders of India that their hesitant approach to land reform did not bode well for democracy. "How long shall we continue to deny equality in our social and economic life? If we continue to deny it for long, we will do so only by putting out political democracy in peril." Caste, as constructed in colonial times and lived in the contemporary moment, is not identical to race, even though both emerge simultaneously as methods to exert imperial control and to justify white supremacy. Nevertheless, the agenda for social justice is not identical, since the social context of the fights are separate: where the human rights agenda of civic justice may be more important in one context, the fight for land rights may be central in the other. To collapse the contexts of social justice in the service of internationalism and solidarity is to harm all our struggles.

REFERENCES

Barbara R. Joshi, *Untouchable!: Voices of the Dalit Liberation Movement*, Zed Books, 1986.

Gail Omvedt. *Dalits and the Democratic Revolution - Dr. Ambedkar and the Dalit Movement in Colonial India*, Sage Publications. 1994.

Mulk Raj Anand. *An Anthology Of Dalit Literature*, by 1992, Gyan Books.

Rajshekhar. V.T. *Dalit - The Black Untouchables of India*, Clarity Press, Inc., 2003.

9

Development of Scheduled Communities

The Depressed Classes, as the SC&ST Dalits were known those days, during their long struggles were demanding not for a token foothold, but a formal Representation in the Administration, due Presence in the Bureaucracy, full Participation in the Govt, and for their Share in the Governance of the Country. They were ably led by the well learned indomitable Baba Saheb Dr Ambedkar.

The presence of some SCs&STs in Services, including the Central Secretariat at Delhi is a fact, even though the SC&ST Communities have not yet really got their Dues, or a real and true Share of Power or Responsible Part in the Governance of the Country. Even this small presence, has now become possible, only because of Dr Ambedkar's Statesmanship Vision Foresight, and his Insistence for Preserving and Continuing in Free India, if not more, at least the motheaten Reservations for the Depressed Classes, to which he was forced to agree by Gandhi in 1932, and entered into a formal Pact, a written and signed Solemn Agreement with the caste hindu leaders, on behalf of the Depressed Classes. And it is these, and particularly because of Dr Ambedkar and his Reservations—that while the Anglo-Indians, Other Christians, Muslims, Parsis etc of the British India, have either faded or vanished from the Central Secretariat, the then rare SCs&STs have gained some presence in Free Independent India, the caste hindu dominated India, as many Minority and Backward Class Leaders of those days including Dr Ambedkar also, rightly predicted and feared. Even this small presence of SCs&STs in the Central Secretariat today, is not a small achievement. And this, in short, is what the Policy of Reservation has achieved.

Many poor Backward Castes with Social Conditions, Economic and Political Standards, comparable or at times at least in some ways bad if not worse than that of the SCs, who in the early days of Independence of the Country refused and fought bitterly against any proposal or suggestion or even an idea to include the names of their Castes into the list of SCs, when the Govts in the States were considering and enumerating various Castes to compile and declare the Lists of the Scheduled Castes for the States, have come around and made a complete about turn, clamouring for their respective individual Castes to be included in the List of Scheduled Castes.

The demand by the Other Backward Classes and also many others, and their claim to be declared as a SC, or at times at least as a ST, even by hook or crook was going on silently almost all the times. This, even though they were all otherwise publicly opposed to the SCs&STs, and were running the SCs&STs down badly as if they were outsiders and their enemies. They were also denigrating the SCs&STs, calling them names and humiliating them openly. The others were opposing all forms of Reservations, specifically any assistance or help by the Govt to the SCs&STs. And they were the bitter critics of the whole Scheme of Reservations, particularly Caste based Reservations. They were arguing that the Reservations should not be on the basis of Castes, even though they were specifically asking for inclusion of their Castes in the List of SCs, only and in order to get the benefits of Reservations for themselves and their own Castes. In the public, they were always critical of Reservations, even when demanding Reservations for themselves. Such were and still are, the double standards of the hindu society. They were claiming that the Reservations were there, and in fact were conceived only to please the SC&ST Dalits, with an eye on the hustings. They were, as the caste hinds today still are, cribbing that the Politicians upheld Reservations only due to the compulsions of electoral necessities. Thus, they were and others are, so foolish even to criticise and blame Democracy, and the processes of choosing the Peoples' Representatives for sending them to the Panchayats, Legislatives and the Parliament through Adult Franchise. In the end, finding the doors of entry and inclusion of their Castes into the List of the SCs closed, or at least closed tight, some of them came around to open a new front or line of similar Reservations in the name of Backward Classes.

Constitution facilitates the Govt to provide for, Reservations to Other Backward Classes, who are not Represented in Govt. But the dominant castes who appropriate everything and take all good things in life for themselves, have been effectively and systematically blocking the Reservations for the Backward Classes all these years. Many of them had gone up in the offices and in their lives. Many others, with the connivance of the officials themselves, even today appropriate and continue to enjoy the benefits meant for the SCs&STs, with the help of bogus SC/ST Certificates they manage to obtain falsely, and or by falsification of facts, about their birth or that of their parents, or just by paying bribes to the caste hindu peons, clerks and the Caste Certificate Issuing Authorities in the States and UTs. This, only because of the all round realisations that Reservations really help, and help even the lowly placed, despised, marginalised, socially suppressed, culturally physically politically, educationally and economically oppressed weaker sections and communities like the SCs&STs. Almost all the authorities and other officials are totally opposed and are against the SCs&STs and their Development, or are jealous and intolerant of the SCs&STs getting even an iota of Progress, little Liberation, inch of Freedom, or at least a bit of Justice.

Reservations are really and truly beneficial not only to the people concerned like the SCs&STs and OBCs, but also to the whole Nation and the Society for the overall and just Development. Also, the Country's Economy gets benefited, and can achieve better and quicker results through all-round Growth and Progress. Whatever may be the shortcomings and oppositions, or behind the screen schemings that go against Reservations, the Reservations had served well, the Nation and the Indian Society. With the part acceptance in 1990, of Reservations for the Backward Classes recommended by the Mandal Commission, Reservations have come to stay, in spite of all the fury and all-round oppositions. Reservations now have become permanent. Nobody in the Country now has the courage or the guts to scrap them, however much they may dislike Reservations and or hate the SCs&STs and OBCs. Now, there is a flurry of rush by individuals and castes to include themselves and their castes as Backward Castes. Reservations have been accepted by all, as the sure means to develop even the badly disadvantaged despised and marginalised sections of the society. In fact, the Reservations for long have been recognised as a reliable mechanism to help the Weaker Sections of the Society anywhere in the World. And there is no better Model, to Uplift the Backward the Helpless the Marginalised and the Neglected Communities. It is only for this reason that, there is so much of fury and oppositions to Reservation Policy on the one hand, and the silent sabotage and subversions that we see on the other in the actual implementation. The specific details of Reservations, the mechanisms and processes of operating and enforcement of the Reservations, are silently and cunningly derailed by those who are jealous and intolerant of the Growth Development and Progress of the SCs&STs.

The Reservations for OBCs had multiple effects. They are yet to be felt or realised in full. But the immediate effects are that the dominant castes had lost their control over the OBCs, and thus an effective tool to oppress the SCs&STs, and focus their tirade against the Reservations for the SCs&STs. They had lost an effective excuse to keep the OBCs captive anymore. They could no more turn the attention of the OBCs away from the fact that, they have always been taking away the opportunities, shares and dues of others including the OBCs, and thus have all along deprived the growth development and progress of the OBCs. They could no more divert the anger of the OBCs against the SCs&STs, to escape from the same. Hence they could no more succeed in keeping the OBCs and the SCs&STs the Deprived Sections of the Society—divided, and hold down the SCs&STs by using the OBCs to keep the SCs&STs suppressed.

The dominant castes till now had only contempt for the SCs&STs, and had only occasionally shown their intolerance and hatred for the Reservations They were only Jealous of the Development of some SCs&STs in spite of all the oppositions and hurdles for growth. They rarely had to deal directly with the SCs&STs, or oppose Reservations by themselves. That task, they had effectively managed to put on the OBCs. They were only operating from the back, by manipulating the Details and the Methodologies of Reservations, and the actual Processes of Implementation. With the Reservations for the OBCs, their hatred had increased, and the targets of hatred had enlarged from the just hopeful expectant SCs&STs, to the restless and aggressive but at the same time unorganised OBCs also. Now they had to confront both, almost at the same time and on the same issues. At the same time, they had to also carry on by themselves on their shoulders the burden of opposing the Reservations, and also keep manipulating the Reservations, so that the Reservations don't actually benefit either the SCs&STs or the OBCs. They are thus actually playing with fire. What will happen when the OBCs fully wake up, organise themselves and get united? What will they do to face the fury of the organised OBCs? And what will happen if the SCs&STs also join them? The dominant castes apparently are not thinking beyond the immediate, and are making a great mistake.

The significant is the fact that the caste hindus have developed in their minds a great fear about the grouping, coming together, possible unity, and combination of the OBCs and the SCs&STs, at least as the Beneficiaries of Reservations. But instead of finding a practical and lasting solution, they still want to play their games. They don't want change or mend their ways. They want to continue with their manipulations. That is the reason why they have Administratively and through the Courts, limited the Reservations for the OBCs, to only Appointments in Public Services by Direct Recruitments alone, and not in Promotions. Therefore, they want to avoid the OBCs and the SCs&STs joining hands, and prevent them from fully coming together. Hence, they want to preserve many areas of divergence between the OBCs and SCs&STs, and thus the disunity and conflict, particularly in Admissions to higher and professional education, at least in the Central Institutions and in Promotions in Services.

Today, the fear in the minds of the caste hindus had grown so intense that all the dominant castes, almost without any exception, feel threatened that their days are counted, and that their dominance now is really at stake. Therefore, even some of those well placed fellows, and happy satisfied comfortable and self contented individuals, who had in the past shown some sympathy for the poor bright or the helpless and needy or capable and promising individual SCs&STs, have no more empathy left in them for the later. Their fear is now so great, intense and total. As they are in power, and in full control of the Govt, Bureaucracy, and the Administration of Public Affairs, the heat is increasingly being felt now, by most of the SCs&STs.

9.1. Reservations for the SCs&STs

Many things! And at the same time the Reservations had failed to achieve much more essential things! They have proved to be a great disappointment to the SC&ST Communities as a whole! They have failed the SCs&STs almost in all the fronts and every walks of the life! It is not that Reservations are bad, but those who have been called to work them have proved to be really bad! The learned officials, the Public Servants of the Country, in whose hands the responsibility of implementing the Reservations rest, have deliberately let down the still poor and helpless SCs&STs! They really have no heart, neither any compassion or concern for the poor helpless and the weak, nor any interest in the Welfare Growth and Development of the People, the Society, the Country and the Nation!

We have adequate and reasonably reliable data on the Reservations for SCs&STs, and there are lots of Reports and other Writings on their actual effects. But sadly, after five decades of operations of Reservations for SCs&STs in free Indian Republic even if we neglect the period between 1935 Govt of India Act and 1950 when the Constitution with Special Provisions for the SCs&STs including various Reservations for the SCs&STs, in different and related spheres of Politics Education Employment and Economic Activities, like Development Growth Housing Welfare etc came into force—the achievements are not really worth recounting. As a result, in the significant areas of Education and Employment, there is nothing we can talk of proudly, or the Govt can take credit of.

Today, fifty years after Independence of the Country, there are only two SC Secretaries to the Govt of India—one an IAS Officer, and the other the Law Secretary to the Govt of India. There is no ST who is a Secretary to the Govt of India. Not very long ago, there were about ten SC&ST Secretaries to the Govt of India—about six or seven SCs and two or three STs, and nearly half a dozen Additional Secretaries as well as more than a dozen Joint Secretaries in the Central Secretariat. And what is worse, there is no worthwhile effort to improve the situation. On the other hand, there is a strong animosity against SC&ST Officials, particularly against the intelligent hardworking honest capable and result oriented ones. Practically every one of them are suffering, have suffered and will suffer more and more problems in the days to come.

Why is This So? The answers are not far difficult to find. One need not even search for them. They are readily available before us, and are clearly visible. They are obvious to everyone. Both the Bureaucracy and the Judiciary have been gunning for the SCs&STs, and the Reservations for them. They are aggressively intolerant, jealous and have been openly working against the Development Growth and Welfare of the SCs&STs. For reasons they can not clearly explain to themselves, or honestly speak out, or perhaps out of total ignorance, or shear stupidity and bull headedness, they are still opposing the Reservations for the SCs&STs and OBCs. And what is worse, there is no more empathy towards the SCs&STs.

Today's Political Party Leaders don't have any concern, or even show any lip-sympathy towards the SCs&STs, even for public and political reasons. They feel that they need not bother at all, or show any concern for the weak and the helpless, like the SCs&STs, Backwards and Minorities. Hence they just don't care now for anyone. They are very sure that they can manage all of them with out really doing anything good or positive for them.

9.2. SCs&STs in Public Services

SCs&STs taken together form nearly 26% of the Indian Population. In absolute numbers they are more than 260 million today. It is not only significant, but is a very large Population. Most of the Nations, barring China and India are not that big. But such a large People have no place or Representation in the Country even today. In fifty years of the Indian Republic, there was only one Vice President, and only just now we have a President from the SCs. There has never been anyone in these Offices from the STs. During the same period, there were hardly two or three Tribal Cabinet Ministers at the Centre. There has never been a SC or ST Prime Minister. Hardly ever been there any SC/ST Chief Minister in the States and UTs, and the rare ones also were not allowed to stay in office even for one or two years. The only exceptions have been in the inevitable North Eastern States. There too, the SCs&STs of Manipur and Tripura have a very bad experience to narrate.

In thirteen Planning Commissions that we have seen so far, there never was a regular SC Member, and only one ST was a Member, twice with tenures of less than one year and five years, from 1990 to 1991, and again from 1991 to 1996. The Planning Commission of India at the Centre, surprisingly does not yet have a Separate Department or even a small Cell for either the SCs&STs taken together, or for the larger group of the SCs, or for the special groups of STs, even though the conditions of the SCs&STs are pitiable all over the Country, and is going from bad to worse with each passing day, as the overall Planning and Development of the Country, Market Forces, as well as the growing numbers of greedy social elements are squeezing and forcing the SCs&STs out, even from their own traditional lands and homes. But this is not at all shocking, given the still prevailing prejudices and biases in the Indian Society, particularly in the hindu mind against the SCs&STs.

The Representations of the SCs&STs in the Judiciary are woefully poor, and that again shows the prevailing awful animosity against the SCs&STs in the minds of the so called learned Judges, and other highly placed Jurists Authorities and the Govt, who choose consider select recommend and make appointments of the Judges, especially to the High Courts in the States and also to the Supreme Court of India. Some of them are not only against the SCs&STs as Judges, but are openly and blatantly against the SC&ST Communities as a whole. With such animosities biases and prejudices, what type of Justice can they do or what sort of Judgements will they deliver? No one has yet made any study of the damages they have done to the creative hard-working SCs&STs, and thus to the Country. In fifty years, there were only three SC Judges in the Supreme Court at different points of time, and not even one ST. Now no one is there, and hardly anyone is likely to be allowed to come in there in the near future. Such is the opposition against them. They throw out their Cases, don't have patience or want to listen anything from the SC&ST Lawyers, even for the sake of appearing to be just and show off that they have heard the Case, and are doing and would do Justice, both to the Lawyers and the Parties they represent in the Case before the Court.

9.3. SCs&STs in Academics and Education

The Representations of the SCs&STs in Academics, either as Students or Employees in Schools, Colleges, Universities, other Autonomous Institutions or Centres of Higher Learning are still very poor.

Thousands of qualified Job-Seekers are deliberately refused employment in the Schools Colleges Universities etc. Hundreds and hundreds of SC&ST Students aspiring for higher studies are turned out every year denied admissions, or even after admissions are thrown out or forced to get out under some pretext or the other from the Colleges, Universities, Autonomous Institutions and other Centres of Higher Education.

The Opportunities for Studies Abroad available to Indian Students are by and large still kept as a secret from the SCs&STs, even though hundreds of Indian Students are to be found in many Foreign Countries with various Scholarships and other Schemes that help them to pursue their studies abroad, without taxing their families. Even Dr Ambedkar's Dream of educating select SC&ST Students Abroad, accepted by the then British Indian Govt, has been badly twisted beyond recognition by the Welfare Ministry over the years. A similar Scheme of Dr Ambedkar Overseas Fellowships for Students to study abroad, through Dr Ambedkar Foundation has been in the cold storage for quite sometime, and many students already selected for the Award of the Fellowships have not been permitted to avail of the Fellowships. A silent effort is said to be in the offing, to turn it as a facility only for SC&ST University and College Teachers already in job. Thus, the Scheme meant for the Students is being distorted, and at the same time, the UGC and other authorities would be washing off their responsibilities in providing opportunities to Train Abroad, the SC&ST Lecturers and Professors working in the Colleges and Universities. Thus by one change, two opportunities available to SC&ST Students and the SC&ST Teachers are now being cleverly and silently closed.

The numbers of SC&ST Lecturers, Senior Lecturers, Readers, Assistant Professors, Associate Professors, Professors etc in the Colleges, Autonomous Colleges, Universities, Deemed Universities, Research Centres and other Institutions of Higher Learning in the Country are extremely poor. This in spite of the fact that, Delhi attracts professionals scholars and teachers from all-over the Country. Yet, the authorities have managed successfully so far to keep the SCs&STs at a very far distance away from Delhi. In this, the negative role being played by the University Grants Commission etc can not ever be discounted or forgotten.

The UGC is not even allowing or facilitating the SC&ST Students to acquire the requisite Higher Qualifications of M Phil and Ph D essential for Teaching in the Universities and Colleges. They do not provide them any Scholarships and Fellowships to pursue these long and costly studies. The Govt and the Ministry of Social Justice and Empowerment is not helping the poor SC&ST Students wanting to go for such essential higher studies.

Perhaps India is the only Nation in the World where the Teachers instead of teaching the poor are denying them education, instead of equipping them with knowledge are condemning them, turning them as unfits and deliberately rating them low. In fact this has been the history of India. One could not ever afford to forget Egalivya.

9.4. SCs&STs in Government Services

The Representations of the SCs&STs in Govt Services, even on the overall reckoning is extremely poor, in spite of operating the Reservation Systems for the last fifty years. And this, with so many brilliant and highly educated and qualified SCs&STs, duly examined and certified so, by all those caste hindu controlled Universities and Educational Institutions, always knocking at the doors of the Govt Offices and various Recruiting and Appointing Authorities for Jobs and Employment. The overall Representations of the SCs&STs in the Central Govt Services all-over the Country, as on 1st January 1995 are:

i) 10.15% SCs and 2.89% STs in Group A(Class I) Services and Posts

ii) 12.67% SCs and 2.68% STs in Group B(Class II) Services and Posts

iii) 16.15% SCs and 5.69% STs in Group C(Class III) Services and Posts

iv) 21.26% SCs and 6.48% STs in Group D(Class IV) Posts

Even in the Group C(Class III) Services and Posts, the Representations of the SCs and STs in the higher grades are very poor. Even these small Representations of the SCs&STs in Services, most of the caste hindu authorities are unable to tolerate and digest. They therefore, go after the blood of even these small numbers of SCs&STs in Service.

All the observations and empirical data available today indicate that, on an average more than 90% of Vigilance Cases are against the Employees and Officers who are weak, susceptible and are vulnerable, such as those about to retire, due for promotions, and are SCs&STs. And what is more surprising is that, more than 60% of the Employees and Officers facing Vigilance Cases, or are under Suspension, caught up in Inquiries, suffering Punishments of loss of increments, reduction in pay or pay-scales, withheld increments, withheld promotions, denial of promotions, downgrading in rank or termination, are the helpless and godfatherless SCs&STs. Since these are Vigilance Cases, none is generally forthcoming or are in a position to extend any helping hand to them. But, the losses, being suffered by so many SC&ST Employees and Officers all around, and their Families in Physical, Psychological, Mental, Social and Financial Terms are immense and colossal. In fact it is a serious and major economic loss to the Country and a criminal wastage of well qualified highly trained productive responsible and useful manpower.

Those who get poor Assessments, Reports, Gradings, and hence as a result miss their Promotions often times and repeatedly, are almost exclusively the SCs&STs. This, in spite of the fact that, many of them have been recruited through All India Competitive Examinations by the UPSC or other Commissions/Agencies. It is often an humiliating experience for them, which get further compounded, when they find that they have lost the race for promotions and seniority, to those who are far far juniors to them in service, and many times to those who are not even qualified and are from the ranks, but have managed the promotions only because they are caste hindus and hence are well connected having direct access to their seniors who matter, either directly by themselves or through their families or with the help of other relatives, friends, or the ever important caste circles.

In the sphere of Sweeping, a category of cleaning jobs as Sweepers, an area and occupation exclusively Reserved by the hindu society for the SCs, others are today making inroads edging out the poor SC Sweepers, even when they are unwilling to work as Sweepers. They are coming in as Sweepers, not to Sweep and work as Sweepers, but to take by hook or crook a well paid Govt Job in Govt Offices, where they can easily and safely avoid work, if they even otherwise choose not to work or don't want to work. For them, the job of a poor

Sweeper is a convenient backdoor entry into Govt Offices, which they are otherwise unable to enter for want of requisite education, training, experience, intelligence, capabilities and such other qualifications required for direct recruitment to the jobs they desire to take. Hence their attempts to take jobs of Sweepers is farce, and is a fraud on the Sweepers and Govt. They therefore, always refuse to work as Sweepers even for a second, and avoid touching the broom ever, even though they had applied for and joined service as Sweepers, hold the job of Sweepers, mark attendance as Sweepers, take salaries as Sweepers, ask for special facilities as Sweepers and promotions as Sweepers. Once in the Govt Offices as Sweepers, these others with the open support help and connivance of their caste hindu superiors hold for namesake the job of Sweepers. They get their work done through other Sweepers in the office, or act informally as Sweeping Contractors or Suppliers of Casual Manpower for Sweeping on their behalf the offices as also for keeping clean the premises and the areas allotted to them for cleaning, for a paltry token payment which they pay from out the full Govt Salaries they take as Sweepers.

In many offices, the system of exploiting and cheating both the Govt and the poor lowly paid Sweepers has been formalised, and the caste hindu Contractors are given regular Contracts to Supply Casual Sweepers regularly to the office, or get the sweeping done on a regular basis on Contract.

It is because of the ingenious dubious practices, cheating and exploitation of the helpless Sweepers, by the educated and well employed superior officials, and the realisation of the same by the regular Sweepers, the regular Sweepers are on an unnoticed continuous strike, and they are now adopting a noncooperative go slow tactics, that they don't take their work anymore seriously. Thus, the quality of their work is poor. Hence the sweeping work suffers. It is because of these that, the maintenance of Cleanliness and Hygiene in Govt Offices and their surroundings are very poor, and the Corridors awfully stink even many paces away from the toilets and waste bins anywhere, that sensitive and conscious individuals cannot pass by them easily.

Unless the Govt makes peace with the Sweepers, genuinely and sincerely look into their grievances, end all forms of cheating and exploitations, and put a complete stop to the present dubious methods of employing others, the overall cleanliness and hygiene not only in the Govt Offices but in the Country will suffer very seriously, particularly when we take into consideration the peoples lack of consciousness and attitudes of not maintaining general cleanliness in their places of work/ living and surroundings.

With acceptance of some Reservations for the OBCs, consolidation of the OBCs which was inevitable and taking place even before the Reservations for them was accepted, and the growing consciousness of the SCs&STs, the caste hindus are today a worried lot. Even then, they don't want to rest, or change and mend their ways. They don't want to adopt reasonable just and fair Civilised Methods of working, and managing the affairs of the society. Since the caste hindus are still in positions of power, and always speak for the Nation, on behalf of the Nation, as if they are the Nation, they adopt such policies and practices that it appears the Nation is hitting back at the SCs&STs, the OBCs and the Reservations. Yes, they are under attack, and the attacks though systematic severe and total, are meted out silently. They are being hit below the belt and in the back at unexpected times.

It is the considered opinion of the SCs&STs and the OBCs that, the Country had adopted the path of Liberalisation, Globalisation, opted for opening up the Economy, and had slowly begun the privatisation and selling of the Public Sector Govt Enterprises built up so laboriously over a long period, with the hard earned money and great savings of the people, only because they want to avoid Reservations at any cost, and are unwilling to part with the Jobs and Employment there, rightly due to the SCs&STs and OBCs.

As a result of the above, the SCs&STs and OBCs today are foxed. There are in principle, on paper, Reservations for them in Employment and Jobs, but in practice there is no Employment Opportunities and no Jobs! The Govt Offices and PSUs themselves are vanishing! Employment and Job Opportunities are shrinking sharply and abruptly for the Public. Private Sector Companies do not believe in Public Employment. They make recruitments silently and privately, with out any knowledge or information to the public. Even if there is any information, the claims of the public are crudely brushed off and set aside. For, they make appointments based on personal contacts and through their own private and secret arrangements.

We talk about the steps to integrate Scs&Sts into the Main stream? The SCs&STs are now at the Cross Roads. Their hopes and aspirations are getting frustrated. Their sufferings and miseries are on the increase. They don't see any signs of change. And there is no such possibility in the near future. The atrocities against them, the crude criminal premeditated oppressions and offences in the Rural Areas and Urban Slums, the sophisticated silent planned white collar suppressions by the educated superiors in Educational Institutions, Govt Offices etc are rapidly on the increase. Their patience is already running out. They may now go in any direction, and take any path. One side, they want to stick to the Path of Peace and Constitutional Methods, shown to them by Baba Saheb Dr BR Ambedkar, and follow his ways.

On the other hand, will the SCs&STs stray away in future from the Constitutional Methods of achieving the Economic and Social Objectives of the People, the Aspirations of the Society, the Goals of the Nation and the Dreams of the Founding Fathers of the Constitution pointed out by their Messiah Dr Ambedkar, and opt out in frustration to Unconstitutional Methods of Change and bloody Revolutions warned by Dr Ambedkar himself many a times? The signs of these are already in air, in various pockets in almost different parts of the Country. Will SCs&STs radically choose to alter the Economic, Social and Cultural Orders of People in the Society, and the Political Structure of the Country, or go for balkanising and break away from the Nation, as we see many frustrated impatient Sections of various societies are already doing in different parts of World? Will there be Social Unrest endless Law and Order Problems, as we already experience, in our Cities and Metropolises? Will there be an avoidable Civil War? We don't know! The real answers to these unanswered potentially dangerous and virtually explosive questions, ultimately depend upon the choices the Society makes and the Govt Leaders now take, to establish a just fair and equitable Economic Order and build an Egalitarian Social Structure. And it needs to be thought as to what can We the People or the Govt, the Country, the Society and the SC&ST themselves do? We have to find an answer, and find it quickly. For, the time is really running out for all of us and the Country as a whole.

What we need more urgently now, is not Liberalisation of the Economy but Liberation of the People, the downtrodden the weak and the marginalised; not Globalisation of our Economy but Universalisation of Human Rights in favour of the poor and the helpless like the SCs&STs.

The SCs&STs are poor weak marginalised and powerless. They need Education and Employment. They want Development and Growth. They are still to get their Independence and Freedom. They are eagerly looking forward to the Day of their Deliverance. They are seeking Liberty and Equality. They have waited all these days with great hopes and patience. They are now demanding Justice and Human Rights. They want Human Rights and Life with Dignity. They are thirsting for Individual Recognitions and Equal Opportunities. They are asking for Self Respect and Fairness in Social Life. They need Good Jobs and Decent Salaries. They look for Helping Hands and Respectful Wages alright. There is also a need to force the private sector companies and the Indian and Foreign Multi National Companies, to make their Recruitment and Appointments public and fair, through open advertisements and without any secrecy. They should be asked to give Representations to different Sections of the Society. After all, these are the ways of any Civilised Nation and all Civil Societies of the World. Secret Selections and Private Appointments based on personal contacts and private considerations are not the ways of a decent World.

If Reservations here in the Country are the due Rights and Shares of the SCs&STs and the OBCs in the Nation Building, Administration and Governance of the Country, even in the Mecca of the Free World and the fountainhead of all the new waves of Liberalisation and Globalisation sweeping the World now, there is Affirmative Action for the Blacks enforced by the Govt. The American Educational Institutions, Universities, Seats of Higher Learning and Centres of Research, and also the big powerful and rich MNCs there, are vying with each other to show to their Society and the World their achievements in this respect. Why should the caste hindus here then not honourably accept their own educated sisters and brothers from the

SC&ST and OBC Communities? Why should they resent the SCs&STs and the OBCs even today, or feel jealous of the alters' progress or become envious of their development?

The caste hindus are now forcibly taking away, what they used to silently steal all these days. Now they are openly grabbing the shares and dues of the SCs&STs and also the OBCs, in the name of Excellence, National Interest, National Security, Defence, Science, Technology, Research, Higher Studies, Super Specialities, Development of Excellence to International Standards, rapid or accelerated Economic Development, Opening up the Economy, Privatisation, Liberalisation, Globalisation, Structural Adjustments, Financial Discipline, and the frauds of their Special Merits and Efficiencies. These are nothing but an open fraud to cheat the people, shield and cover up all their inefficiency, blatant nepotism, shameless favouritism, violation of rules and regulations as well as the norms and procedures/precedences, open corruption, lack of respect for fair open honest selections/recruitment/promotions and appointments.

The latest cruel joke of caste hindus is that, they are all now waking up after fifty long years, to talk about the need to produce and support the specialists in the making, comparable to International Standards, but only from the dominant castes. What were they doing all these five decades? What happened to all those meritorious sons and daughters of theirs, whom they freely selected all these years, saying that no suitable SC/ST was available, and without giving any Reservations to the OBCs? Why should they get this urge now, when the SCs&STs have already grown up to become Specialists, and are doing extremely well in Serving the Country with out fleeing to foreign shores, and as the OBCs are getting their Opportunities? Even now, why don't they produce such International Class Specialists from their top most meritorious scholars? Do they have no faith in their most meritorious fellows, who come at the top in the assessment of merits as per their own methods, standards of evaluations and the scheme of norms and scales? Do they want to play a game of choices, and gamble on those who miss out in the race, that they want to bring them in the places of the SCs&STs and OBCs? Would they then wait, hope, pray, or dream that at least one of their third-rate scholars, who had come in through the back doors, to the professional and super-speciality courses, in place of the poor SCs&STs and OBCs, to become an

International Expert par-Excellence? Should we or can anyone believe them?

Govt should now come out with a Comprehensive Reservation Policy for the whole Country covering Govt, Public Sector Enterprises, Banks, Financial Institutions, Colleges, Universities, Centres of Higher Learning and Research, other Educational Institutions, Autonomous Bodies, Non-Governmental Organisations, Voluntary Organisations, and Private Enterprises including Indian and Foreign Multi-National Companies in the Country.

9.5. Law on Reservation

SCs&STs of the Country strongly feel that there is no point in believing and trusting that the caste hindus in the Govt, in Govt Offices, and the Courts would ever be honest to implement the Reservations in an honest and fair manner. Hence there is a need to bind them legally. The present Reservations are only Govt Orders, Departmental Rules and Regulations, and Office Memorandums. Therefore, the Govt of India should bring in urgently, without any further delay a comprehensive Reservation Bill, and enact a Law on Reservations. This Reservation Law should, amongst other things provide for:

1) Incentives and Financial Assistances to individual SCs&STs, wanting to pursue Higher Studies, particularly Post Graduate Studies in Professional Spheres like Architecture, Engineering, Medicine, Management, Law etc, and take up Advanced Courses like M Phil, Ph D and Post Doctoral Studies and Specialist Trainings
2) Incentives and Financial Assistances to the Families, for encouraging individual SCs&STs to pursue Higher Studies
3) Incentives to individual Teachers, Professors and Officials for encouraging helping developing and training SC&ST Students, Professionals, Employees and Officials
4) Incentives to Schools, Colleges, Universities and Government Departments/ Ministries/ Public Sector Enterprises, Banks, Financial Institutions, Autonomous Bodies and Private Sector for teaching employing and encouraging SCs&STs

5) Penalties for the Teachers, Professors, Officers and Schools, Colleges, Universities, Offices and other Establishments who/which do not follow and fail to implement the Reservations, and discourage SCs&STs
6) Reservations in all Govt Offices, Public Sector Enterprises, Banks, Financial Institutions and Autonomous Institutions without any exceptions
7) Reservations in every Public Service, Post, Grade and Level, right from the top most Public Office to down below, without any exemption whatsoever
8) Reservations in all Educational Institutions Govt or Private, in Admissions of Students and Scholars, and also in the Recruitments and Promotions of Teaching Faculty as well as the non-Teaching Staff
9) Reservations in the Joint Sector Organisations
10) Reservations in all Establishments where the Govt and the Public have a share
11) Reservations in all Establishments which make use of Public Facilities created with Public Funds, or created for the use of the People
12) Reservations in all Establishments making use of Land and other Natural Resources of the Country
13) Reservations in Employment in all Private Sector Establishments
14) Reservations in all Courts, including Law Officers and the Judiciary
15) Lateral Entry of SCs&STs into various Services and Cadres at higher Levels Grades and Posts, to improve and ensure their full Representations at every level
16) Free mobility of SC&ST Professionals and Academicians, between and across Govt, Bureaucracy, Administration, Public Sector, Joint Sector, Private Sector, Voluntary Organisations and into the Universities

This Reservation Law should be placed in the Ninth Schedule of the Constitution, and be beyond the purview of the Courts. The People are Sovereign in a Democracy. India is a Democracy, a Socialist and

Secular Democratic Republic. Hence the People, their Representatives and the Parliament have the ultimate Power to make Laws. The Courts can legitimately interfere on behalf of the People when the Govt fails to act and Govern or Govern properly, but can not go against the People, the will of the People, and poke their nose into the Parliament. Of late, the Courts have been interfering too much and too frequently against the SCs&STs, their Development and with the Reservations for the SCs&STs, and the Govt Policies and Procedures in this regard.

It is hightime that the Govts take some specific steps and positive action beyond Reservations. Fifty-three years of Independence had already passed. Fifty years after the establishment of the Republic, had also rolled by. We have wasted precious long time. We can not afford to sleep any further. Otherwise, the poor people would soon lynch us all alive. It is necessary to think what we need to do, and at the sametime act fast. Honestly speaking, we have not yet really started thinking of Development of the Weaker Sections. We have only been playing soft balls with them all these days. Let us get serious now, at least a bit. The Govt of India therefore, should bring in the learned SCs&STs and thinkers amongst them, to chalk out real Plans and Action Programmes for their Social, Economic and Cultural Development. As Baba Saheb Dr Ambedkar had long ago rightly said, it is only the servile class who can lead them. Definitely not their antagonists, nor the class room city products of just the Universities, or those with foreign education, or WB and IMF trainings and mandates. The Govts at the Centre and the State/UTs should at least now establish -

1) National and State Level Administrative and Professional Training Establishments for the SCs&STs, to develop and improve their Administrative and Professional Competence and Capabilities
2) National SC&ST Housing Finance and Development Corporations
3) National and State/UT Level Centres for SC&ST Development
4) National Level Centres for Planning for, SC&ST Education and Employment
5) National and State/UT Level Task Forces, for Entrepreneurship Development amongst the SCs&STs

6) Separate Tribunals to look into and expeditiously dispose off the Cases of SC&ST Employees
7) Separate District Level Courts to expeditiously hear and decide the Cases of SC&ST Lands taken away by others
8) A Special Judicial Commission to exclusively look into the Judgements of the various Judges, who have a tendency to decide cases against SCs&STs, and make specific recommendations to the Govt to protect the interests and Welfare of the SCs&STs
9) A Special Committee to visit and look into the working of SC&ST Student Hostels and make appropriate Recommendations to the Govt to improve the Conditions and Working of these Hostels

The Govt at the Centre should also Institute -

1) Awards for Selection, Recruitment and Promotion of SCs&STs, similar to those for the physically handicapped
2) Recognition of Individuals and Institutions, working for the Development and Integration of the SCs&STs
3) Special Insurance Schemes, to protect and also provide succour and help to the SCs&STs, from suspensions terminations and non-payment of salaries and wages
4) A Cadre of Rural Welfare and Labour Officers, to look into and expeditiously solve the Grievances of the Workers in the Rural Areas and in the Unorganised Sectors
5) Special Social Security Schemes, for the SCs&STs, especially the educated and unemployed
6) Special Tax Concessions, to SCs&STs to educate their Children, and for sending them for Higher Studies or Studies Abroad, and or for Specialist and Advanced Courses and Trainings
7) Special Concessions, to SCs&STs for building their own homes, to eliminate the slums and the growing problems associated with them that dehumanises the people
8) Special Schemes and Concessions to SC&ST Entrepreneurs taking up self-employment, starting their own business, and setting up their own industries

9) Special Programmes, to harness and utilise the talents, knowledge and experiences of retired SC&ST Professionals, for the Development and improving the Standards of Life of the SC&ST Communities

The Govt should also regularly Constitute an High Power Committee, at least every two years, to review the Allocation, Utilisation, Appropriation and Diversion of the Funds meant and Budgeted for the Education Welfare and Development of the SCs&STs both in the States/UTs and at the Centre.

Similarly, in the STATES and UTs also, appropriate Committees should be constituted, to look into the Funds earmarked, actually made available, utilised, surrendered and or diverted by the STATE/UT Govts, Zilla Parishads and down at the Village Panchayats.

Govt should regularly review, assess and change from time to time, both the long term and short term SC&ST schemes and Programmes to Evolve better Schemes and Programmes. There should also be Schemes and Programmes, evolved and structured to suit Specific Communities/ Castes/ Tribes, and also sub-Castes, sub-Tribes and Part of the Castes and Tribes living/ settled in different areas.

Govt should classify the schemes and programmes meant for the SCs&STs, into specific categories. Adequate funds have to be separately earmarked for poverty alleviation, ameliorative, assets creation, welfare, infrastructure development, education including grant of various freeships scholarships fellowships and provision of hostels and messes, entrepreneur development, financial assistance for purchase of land/ house building/ starting business, and for establishing cottage/ mini/ small-scale/ medium/ big/ large industries, and such other identifiable schemes and programmes. Similarly, funds should be separately budgeted, allocated and released to ngos run by others for the welfare and development of the SC&ST dalits, to ngos headed or patronised by SC&ST leaders and individuals, and to ngos run and personally managed by the SC&ST dalits themselves. Only this could ensure a real help to SCs&STs, today at different stages of life, and in various levels of development and growth in different Regions and Parts of the Country. The present Practices of allocating Consolidated Funds, and leaving them in the hands of Govt Officials who are only interested in their jobs, perquisites and or the privileges of their offices and future/ promotions; or in supporting, helping and patronising their friends, relatives, colleagues, neighbours etc, are not going to deliver any results, or ever Develop and Liberate the SC&ST Dalits still living and believing in this Country and the Govts.

References

Eleanor Zilliot, *From Untouchable to Dalit - Essays on the Ambedkar Movement*, Manohar, 2005.

Michael. S M, *Dalits in Modern India - Vision and Values*, Sage Publications, 2007.

Pradeep K. Sharma, *Dalit Politics and Literature*, Shipra Publications, 2006.

Ranabira Samaddara, Ghanshyam Shah, *Dalit Identity and Politics*, Sage Publications, 2001.

10

Contemporary Relevance of B.R. Ambedkar

On December 27, 2006, Indian Prime Minister Manmohan Singh became the first sitting prime minister to openly draw a parallel between the practice of "untouchability"—the imposition of social disabilities on persons by reason of their birth in certain castes—and apartheid.

The analogy is an apt one on many levels, and an uncomfortable one on others. Like South Africa, those who sit atop the caste pyramid are a numerical minority. When combined, the population of Dalits, "tribals," "Other Backward Classes," and religious minorities far outnumber those of "upper-caste" Hindus. But the analogy reveals something far deeper, that the system of "untouchability" in India continues to operate as though a form of legal apartheid were effectively still in place.

In many ways the Dalit condition naturally invites such comparisons, and in others it is a singular category, cutting across the Indian subcontinent, but categorically different than discrimination on the basis of race. To begin, the visual cues that accompanied apartheid in South Africa, or racial discrimination in other parts of the world, are lacking in India. Caste is like oxygen—it is both invisible and indispensable.

The Indian government has taken great pains to insulate itself from international scrutiny by repeatedly pointing out that this is not discrimination based on race, as though such confirmation nullifies the abuse in question. Regardless of how the abuse is defined, its noxious and pervasive character should be sufficient to invite international attention and condemnation.

Though scholars have pointed to the racial dimensions of caste, this is not a Black and White issue, or a clear Black and Brown issue. The caste system is one of *graded inequality* that invites people to share in the spoils of iniquity even as they suffer from it. By offering individuals a rank in a pecking order, the system strengthens itself and keeps the equality revolution at bay.

India is also an example of injustice in the extreme: the numbers affected are greater, the poverty is deeper, the atrocities are an every day affair, and enforced servitude and segregation is the norm. The population of Dalits equals more than half the population of the United States. A majority of Dalits live on less than US$1 per day. Every week, thirteen Dalits are murdered and five Dalit homes are destroyed. Three Dalit women are raped and eleven Dalits are assaulted every day—a crime is committed against a Dalit every eighteen minutes. But, as discussed below, a number of contemporary commonalities do exist.

The cross-fertilization of ideas between India and the United States on approaches to ensuring equality is not new, nor is it surprising. As two of the world's largest democracies and as common law countries with a profound history of *de jure* discrimination, India and the United States have learned much from one another. As written by one commentator: "Ambedkar's revolution for the emancipation of untouchables was significantly influenced by American ideals of equality." In 1947, the constitutional drafting committee's advisor B. N. Rau visited the United States and solicited the views of leading American judges and scholars. Almost every fundamental right in the Constitution of India finds its corollary in its American counterpart. Moreover, according to some scholars, the process of drafting the Constitution of India took into account not only the textual wording of the American provisions, but also the eventual interpretation of those provisions offered by American courts.

Both countries also continue to be mired in the politically charged debate around affirmative action as either a suitable remedy to compensate for past injustices or as a means to level a playing field tilted in favour of whites and "upper-caste" Hindus. Indian judges have often cited U.S. affirmative action decisions and law review articles in their opinions, although U.S. case law has not been cited as legal precedent.

It comes as no surprise that the richness of the field of comparison has invited critical and thoughtful comparative legal scholarship on the Indian and American experience with affirmative action. Less well-considered are the contemporary struggles faced by both movements to counter the mechanisms and rhetoric through which the objectives of that legal framework now stand to be defeated.

The narrative of oppression, and of racist and casteist denial, is strikingly similar from continent to continent and each country's equality project is decidedly unfinished for similar reasons.

Inviting American scholars and advocates to turn to India and the lessons it offers to illuminate their own racial justice project is not an anomaly, it is the natural continuation of a long tradition of inspiration and solidarity shared between Indian and American civil rights leaders and movements.

In 1936, Howard Thurman, a famous black preacher and educator, visited Mahatma Gandhi in India—who at the time was waging India's civil disobedience campaign against the British—to discuss issues of racial segregation and voting rights in the United States. Better known is the fact that Martin Luther King, Jr. utilized the Gandhian concept of "Satyagraha" or "nonviolent direct action" in his teachings and leadership. Less well known, but equally significant, is the relationship Ambedkar forged with W.E.B. Du Bois during the founding year of the United Nations. In efforts to take the struggle for racial justice to the international level, Du Bois used Ambedkar's example in appealing to the Secretary of the National Association for the Advancement of Colored People ("NAACP") to lodge a petition with the newly formed United Nations General Assembly concerning the plight of American Negroes.

Formed in the Indian state of Maharashtra in the 1970s, the Dalit Panthers aligned themselves ideologically to the Black Panther movement in the United States. Dalit Panthers visited "atrocity" sites, organized marches, election boycotts, and rallies in villages, and raised slogans of direct militant action against their "upper-caste" aggressors. Panther leaders were often harassed and removed from districts for speaking out against the government and Hindu religion. And like the Black Panthers, the Dalit Panthers became frequent targets of police brutality and arbitrary detentions.

Like the civil rights struggle that began in the 1950s and was led by African-Americans, Dalits in the twenty-first century are forming human rights movements, challenging local governments, and demanding equal access to services and equal protection before the law, often in alliance with international partners. In 2001, African-American and Dalit activists found themselves sharing the same contested space at the World Conference against Racism in Durban, South Africa. Both groups faced the racist and casteist denial of their respective governments who either refused to allow consideration of their concerns in the international forum or diluted their delegation's involvement to the point that their participation was rendered meaningless.

As the battle lines are drawn once again in the debate around affirmative action in both countries, the same ideologies are used to discredit the state's use of race or caste-conscious measures to ensure real equality of opportunity for minorities in the United States and Dalits and other "lower-caste" groups in India. Affirmative action is attacked as either having sufficiently served its purpose, or as not being up to the task of alleviating a broad-based social problem. In the latter category, the alternatives that are offered in its place rarely find traction, let alone implementation in policy terms. Reservations, once the mask that India wore to hide the real face of caste oppression, are now being attacked as an affront to (formal) equality and a barrier to achieving a caste-blind society. Yet formal equality assumes a level playing field—which it certainly is not for minorities in the United States or for Dalits and other marginalized communities in India.

African-Americans and Dalits are also now made to compete against other marginalized communities in their respective countries for sufficient attention to their demands and their rights. It seems the small slice of the pie reserved for non-whites and non-"upper-caste" Indians has not grown much bigger, and attempts to broaden the collective share invites swift protest and condemnation in the conservative media, on the streets, at the polls, and in the courtroom. Regrettably, the attendant claims of women in both struggles, and the compounded discrimination they face, get lost in the debate.

Like the United States, India exhibits a temporal tension between striving for equality as a space where caste categories do not matter, and the need to continually identify and name the categories that have been used to create hierarchy or exclusion for the purposes of ensuring social inclusion. Such a tension is reflected at the level of policy, of social movements, and of political discourse, both for and against caste-conscious measures to ensure social inclusion.

In both countries, caste- or race-based stigma has not been erased by upward class mobility. Even for the minority of Dalits who have managed to defy their religiously proscribed economic lot, social oppression has not fallen away.

The inter-category diversity among Dalits that comes about as a result of the creation of a new Dalit middle class is cited not as the success of affirmative action that it represents, but as the reason to now defeat the affirmative action project. Class operates in both countries as a displacement strategy. And in both countries the criminal justice system and its application to particular groups suffers from the twin malaise of over- and under-enforcement. Dalits are routinely rounded up for crimes committed in their vicinity, yet summarily ignored when they themselves are the victims of abuse.

Like the United States, India's social transformation project is stunted by its increasing dependency on courts as a source of redress; its recourse to the legislature and courts is seen as the dominant avenue for social reform. The disproportionate focus on proportional representation—or policies that aim to increase the representation of marginalized groups in the legislature, institutes of higher education, and now the private sector—is where this conversation gets debated and defeated. Even more neglected is the work that must be done on both continents to dismantle the racist and casteist mindsets that fuel the discrimination and generate inequality.

The social transformation project—that began in India with adoption of the constitution in 1950, and in the United States with the civil rights struggle leading up to and following the landmark case of *Brown v. Board* in 1954—has left some with greater opportunity and political mobility but has "transformed" little. The gap between constitutional vision and social reality is therefore far greater in India where the progressiveness of the constitution and the broader legal framework is belied by its almost complete under-enforcement. The rule of law lives in the shadow of the rule of caste. Though crafted as a bulwark against caste discrimination, the juxtaposition of egalitarian laws against an inherently unequal system acts as an open invitation to frustrate constitutional intentions.

As a case study, the condition of Dalits in India brings into clear view the limitations of the law and economic growth as antidotes to inequality. India's high levels of poverty concentrated among particular social groups, its epidemic of violence meted out in the name of upholding caste-based norms and traditions, and the prevalence of Dalit segregation, exploitation, and untouchability as the rule, rather than the exception, all expose the ways in which discrimination wears poverty as its mask.

Poverty is deceptive. It makes one conclude that all suffer from it equally. Poverty also masks a lack of political will to change the status quo by shifting the debate to a lack of resources. A closer look at victims of violence, bonded labour, and other atrocities also reveals that they share in common the lowest ranking in the caste order. Poverty in India is, of course, not limited to Dalits, but as is the case with African-Americans in the United States, if you are a Dalit in India, you are far more likely to be poor.

In both countries, economic progress has not led to equitable growth. In the United States— which is the most economically powerful country in the world—and India—whose economic growth is celebrated as a success of the ethos of economic liberalization—the rising tide has not lifted all boats; rather, it has caused many to drown, in some cases all too literally. Dalits are particularly susceptible to loss of life and property in times of natural disasters due to the precarious conditions in which they live. A survey conducted by the National Campaign on Dalit Human Rights ("NCDHR") following catastrophic flooding in the eastern state of Bihar in August 2007—which affected 14 million people in the state and killed 2,253 in the region—found that Dalits were the worst hit. Relief rarely reached Dalits, testifying to the fact that "[t]he culture of discrimination which runs through Indian society intensifies in times of crisis." In some cases, Dalits were forced to wait for their share of relief supplies until all other groups had received aid.

Even during moments of shared hardship, communities are divided by race or caste. Similarly, caste-based inequality, like racial inequality, survives dramatic economic growth. Even as India celebrated its triumphant testing of nuclear weapons, exploding them underground in the deserts of Rajasthan, Dalit manual scavengers were being manually lowered into open sewers without protective gear to unblock toxic and noxious sewage. The militarism and jingoistic nationalism of both governments has also depleted state coffers in the name of ensuring "national security" and fighting the global "War on Terror"—a fight in which both states are now staunch allies—to the detriment of the poor in both countries who enjoy neither physical nor economic security.

Inequality, Indian-style, is a valuable case study for a variety of reasons: it exposes the pitfalls of relying on the "rule of law" as a self-fulfilling prophecy, or on the "neutrality" of the state as a guarantor of social justice. The case of Dalits in India also serves to counter prevailing global narratives that an insufficiency of resources is solely to blame for the economic woes of the dispossessed, or, its sister argument, that allowing for aggressive market reforms in the name of promoting economic growth will reduce poverty and lead to equitable development. Such lessons are particularly apt for general inquiries into the need for and/or legitimacy of affirmative action. Inasmuch as affirmative action around the globe is under attack as an affront to liberalism and "meritocracy," the intrinsically anti-merit nature of the caste system offers an alternative space in which conversations about "merit" can take place.

India also presents a unique challenge for those human rights lawyers and advocates who operate exclusively in the framework of international human rights law as a mechanism for achieving social change. International human rights laws and mechanisms, with their over-reliance on the role of the state, and their almost unquestioned faith that the right laws will do the trick, are ill-equipped to take on systems that define equality in the inverse, and in which human beings are born inherently *unequal*.

10.1. Caste-based Inequalities

India's caste system is perhaps the world's longest surviving and most rigorously enforced system of social hierarchy. The caste system encompasses a complex ordering of social groups on the basis of ritual purity. Caste is descent-based and hereditary in nature. It is a characteristic determined by one's birth into a particular caste. While the particular ranking of castes may vary among regions, the extremes of the spectrum are fixed with Brahmins sitting atop the hierarchy and Dalits, or so-called untouchables, at the very bottom.

The caste system is an intrinsic part of Hinduism, the dominant faith practised by Indians. According to Hindu scripture, individuals are born inherently unequal into a graded caste-based structure that defines their status and opportunities in life. Caste-based discrimination is also openly practised by Sikhs, Christians, and Muslims against Dalits who have converted to these faiths in an effort to escape their persecution.

Though the origins of the caste system have long been a subject of dispute, as has the question of whether it tracks racial groupings, the following theories are worthy of note. Caste is said to have its basis in the Hindu religion, as it is referred to in scripture. In the *Bhagavad Gita*, Lord Krishna proclaims: "the four castes have been created by Me;" similarly, the *Manu-Smriti* sets out the main castes as each having been created from a different part of God's form, and codifies the respective God-given duties of each of these castes. Alternative sociological theories posit the caste system as a ritual solution to the Vedic cultural preoccupation with distancing oneself from pollution.

Differences in status are traditionally justified by the religious doctrine of *karma*, a belief that one's place in life is determined by one's deeds in previous lifetimes. Traditional scholarship has described this more than two thousand-year-old system within the context of the four principal *varnas*, or large caste categories. In order of precedence these are the Brahmins the Ksyatriyas the Vaisyas and the Shudras. A fifth category falls outside the varna system and consists of those known as "untouchables" or Dalits; they are often assigned tasks too ritually polluting to merit inclusion within the traditional varna system.

Though most closely associated with Hinduism, the practice of untouchability—the social imposition of particular disabilities against individuals deemed to be untouchable—permeates all major religions in India and the entire subcontinent. Within the four principal castes, there are thousands of subcastes, also called *jatis*; endogamous groups that are further divided along occupational, sectarian, regional, and linguistic lines. Collectively, all of these are sometimes referred to as "caste Hindus," those falling within the caste system. Even as outcasts, they themselves are divided into further subcastes and practice untouchability against those ranked below; the discrimination is wholly internalized giving way to what Dr. Ambedkar termed a system of "graded inequality."

Whereas the first four varnas have over time enjoyed significant occupational mobility, a majority of Dalits in India continue to involuntarily inherit occupations assigned to the caste into which they are born—occupations deemed too filthy or polluting for others to carry out. In much of South Asia and India in particular, caste has become coterminous with race in the definition and exclusion of distinct population groups on the basis of their descent. For over 167 million Dalits or "untouchables" in India, caste remains the determinative factor for the attainment of civil, political, social, economic, and cultural rights.

10.1.1. Living Below the Pollution Line

The practice of "untouchability"—the imposition of social disabilities on persons by reason of their birth into "untouchable" castes—continues to blight the lives of millions of Indians today who are relegated to life below the "pollution" line. The manifestation of such oppression has taken and continues to take many forms. Age-old customs included prohibiting Dalits from walking public streets lest their "polluting" shadow should fall on an "upper-caste" Hindu, and requiring Dalits to mark themselves with black bracelets; string a broom around their waists so as to sweep the "polluted" dust they walked on; or hang an earthen pot around their necks "lest [their] spit falling on the earth should pollute a Hindu who might unknowingly happen to tread on it."

Modern India has improved little by way of untouchability practices. Dalits are still prohibited from entering temples, are segregated into Dalit ghettoes, and in some areas are still forced to get off their bike or take off their slippers when walking past non-Dalit homes—gestures that force Dalits to repeatedly self-affirm their inferior status. Dalits are denied access to land, forced to work in degrading conditions, and routinely abused at the hands of the police and "higher-caste" groups that often enjoy the state's protection. In what has been called India's "hidden apartheid," entire villages in many Indian states remain completely segregated by caste. As noted by Ambedkar, "India is admittedly a land of villages and so long as the village system provides an easy method of marking out and identifying the untouchable, the untouchable has no escape from untouchability."

"Untouchability" relegates Dalits to a lifetime of discrimination, exploitation, and violence, including severe forms of torture perpetrated by state and private actors. Because of the castes into which they are born, Dalits are forced to work in "polluting" and degrading occupations and are subject to exploitative labour arrangements such as bonded labour, migratory labour, and forced prostitution. Dalit children are vulnerable to trafficking and the worst forms of child labour in these and other areas. Dalits are also discriminated against in hiring and in the payment of wages by private employers..

Migration and the anonymity of the urban environment have in some cases resulted in upward occupational mobility for Dalits, but the majority continues to perform its traditional or "polluting" functions. A majority of the Dalit rural workforce subsists on the menial wages of landless agricultural labourers, earning less than US$1 per day. Those in urban areas work mostly in the unorganized sector. India's much touted system of reservations or constitutionally reserved quotas for scheduled castes assists less than 1 percent of the Dalit population.

Segregation between Dalits and non-Dalits is routinely practised in housing, schools, and access to public and private sector services. Ninety-nine percent of Dalit students are enrolled in government schools that lack basic infrastructure, classrooms, teachers, and teaching aids. Government schools by and large teach in local languages, as opposed to private schools—whose students are predominantly "upper-caste"—that teach in English. Dalit children also face abuse from teachers and non-Dalit students as well as segregation both in the classroom and in the provision of midday meals. Dalit schoolchildren and teachers also face discrimination from "upper-caste" community members who perceive education for and by Dalits as both a waste and a threat.

Indian economist Sukhadeo Thorat analyses data generated by primary surveys conducted in four regions of India as well as data generated by the National Commission for Scheduled Castes and Scheduled Tribes' all-India annual reports. He argues that the regional data generated by the primary surveys is important because it underscores severe caste-based abuses that may not have been reported to the local authorities and have been left undocumented. The studies highlight persistent patterns such as: denial of Dalits' access to water; refusal of essential and/or public services to Dalits, or provision of such services in a discriminatory fashion; physical violence against Dalits; and Dalit political disenfranchisement. Thorat concludes that "upper-caste" social behavior in rural India is governed by the norms and codes of the traditional caste system.

The practice of economic exclusion and discrimination is also evident in the differential pricing for Dalits in the sale and purchase of items ranging from raw materials to finished goods, and in Dalits being denied the ability to purchase land for both agricultural and non-agricultural use. A study published in 2006 on the forms and prevalence of "untouchability" in rural India—based on an extensive survey of 565 villages in 11 Indian states conducted in 2001-2002—confirmed the extent of "untouchability" practices in rural India today. But contrary to conventional wisdom, "untouchability" is not an exclusively rural phenomenon perpetuated by the uneducated masses.

10.1.2. Endogamy

Strict prohibitions on inter-dining, inter-living, and general social interaction come together with the practice of endogamy as the means for which the caste system is the end. Prohibitions on intermarriage are not only a hallmark feature of the caste system—designed to ensure rigid social norms of purity and pollution—but are essential to maintaining its very existence. As a result, inter-marriages between Dalits and non-Dalits frequently become flash points for conflicts and can result in extrajudicial punishments that include the public lynching or killing of couples or their relatives, rape, public beatings, and economic sanctions. The prevalence of on-line matchmaking sites, which explicitly offer to match individuals according to their caste (both within India and abroad) provides a clear example of the practice of endogamy in its twenty-first century avatar.

10.1.3. Caste and Gender Discrimination

Caste discrimination has a unique and specific impact on Dalit women who endure multiple forms of discrimination. Dalit women are especially vulnerable to violence by the police and private actors. Landlords use sexual abuse and other forms of violence and humiliation against Dalit women as tools to inflict "lessons" and crush dissent and labour movements within Dalit communities. Vulnerability to sexual violence also results from Dalit women's lower economic and social status, leading many of them to turn to prostitution for survival.

Dalit women have unequal access to services, employment opportunities, and justice mechanisms as compared to Dalit men. In relation to employment opportunities, Dalit women are allotted some of the most menial and arduous tasks and experience greater discrimination in the payment of wages than Dalit men. In relation to services, Dalit women have less access to education and health facilities, ensuring that their literacy, nutrition, and health standards fall far below that of Dalit men and non-Dalit men and women. Benefits of various development programs for Dalits, such as distribution of land and other productive assets, have essentially gone to Dalit males and have failed to improve the status of Dalit women. Investment in projects targeted to the development of Dalit women is also far lower as compared to those for men.

The practice of *devadasi*, in which a girl, usually before reaching the age of puberty, is ceremoniously dedicated or married to a deity or to a temple, continues in several southern Indian states including Andhra Pradesh and Karnataka. Literally meaning "female servant of god," *devadasis* usually belong to the Dalit community. The age-old practice continues to legitimize the sexual violence and discrimination that have come to characterize the intersection between caste and gender.

10.1.4. Dalits among Dalits

Dalit women make up the majority of manual scavengers—a caste-based occupation wherein Dalits remove excrement from public and private dry pit latrines and carry it to dumping grounds and disposal sites. Indeed, the "occupation" of manual scavenging is the only economic opportunity available to many Dalit women hailing from scavenger subcastes, with the result that more Dalit women and girls work as manual scavengers than Dalit men. Manual scavengers are situated at the very bottom of the graded inequality structure of the caste system and as a result face discrimination from other non-scavenger caste Dalits who treat them as "untouchables," creating an unquestioned "'untouchability' within the 'untouchables'"

"Though long outlawed, the practice of manual scavenging continues in most states, and will continue as long as dry latrines are used." Similarly, dry latrines will continue to be used as long as there are Dalits forcibly designated to clean them.

Manual scavengers are routinely exposed to both human and animal waste without the protection of masks, uniforms, gloves, shoes, appropriate buckets, and mops, resulting in severe health problems. "Many scavengers have died of carbon monoxide poisoning while cleaning septic tanks." "More than 100 die every year due to inhalation of toxic gases or drowning in excrement." "The fear of being fired by municipality officials keeps manual scavengers from demanding higher wages or sanitary instruments."

The persistence of the outlawed and inhuman practice of manual scavenging speaks to the resilience of caste-based discrimination. That human beings should continue to clean human waste and be lowered into sewers in a country that boasts of technological innovation and prowess demonstrates the stranglehold of caste in India today—a system set up to *enforce* the poverty of those it considers "outcaste."

10.1.5. Unequal by all Measures

Although "untouchability" was officially abolished under Article 17 of the Constitution of India, the practice remains determinative of the social and economic outcomes of those at the bottom of the caste hierarchy. Though "untouchability" is normally considered as a religiously prescribed system of separating the pure from the impure, it is, at its heart, a system to support and sanction an exploitative economic order. While Dalits have achieved some gains across a variety of indicators in the six decades since independence, their socio-economic development continues to lag significantly behind non-Dalits. Broadly speaking, the gap between Dalits and non-Dalits in education, health, income, and land ownership has either remained constant or widened.

The practice of "untouchability" in schools has contributed to an alarmingly high dropout rate and illiteracy level among Dalit children, particularly Dalit girls. According to the 2002 India Education Report, school attendance in rural areas in 1993-94 was 64.3 percent for Dalit boys and 46.2 percent for Dalit girls, compared to 74.9 percent among boys and 61 percent for girls from other social groups. According to a 2001-2002 report prepared by the Indian government, "the dropout rate in Scheduled Castes during 1990-91 was as high as 49.35 percent at primary stage and 67.77 percent at middle stage and 77.65 percent at secondary stage." The statistics for higher education are just as alarming the same government report states that enrolment of Dalit students at graduate, postgraduate, and professional/research/PhD levels is "abysmally low," at 8.73 percent, 8 percent, and 2.77 percent respectively.

Discrimination in schools and the resulting dropout rates for Dalit children are intimately linked to child labour. Illiteracy results in a lack of gainful employment options for Dalits. Even educated Dalits face discrimination in the labour market, as seen through the systematic exclusion of Dalits from jobs that they are considered too "impure" or unintelligent to perform. Selective inclusion of Dalits in various employment sectors still results in unequal treatment in the payment of wages, in different terms and conditions applied to their work in discriminatory treatment in the workplace, and in the prevalence of compulsive or forced work governed by traditional caste-related obligations.

There are an estimated 40 million bonded labourers in India, of whom 15 million are children. The vast majority of these labourers are Dalits or tribal community members. Bonded labour is sustained by the caste system, in particular through the traditional expectation of free labour and/or inadequate remuneration for work, and by the lack of Dalit ownership of land. Landlessness encompassing a lack of access to land, inability to own land, and forced evictions constitutes a crucial element in the subordination of Dalits. When Dalits do acquire land, their right to own property including the right to access and enjoy it is routinely infringed.

As a result of their poverty and discriminatory treatment, Dalits also fare poorly in health indicators. Over half of India's Dalit children are undernourished, 18.5 percent are classified as "severely underweight," while 8.8 percent die before their fifth birthday. Dalits are often refused admission to hospitals, access to healthcare, and medical treatment. In addition, caste-based occupations that Dalits are made to perform, such as manual scavenging and forced prostitution, frequently expose Dalits to serious and sometimes fatal health hazards.

10.1.6. Incredible Shrinking Indian State

Beginning in 1991, and under the direction of the International Monetary Fund ("IMF") and World Bank's Structural Adjustment Programme, India's New Economic Policy introduced dramatic shifts in macroeconomic policy and aggressively pursued the privatization of industries and the liquidation of policies and controls in economic planning and regulation. While these reforms may have ushered in an era of astounding progress in the areas of technology, infrastructure, machinery, space, and even nuclear research, much of this progress has meant little to Dalits; most continue to live in grinding poverty, lacking food security, and without the basic amenities of electricity, sanitation, and safe drinking water. Unprecedented economic growth has coincided comfortably with a post-reform reversal in poverty reduction trends. Economic liberalization, for Dalits at least, may be fuelling economic inequality.

As liberalization leads to a capital-intensive mode of production requiring a greater proportion of highly skilled workers to manage automated production processes, a large migration of unskilled labour to the agricultural sector has led to lower wages for agricultural workers as a whole. In addition to a reduction in agricultural subsidies, Dalits are also affected by the increased acquisition of coastal lands by multinationals for aquaculture projects. Dalits are the main labourers and tenants of coastal land areas and are increasingly being forced to leave these areas—to live as displaced people—as foreign investment rises.

A reduction in the budget and fiscal deficit, devaluation, privatization, the elimination or reductions in subsidies, and export promotion have all contributed to inflation. As is true the world over, inflation hits the poorest the hardest. With most of their earnings spent on food, shelter, and clothing, any rise in prices has had a direct negative effect on Dalits' level of consumption.

Empirical studies seem to confirm that poverty rates are uniformly higher in Dalit households. Eighty-five percent of Dalits live in rural areas while over 75 percent of Dalits perform land-connected work; 25 percent as marginal or small farmers and over 50 percent as landless labourers earning less than US$1 per day. Though only 16 percent of the population, Dalits comprise 60 percent of those below the poverty line.

According to government estimates in 2000, the unemployment rate for Dalits and tribal groups was double that of non-Dalits/tribals. Additionally, public sector divestment to private owners is estimated to have left two hundred thousand Dalit employees jobless. Economic liberalization has not translated into economic liberation for Dalits and other marginalized communities in India. The market, in short, has not served as an equalizing mechanism. Economic reforms must be scrutinized for the work that they leave undone and for the inherent assumption that such work can be done by either economic or legal means.

10.2. Policies for Redressing Caste Discrimination

The Constitution of India, often heralded as a landmark document, was inspired by the emancipatory vision of its chief architect Dr. B.R. Ambedkar—a Dalit leader who himself suffered severe discrimination and who sought to ensure equal protection and substantive equality for Dalits in independent India. As a document, the constitution combines broad social purpose, stemming from the social content of the Independence Movement, with practical administrative detail, based on the Assembly members' experiences in government and on the events around them.

Ambedkar cautioned against adopting too "Western" a vision of what constitutional democracy in India should look like. Indian constitutionalism attempts, however imperfectly, to balance liberty and equality interests and in so doing foreshadows the delicate balance between formal and substantive conceptions of equality in international human rights law. Chief among these fundamental rights is the right to equality. Article 14 of the Constitution of India reads: "The state shall not deny to any person equality before the law or the equal protection of the laws within the territory of India."

The clause marks a significant departure from the American model on which India's equality provision is based and constitutionalizes the validity of affirmative action in the Indian context. The Indian model is also one of substantive equality.

The Court has interpreted Article 14 on a number of occasions as charging the state with ensuring that there is equality among equals.

As noted above, Article 17 of the constitution abolishes the practice of "untouchability" and punishes the enforcement of any disability arising out of the practice. Article 21 guarantees the right to life and liberty. The Indian Supreme Court has interpreted this right to include the right to be free from degrading and inhuman treatment, the right to integrity and dignity of the person, and the right to speedy justice. Article 23 prohibits traffic in human beings and other similar forms of forced labour. Similarly, Article 24 provides that no child under the age of fourteen shall work in any factory or mine or engage in any hazardous employment.

Article 43 calls on the state to secure to all workers, agricultural, industrial, or otherwise, a living wage and conditions of work ensuring a decent standard of life. Article 46 comprises both development and regulatory aspects and stipulates that: "The State shall promote with special care the educational and economic interests of the weaker sections of the people, and in particular, of the Scheduled Castes and the Scheduled Tribes, and shall protect them from social injustice and forms of exploitation." Article 15 prohibits discrimination on the grounds of religion, race, caste, sex, or place of birth while Article 15(4) empowers the state to make any special provisions for the advancement of any socially and educationally backward classes of citizens, or for scheduled castes and scheduled tribes.

Article 330 provides reservations for seats for scheduled castes and scheduled tribes in the Lok Sabha while Article 332 provides for reservations in the state legislative assemblies. Through Article 16(4) the state is empowered to make "any provision for the reservation of appointments or posts in favour of any backward class of citizens which, in the opinion of the State, is not adequately represented in the services under the State." Accordingly, under constitutional provisions and various laws, India grants Dalits a certain number of rights, including reservations in education, government jobs, and government bodies. India's policy of reservations is an attempt by the central government to remedy past injustices related to "low-caste" status.

To allow for proportional representation in certain state and federal institutions, the constitution reserves 22.5 percent of seats in federal government jobs, state legislatures, the lower house of 181 parliament, and educational institutions for scheduled castes and scheduled tribes. An amendment to the constitution also enables reservations for scheduled castes and scheduled tribes in village councils (*panchayats*) and municipalities, with no less than one-third of reserved seats to be allocated to scheduled caste and scheduled tribe women. Under the premise of proportional representation, OBCs are entitled to 27 percent reservations in public sector employment and higher education.

10.2.1. Protective Legislation

In addition to constitutional provisions, the government of India has pursued a two-pronged approach to narrowing the gap between the socio-economic status of the scheduled caste population and the national average: one prong involves regulatory measures which ensure that the various provisions to protect their rights and interests are adequately implemented, enforced and monitored; the second focuses on increasing the self-sufficiency of the scheduled caste population through financial assistance for self-employment activities through development programs to increase education and skills.

10.3. Social Exclusion

A caste system is the major feature of Indian society, it is not only reflects in social life of Indian people but also economic and political behaviour of people are governed by the caste system. Caste is the identity of a person in Hindu society. In India, exclusion or inclusion in the economic activities such as production, distribution or any gainful job to a particular person depend by his caste. The unfavourable inclusions with unequal treatment may carry the same adverse effects as unfavourable exclusion.

Caste is a term derived from a Portuguese word, casta, meaning breed, lineage, or race. It is a term used to identify the different social segments within the caste based Hindu society. Each caste has its own customs, rituals, family deities and food habits. According to Dr Babasaheb Ambedkar, it is mainly the custom of endogamy that has preserved the castes and prevented one caste from fusing into another. Almost all the writers and scholars conform to this view of Dr. Babasaheb Ambedkar. Sociologist G. S. Ghurye following features of caste

i) Segmented division of society

ii) Hierarchies

iii) Restrictions on feeding and social intercourse

iv) Civil and religious disabilities and privileges of different sections

v) Lack of unrestricted choice of occupation

vi) Restrictions on marriage

Prof. Ghurye holds that caste in India is a Brahminic child and that endogamy, the outstanding feature of caste was first developed by the Brahmin. The functions of caste can be understood only with regard to the caste system. The caste system is the foundation on which Hindu society is built. Dr. Ambedkar says: by the Hindu social system the communities are placed in an ascending scale of reverence and a descending scale of contempt. According to him, Brahmins were the originators of this unnatural institution founded and maintained through unnatural means. Brahmin class first raised the structure of caste while making themselves into caste, the Brahmins by virtue of this, created non-Brahmin caste. The government of India's Anthropological Survey of India (ASI), under the leadership of K.S.Singh, brought out a series of publications titled 'The People of India'. This historic verdict of the ASI project did not get any publicity in India's press because our ruling class is shy of admitting this fact which has made them the rulers. Dalit Vice editor Mr. V. T. Rajshekar says, "Almost all political party leaders be they nationalists, socialists, communists and Hindu Nazi have uniform opinion on caste 'caste is bad and hence it has to be destroyed; Indian scholars and researchers have produced mountains of literature to prove that caste is non-existent'. They believed and made others believe that with economic development, the superficial "caste" could be eradicated. Our planners and rulers, based on this belief, introduced hundreds of welfare schemes and invested thousands of Cr. of rupees on these schemes. All these economic programs proved an utter failure. But they conveniently forget that this antisocial spirit is the worst feature of their own caste system. The caste system's fundamental characteristic of fixed civil, cultural, religious and economic rights for each caste by birth, with restrictions for change implies forced exclusion of one caste from the rights of castes. Exclusion in economic spheres such as occupation, education and labour employment is therefore, internal to the system, and a necessary outcome of its underlying principles. Therefore, in our country all major assets of production are own and concentrated in the hands of upper castes Hindu and lower strata of society particularly depressed classes (SC/ST) are assets less people. The unnatural distribution of national wealth forced depressed classes to depend on for their survival on upper castes Hindu at large extent; this is the main reason for their socio-economic exploitation in India.

Discrimination is the main function of caste system in India. Though the Indian constitution provides for a slew of preferential schemes designed to end discrimination against the scheduled castes/ scheduled tribes yet, atrocities against them continue unabated. The provision in the constitution resolves, 'to secure to all citizens: justice, social, economic and political, liberty of thought, expression, belief, faith and worship; equality of status and of opportunity, and to promote among them all fraternity, assuring the dignity of individual and unity.'

In the directive principles it adds that 'The state shall promote with special care the educational and economic interest of the scheduled castes/tribes and shall protect them from social injustice and all forms of exploitation'.

In spite of all these provisions discrimination on basis of castes is still continue till to date. Because, to implementations of provisions made in the constitution are not in the capacity of depressed castes the political, social and economic powers are vested in the hands of upper castes Hindus. As upper castes Hindu could control all powers by the virtue of castes system they do not want to implements the constitutional provisions for their vested interests. But the Hindus have never felt ashamed of it. This is a phenomenon which in my view is quite unparalleled". Thus, biases within the law-enforcement machinery and the political class have combined to prevent the depressed castes from utilizing programs designed for them. Caste discrimination not only hinders SC/STs children from attending school but also affect the quality of education they receive. Therefore, the progress of schooling among Dalit children between the ages of 6-14 has been low and dropt out rate among them is very high compared to that of the general population.

Several such facts have been revealed in the 'Indian Education Report'. Upper castes teachers refuse to touch scheduled castes students. At the same time they make these children special targets of verbal abuse and physical punishment. Such behavior of teachers affects adversely on the educational desire among the scheduled castes children. According to Dr Babasaheb Ambedkar the capacity to appreciate merits in a man apart from his caste does not exist in a Hindu. There is appreciation of virtue but only when the man is a fellow caste-man. It is not a case of standing by virtue and not standing by vice. It is a case of standing or not standing by the caste. Have not Hindus committed treason against their country in the interests of their caste? This is the question raised by Dr. Babasaheb Ambedkar is very much relevant in present context. Dr. Ambedkar was a social reformer of 20 century he rightly said "Enlightened high caste Hindus, who did not feel the necessary for agitating for the abolition of caste or had not the courage to agitate for it". The root of untouchability is the caste system; the root of the caste system is religion attached to varnashram; and the root of varnashrma is the Brahminical religion; and the root of the brahminical religion is authoritarianism or political power. He proved that deprivation of human rights resulted in untouchability and casteism. A country of castes is a country of stagnation and underdevelopment.

Thorat committee was appointed by the government to find out the reported discrimination in India's most reputed All-India Institute of Medical Sciences (AIIMS) in New Delhi. The report revealed that, the struggle that SC/ST students face to enter premier institutions of higher learning seems mild compared to what they have to put up with later. On top of coping with academic challenges and a totally unfamiliar environment, many dalit students have to deal with the hostility that comes with being a 'reserved category student'. Most of the students complained that teachers were inaccessible and plain indifferent towards them. The committee found that over a period of time, SC/ST students have moved from their allotted rooms to be closer to other SC/ST students. Many of the students said they moved because their rooms would be locked from outside repeatedly while they were in, vulgar abuse would be scrawled on the doors and it would be made clear that this would stop only if they moved to floors where other SC/ST students stayed. They also faced social isolation, refusal to share books and notes and objections to sharing seats in class.

There are preconceived notion about academic caliber of the SC/STs students and hence they are labelled as 'academically backward'. Today in college these student identity manipulated as 'reserved quota' students. Thus, in spite of academic competence comments like 'these reserved chaps will never be as good as us' are passed. Another issue is the non-admission of 'merit' students in the 'open' category, despite a central direction that they must be. It is always thought why enrol an extra low caste student when we already have to admit a certain number of them? This follows two consequences, it brands a brilliant student as one coming from the reserved category and it deprives another needy SC/ST student of a seat. Their contribution is not recognized in any area; they are always put in an environment which will hamper their personal development and performance. The major objective of such discussion is not to find out the ideology of the state behind the measure, but to create hatred among the students and employees in organizations. The worth of SC/STs is not prized at work place, though they have potential. No one can deny that backwardness very substantially arises from lack of access to economic resources and facilities like quality education and employment opportunities.

The Maharashtra state is known as socially progressive state, political leaders always talk about social reform on the name Phule, Ambedkar yet Khairlanji massacre happen in Maharashtra recently on September 29, 2006, four members of the Buddhist Bhotmange family Surekha, her daughter Priyanka and sons Roshan and Sudhir were killed near their house in Khairlanji in full public view, by an angry village mob, allegedly out of caste hatred.

10.4. Economic Implication of Caste System

India is recognized as an economy with a 'stunning' but jobless growth' and a 'booming economy with growing gaps' where the spectacular successes made have not been shared by all equally. The planning commission has also realized that economic growth has failed to be sufficiently inclusive, particularly after the mid 1990, it noted in the approach to the eleventh five year plan. For too many people still lack access to basic services such as health, education clean drinking water and sanitation facilities without which they cannot be empowered to claim their share in the benefits of growth. A poor Brahmin, Rajput or Bania may be deprived of good education for reasons of poverty, but his or her whole lifestyle radiates a degree of confidence which a low caste person from an economically well-off background is hard put to match. In India those who are not in the growth process they are particularly SC/ST/OBC and Muslims. While some occupations are valued by society, others are devalued and are considered polluting, impure, and therefore socially degrading. The social stigma of impurity and pollution attached to occupations such as scavenging and leather-making reduces the social status of the persons engaged in them. There are many occupations in India which on account of the fact that they are regarded as degraded by Hindus, provoke those who are engaged in there is a constant desire to evade and escape from such occupations which arises solely because of the blighting effect which they produce upon those who follow them owing to the slight and stigma of caste on them by Hindu religion what efficiency can there be in a system under which neither men's hearts nor their minds are in their work, public life in India is controlled by caste identities. This is the one of the main reasons of low productivity and production in India. The implication of such tendencies is the results of under utilization of resources and under production.

10.4.1. Worst Condition of Unorganized Sector' Workers

SC/STs are predominantly working in unorganized sector and their conditions are miserable there it is reported in various commissions' reports appointed by the government of India. The report of the Commission on the condition of unorganized sector workers revealed that, the number of people below the poverty line may have come down, but 79 per cent of unorganized workers 88 per cent of SC/ST, 80 per cent of OBC population and 84 per cent of Muslims belong to the "poor and vulnerable group".

The finding of Kevin Watkins, who edited the United Nation's Human Development Report, said that despite growing prosperity brought on by a sustained boom, child malnourishment in India is higher than Ethiopia and well above the African average of 28 per cent. In India four in every ten children are malnourished despite the country's economy growing at an average rate 9 per cent per year. Report further said, when it comes to economic growth India is a long way ahead of Bangladesh but when it comes to child survival rates, it lags behind. Both Bangladesh and Nepal are far poorer than India, but India still has a higher child death rate then both the nations:' said Watkins. Poverty has also been falling far more slowly in India than in other high- growth developing countries, such as Vietnam and Brazil. Watkins believes that part of the problem is that the benefits of growth have been "highly skewed'. Secondly from the side of government agencies there is height of negligence's to implements the prescribed policies made for SC/ST.

10.4.2. Government Institutes

It is reported in review of the state corporations, the National Institute of Financial Management (NIFM) in 2006 paints a shocking picture. Most of these agencies have parked their funds in fixed deposits instead of giving loans to needy SC/ST it's on an average; their equity–debt ratio was 65:35. The report says that there is widespread irregularity in selection of beneficiaries–cases of submitted lists not matching actual recipients have been recorded. Most state corporations have not prepared accounts for anything between 6 to 16 years. Another problem is declining allocation and even lower utilization. In the past decade, central government spending on welfare of SC/ST and OBC declined from a tiny 0.005% of the total non- plan revenue expenditure to 0.004%. Plan expenditure for this purpose declined from 2.4% to 1.6% over the same period.

10.4.3. Special Component Plan

For raising SC/STs families above poverty line, there is a Special Component Plan (SPC) under which each central ministry and all state governments are supposed to allocate funds in proportion to the scheduled castes population. According to the Mid-Term Review of the 10 five year plan (2002-07) only 14 out of 37 central government ministries had complied with this.

10.4.4. Bank Credits

Bank credits to SC/ST to run their own businesses have also declined. Data from RBI shows the amount of credit per capita received by SC/ST declined from Rs 495 in 1993 to Rs 285 in 2001 and further to Rs225 in 2004. In fact the number of small borrowable accounts of them declined from 77 to 23 per thousand.

The Indian system of exclusion on the basis of castes has also been clearly reflected in the National Sample Survey Organization's (NSSO) Report (2004-05). It is revealed from the report that 40.94 % out of total population are OBC, 19.59 % are SC and 8.63 % are STs. Approximately 70 % of Indian population is backward castes population as per Hindu Social Order. The second important point revealed by report is that, 91.4 percent of STs, 79.8 percent of SCs and 78.0 percent of OBC live in rural areas. The third point is that, the economic growth seems to be reflecting in the expenditure of urban India, which is spending nearly double the amount on an average compared to the rural areas. The per capita monthly expenses of people living in urban areas were Rs. 1052.36 a month as against Rs 558.78 of those in rural areas.

These are the implications of social exclusion of SC/STs from main stream of development in our country. As an economic organization caste is therefore, a harmful institution in as much as it involves the subordination of man's natural powers and inclinations to the exigencies of social rules. Economic survey says, if people are healthy, educated and adequately skilled, they can participate fully and contribute more to economic development process. However, India's overall performance on human development has been poor in last decade. Infant mortality rate have been much slower than expected. UNDP's global Human Development Report (HDR) for 2005 ranks India at 127 out of 177 countries of the world in term of a composite Human Development Index (HDI) for 2003.

10.4.5. Remedial Measures

Special Central Assistance (SCA) for the special component plan (SCP) is a major scheme for the welfare and development of SCs. Under the scheme 100% assistance is extended to supplement the efforts of the states/ UTs for ensuring rapid socio-economic development of SC specially those living below the poverty line. Allocation for 2005-06 was Rs 407.36 Cr. for economic development of these disadvantaged groups through income generating schemes, special financial institutions have been set up namely scheduled castes finance and development corporation (NSCFDC) National Safai Karmchari Finance and Development Corporation (NSKFDC) National Backward Classes Finance and Development Corporation (NBCFDC) and National Minorities Development and Finance Corporation (NMDFDC) The Protection of Civil Rights (PCR) Act 1955, and the SC/ST Prevention of Atrocities (POA) Act,1989 are two important legal instruments to prevent/curb persistent problems of social discrimination, prevalence of social evils like untouchability and cases of exploitation and atrocities against these disadvantaged groups.

Some of intellectuals among SC/STs and politician, social reformers gather in Bhopal in January 2002 and come with agenda for SC/STs empowerment known as The Bhopal Declaration. Accordingly, ensure that each SC/STs family will own enough cultivable land for socio-economic well-being. The law must be amended to ensure that lengthy litigation with the ulterior motive of denying SC/STs of legal redresses is not resorted to. Enact legislation and enforce the right of SC/STs, agricultural labourers to living wages, to gender parity in wages, to job security, to better working conditions and welfare measures, and ensure punitive measures against offenders. Enforce with stringent measures the Bonded labour system (Abolition) Act, 1976 and abolish forthwith child labour to ensure freedom with dignity for all the SC/STs Make the reservation quota applicable in all the public and private educational institutions from primary to technical and professional levels. Implement effectively in letter and spirit the SC/ST Act, 1989 and Rules 1995, especially with regard to atrocities against SC/STs women, and accordingly prosecute the dominant caste leaders and their minions who stoke the fire of caste clashes and the police officials acting in connivance with them. The state must assume sole responsibility in protecting the SC/ST. Make it statutory for parliament and state Assemblies to debate on the Annual Reports of the National and state level Commissions for SC/ST and Safai karmcharis within the following year, and ensure that these annual reports and the action-taken reports of the government are made public. These are some of the suggestions of the Bhopal Declaration. But unless the mind set of upper caste Hindus changes the implementation of these provisions are not possible.

SC/STs and OBC are in majority in India. They should have their own identity in the Democratic society like India because of self identity all these depressed castes people can organized themselves and fight for justice through democratic ways. Dr. Babasaheb Ambedkar has shown us the path of conversion to Buddhism. All SC/STs and OBC should follow the way shown by Dr. Babasaheb Ambedkar and embraced. Buddhism will be the identity of depressed castes being in majority they can have their own government in democratic society and use the political power to empower themselves and establish the just society based on the principle of liberty, equality, justice, and fraternity.

10.5. Ambedkar's Humanistic Convictions

Humans as the Homo sapience evolved on this planet about 150,000 years before present. Some of the oldest civilizations known in the history of humanity have been dated 10,000 years old. Human Being is a social animal. Social animal has a tendency to govern and to be governed by a set of rules framed by the society itself. There are two fundamental types of human nature. Creative and possessive. Creative humans use human intellect for creative endeavours which enriches human thought; knowledge and wealth thereby contribute to the development of human heritage for the posterity. Possessive people, on the other hand do not believe in the use of human intellect for creative purpose. This type of people posses a strong urge to become the governing class by all means in order to achieve their aims. Lesser the degree of civilization in the society, greater is the probability of succeeding this type of people in becoming the governing class. This is a continuous process in the human society. Karl Marx has scientifically analysed this conflict by applying the principles of dialectical materialism to the sphere of social phenomenon and described it as the historical materialism. Slavery, apartheid, gender bias and caste system are the abominable creations of possessive peoples for the exploitation of creative people. These are man made evils created by man for the exploitation of man. Those, who have raised their voices against these evils and given a relentless fight against the prevailing social order of their times in order to free the creative peoples from the shackles imposed on them have become immortal personalities in the human history. Some of these great persons are better known as founders of religions

Gautam Buddha, Jesus Christ, Guru Nanak Kabeer, Ravidas, Tukarama, Krantiba Jotirao Phoolay, Periyar and Dr. Babasaheb Ambedkar they all belong to the great class of exalted Homo sapience called as Humanists.

Dr. Babasaheb Ambedkar was truly a multifaceted personality. A veritable emancipator of Dalits, a great national leader and patriot, a great author, a great educationist, a great political philosopher, a great religious guide and above all a great humanist without any parallel among his contemporaries. It is only regrettable that the press in the past as well as the contemporary has projected Ambedkar mainly as a great social rebel and a bitter critic of the Hindu religion. Critics of Dr. Ambedkar have ignored his basic humanistic instincts and strong humanitarian convictions behind his every act or speech through out his life. It is important to trace the origin and consolidation of his humanistic convictions.

Dr. Ambedkar's father, Subhedar Ramji was a known follower of the Kabeerpanth. Many of the Kabir's Dohas are the veritable gems of rationalism and the most daring expressions of the humanitarian beliefs. Dr. Ambedkar's mind was thus deeply imbued with Kabeer's philosophy in the childhood days. On passing his matriculation examination, he was felicitated by his teacher and was presented with a copy of a book on the life of Buddha. This gift must have made a profound impact on the mind of young Ambedkar. Dr. Ambedkar stayed in America, the land of liberty, for his higher studies. There he studied the western liberal thought and the humanitarian philosophy expounded by great thinkers such as Prof. John Dewey, who was also his teacher, John Stuart Mill, Edmund Burke, and Prof. Harold Laski to name a few. The contrast between the social milieu which he lived in, and the liberal academic thought he studied could not have resulted in anything but making him an ardent humanist.

Following events in the life of Dr. Ambedkar bears testimony to his humanitarian concerns and convictions.

10.5.1. Mahad Tank Satyagraha

Untouchables were barred however; the animals were allowed to use the water of the Chawdar tank in the Mahad town of Maharashtra. This glaring manifestation of inhuman attitude of the society was challenged by Dr. Ambedkar to usher a new era of social revolution. The procession was attacked by caste Hindus and many satyagrahis were injured by them. There were many ex-military persons among the satyagrahis who had shown their bravery during the World War I. They could have retaliated in a befitting manner. However Dr. Ambedkar appealed to his comrades not to indulge in violence. Only a person who is the humanist to his innermost core can show such steadfast faith in the non-violence in such situation. The name of Mahad town is also permanently linked with human rights because one more reason. Dr. Ambedkar organized a conference of satyagrahis on the 25th December 1927 in which the Manusmriti was burned.

10.5.2. Pune Pact

In the field of politics also, Dr. Ambedkar remain firm with his convictions. Signing the Pune pact is perhaps the ultimate testimony of Dr. Ambedkar's humanitarian credentials. He was fully aware of the reason for Gandhi's fast and also the consequence of signing the pact, yet only on the humanitarian ground to save the life of Gandhi he did it. The essence of his political philosophy, the trilogy of Liberty, Equality and Fraternity he had borrowed from Buddha's philosophy. Many of the current provisions for the welfare and protection of labour have their origin in the manifesto of the independent labour party.

Fundamental rights assured to all citizens of our country is a great leap towards establishing the basic human values in the society that was based on graded inequality. As the chairperson of the constitution drafting committee Dr. Ambedkar was instrumental in the incorporation of the principle of fundamental rights in the constitution.

Dr. Ambedkar was a firm believer in the parliamentary democracy. A few months before his Mahaparinirvana he embraced Buddhism. It was a great tribute of a great humanist to the greatest humanistic philosophy of Buddha. By initiating millions of his follower in to the Buddhist fold, he asserted his faith in the humanistic values preached by Buddha in alleviating the sufferings of his lot. He thus reached the pinnacle of the humanism by becoming a Bodhisattva.

10.6. Vows of Dr. Ambedkar

Dr.B.R.Ambedkar prescribed 22 vows to his followers during the historic religious conversion to Buddhism on 15 October 1956 at Deeksha Bhoomi, Nagpur in India. The conversion to Buddhism by 800,000 people was historic because it was the largest religious conversion, the world has ever witnessed. He prescribed these oaths so that there may be complete severance of bond with Hinduism. These 22 vows struck a blow at the roots of Hindu beliefs and practices. These vows could serve as a bulwark to protect Buddhism from confusion and contradictions. These vows could liberate converts from superstitions, wasteful and meaningless rituals, which have led to pauperisation of masses and enrichment of upper castes of Hindus.

The famous 22 vows are:

1) I shall have no faith in Brahma, Vishnu and Mahesh nor shall I worship them.

2) I shall have no faith in Rama and Krishna who are believed to be incarnation of God nor shall I worship them.
3) I shall have no faith in 'Gauri', Ganapati and other gods and goddesses of Hindus nor shall I worship them.
4) I do not believe in the incarnation of God.
5) I do not and shall not believe that Lord Buddha was the incarnation of Vishnu. I believe this to be sheer madness and false propaganda.
6) I shall not perform 'Shraddha' nor shall I give 'pind-dan'.
7) I shall not act in a manner violating the principles and teachings of the Buddha.
8) I shall not allow any ceremonies to be performed by Brahmins.
9) I shall believe in the equality of man.
10) I shall endeavour to establish equality.
11) I shall follow the 'noble eightfold path' of the Buddha.
12) I shall follow the 'paramitas' prescribed by the Buddha.
13) I shall have compassion and loving kindness for all living beings and protect them.
14) I shall not steal.
15) I shall not tell lies.
16) I shall not commit carnal sins.
17) I shall not take intoxicants like liquor, drugs etc.
18) I shall endeavour to follow the noble eightfold path and practise compassion and loving kindness in every day life.
19) I renounce Hinduism which is harmful for humanity and impedes the advancement and development of humanity because it is based on inequality, and adopt Buddhism as my religion.
20) I firmly believe the Dhamma of the Buddha is the only true religion.
21) I believe that I am having a rebirth.
22) I solemnly declare and affirm that I shall hereafter lead my life according to the principles and teachings of the Buddha and his Dhamma.

10.7. Constitutional Safeguards for Dalits

The important Constitutional safeguards for SCs & STs are mentioned below:

10.7.1. Directive Principles of State Policy

Article 46 is a comprehensive article comprising both the developmental and regulatory aspects. It reads as follows:

10.7.2. Social Safeguards

Article 17. "Untouchability" is abolished and its practice in any form is forbidden. The enforcement of any disability arising out of "Untouchability" shall be an offence punishable in accordance with law.

To give effect to this Article, Parliament made an enactment viz., Untouchability (Offences) Act, 1955. To make the provisions of this Act more stringent, the Act was amended in 1976 and was also renamed as the Protection of Civil Rights Act, 1955. As provided under the Act, Government of India also notified the Rules, viz., the PCR Rules, 1977, to carry out the provisions of this Act. This act known as the Scheduled Castes and the Scheduled Tribes Act, 1989, became effective from 30.1.1990. For carrying out the provisions of this Act the Govt. of India have notified the SCs and the STs Rules, 1995 on 31.3.1995.

Article 23. Prohibits traffic in human beings and begar and other similar forms of forced labour and provides that any contravention of this provision shall be an offence punishable in accordance with law. It does not specifically mention SCs & STs but since the majority of bonded labour belong to SCs/STs this Article has a special significance for SCs and STs. In pursuance of this article, Parliament has enacted the Bonded Labour System Act, 1976. For effective implementation of this Act, the Ministry of Labour is running a Centrally Sponsored Scheme for identification, liberation and rehabilitation of bonded labour.

Article 24 provides that no child below the age of 14 years shall be employed to work in any factory or mine or engaged in any other hazardous employment. There are Central and State laws to prevent child labour.

Article 25(2)(b) provides that Hindu religious institutions of a public character shall be thrown open to all classes and sections of Hindus. This provision is relevant as some sects of Hindus used to claim that only members of the concerned sects had a right to enter their temples. This was only a subterfuge to prevent entry of SC persons in such temples. For the purpose of this provision the term Hindu includes Sikh, Jaina and Budhist.

10.7.3. Educational and Cultural Safeguards

Article 15(4) empowers the State to make any special provision for the advancement of any socially and educationally backward classes of citizens or for SC and ST. This provision has enabled the State to reserve seats for SCs and STs in educational institutions including technical, engineering and medical colleges and in Scientific & Specialised Courses. In this as well as in Article 16(4) the term 'backward classes' is used as a generic term and comprises various categories of backward classes, viz., Scheduled Castes, Scheduled Tribes, Other Backward Classes, Denotified Communities and Nomadic/Seminomadic communities.

Article 330 provides for reservation of seats for SCs/STs in the Lok Sabha.

Article 332 provides for reservation of seats for SCs/STs in the State Vidhan Sabhas.

Article 334 originally laid down that the provision relating to the reservation of seats for SCs/STs in the Lok Sabha and the State Vidhan Sabhas would cease to have effect on the expiration of a period of ten years from the commencement of the Constitution. This article has since been amended four times, extending the said period by ten years on each occasion. This provision was to expire in January 2000.

10.7.4. Service Safeguards

Article 16(4) empowers the State to make "any provision for the reservation in appointments or posts in favour of any backward class of citizens which, in the opinion of the State, is not adequately represented in the services under the State".

Article 16(4A). Nothing in this Article shall prevent the State from making any provision for reservation in matters of promotion to any class or classes of posts in the services under the State in favour of the Scheduled Castes and the Scheduled Tribes which, in the opinion of the State, are not adequately represented in the services under the State".

Article 335. "The claims of the members of the Scheduled Castes and the Scheduled Tribes shall be taken into consideration, consistently with the maintenance of efficiency of administration, in the making of appointments to services and posts in connection with the affairs of the Union or of a State".

Article 320(4) provides that nothing in clause (3) shall require a Public Service Commission to be consulted as respects the manner in which any provision under Article 16(4) & 16(4)A may be made or the manner in which effect may be given to the provisions of Article 335.

10.7.5. Statutes and Legislations

There are a number of laws, both Central and State, which provide for safeguards to SCs/STs. Some of these emanate from the various Constitutional provisions. An illustrative list of such laws is given below:

1) The Protection of Civil Rights Act, 1955.
2) The Scheduled Castes and the Scheduled Tribes Act, 1989.
3) The Bonded Labour System Act, 1976.
4) The Child Labour Act, 1986.
5) Acts and regulations in force in different States to prevent alienation of land belonging to SCs/STs. In some States such provision exists in the Land Revenue Code.
6) Acts in different States for restoration of alienated land to SCs/STs.

Index